Technology and International Trade

Technology and International Trade

Edited by

Jan Fagerberg

Norwegian Institute of International Affairs (NUPI), Oslo, Norway. Professor of Economics, University of Oslo, Norway

Pär Hansson

Trade Union Institute for Economic Research (FIEF), Stockholm, Sweden. Associate Professor of Economics, University of Umeå, Sweden

Lars Lundberg

Trade Union Institute for Economic Research (FIEF), Stockholm, Sweden. Professor of Economics, University of Umeå, Sweden

Arne Melchior

Norwegian Institute of International Affairs (NUPI), Oslo, Norway

Edward Elgar

Cheltenham, UK • Brookfield, US

Published by
Edward Elgar Publishing Limited
8 Lansdown Place
Cheltenham
Glos GL50 2HU
UK

Edward Elgar Publishing Company
Old Post Road
Brookfield
Vermont 05036
US

A catalogue record for this book is available from the British Library

Library of Congress Cataloguing in Publication Data
Technology and international trade / edited by Jan Fagerberg ... [et al.].
    Collection of papers originally presented at a conference on Technology and International Trade, held in Oslo, Oct. 1995.
    Includes bibliographical references.
    1. International trade—Congresses.   2. Technological innovations—Economic aspects—Congresses.   3. Competition, International—Congresses.   4. Comparative advantage (International trade)—Congresses.   I. Fagerberg, Jan.
HF1372.T43   1997
382—dc20
                                        96–26477
                                            CIP

ISBN   1 85898 528 5

Printed and bound in Great Britain by
Biddles Ltd, Guildford and King's Lynn

Contents

Figures

Tables

Contributors

Steve Dowrick, Department of Economics, Research School of Social Science, The Australian National University, Canberra, Australia.

Jørgen Drud Hansen, Department of Economics, Odense University, Denmark.

Jan Fagerberg, Norwegian Institute of International Affairs (NUPI), Oslo, Norway.

Steven Globerman, Western Washington University, College of Business and Economics, Washington, US.

Patrik Gustavsson, Trade Union Institute for Economic Research (FIEF), Stockholm, Sweden.

Pär Hansson, Trade Union Institute for Economic Research (FIEF), Stockholm, Sweden. Associate Professor of Economics, University of Umeå, Sweden.

Juha Honkatukia, Department of Economics, Helsinki School of Economics, Finland.

Lars Lundberg, Trade Union Institute for Economic Research (FIEF), Stockholm, Sweden. Professor of Economics, University of Umeå, Sweden.

Arne Melchior, Norwegian Institute of International Affairs (NUPI), Oslo, Norway.

Fredrik Sjöholm, Department of Economics, Lund University, Sweden.

Anders Sørensen, Economic Policy Research Unit, Copenhagen Business School, Denmark.

Bart Verspagen, Maastricht Economic Research Institute on Innovation and Technology (MERIT), University of Limburg, Maastricht, The Netherlands.

Katharine Wakelin, Maastricht Economic Research Institute on Innovation and Technology (MERIT), University of Limburg, Maastricht, The Netherlands.

Edward N. Wolff, Department of Economics, New York University, New York, US.

Preface

The chapters in this book were originally presented at a conference on 'Technology and International Trade', initiated by the Norwegian Institute for International Affairs (NUPI) and the Trade Union Institute for Economic Research (FIEF), at Leangkollen, Oslo, in October 1995. We, the organizers of the conference and the editors of this book, wish to thank the authors for their patience with the continuous harassment from editors and referees and for their ability to produce revised versions within a very tight time schedule. Thanks are also due to a number of referees who greatly facilitated our editorial task, to Liv Høivik for handling the practical matters concerning the conference and to Jimmy Miller for checking the language. Finally we wish to express our gratitude to the Nordic Council for Economic Research (NEF), the Nordic Academy for Research Education (NorFA) and the Norwegian Research Council (NFR) for their generous financial support.

Jan Fagerberg
Lars Lundberg
Pär Hansson
Arne Melchior
Oslo and Stockholm, March 1996

Introduction

The last decades have witnessed important changes in global trade patterns. The market shares of Japan and other fast-growing countries in Asia have increased at the expense of other countries. At the same time many European countries face sluggish growth and increasing unemployment. These developments have led to an increased awareness among policy-makers, media and researchers of factors affecting competitiveness and employment. Increasingly, many observers have come to stress the importance of technology in this context. For instance, this view has figured prominently in recent policy debates within the European Union.

The objective of this book is to contribute to the understanding of the relationships between technology, competitiveness, trade, employment and growth. The book includes theoretical as well as empirical work, applying different perspectives. The first half of the book – Chapters 1 to 6 – addresses the general issue of the determinants of competitiveness and specialization. Of these, Chapters 1, 2, 3 and 4 focus on the impact of technology on international competitiveness. Chapters 3 and 5 study the role of domestic market size. The consequences of technological progress in the form of learning for specialization are analysed in Chapter 6, while Chapter 7 reviews the literature on trade (openness) and growth. Chapters 3, 8 and 9 focus on national and international flows of technology and the role of multinational firms for the localization of R&D. Chapters 10 and 11 analyse the policy options in open, innovation-driven economies. Finally, Chapters 4 and 12 assess the impact of technology on labour markets.

The idea that technological differences, or differences in productivity, across countries explain specialization patterns is not a new one. In fact, this was the starting point of the most influential trade theorist of all times, David Ricardo. For most of this century, however, theoretical and empirical studies of trade patterns have been dominated by another paradigm, the factor proportions or Heckscher–Ohlin theory, named after the two Swedish economists Eli Heckscher and Bertil Ohlin. According to this theory, comparative advantage is determined not by technology gaps, but by the unequal distribution across countries of various (immobile) factors of production.

The role of technology for competitiveness was never completely neglected. The effects on trade patterns and specialization of factor accumulation and (exogenous) technical change and technology gaps were studied by Johnson (1959) and Jones (1965) within the framework of the traditional factor proportions theory. Basically this approach treated the R&D efforts of a country as an additional resource or 'endowment'. Moreover, some early empirical studies (for example, Gruber, Metha and Vernon, 1967) included measures of technological requirements such as R&D expenditure together with factor proportions variables to explain trade patterns.

However, it is probably fair to say that technology came to the forefront of research in international trade with the formulation of the technology gap and product-cycle theories (Posner, 1961; Vernon, 1966; Hirsch, 1967). Posner's theory was based on the idea that manmade differences in technological capabilities across countries induce trade. Vernon and Hirsch assumed that the competitive conditions of an industry, and hence the factors affecting competitiveness, change through time. The rich countries (the North) were assumed to specialize in the early phases of the life cycle, in which innovation matters most. But as the industry matured the North would be outperformed by the imitating South, exploiting cost advantages. The lessons for the rich part of the world were summarized by Paul Krugman (1990, p. 147): 'Like Alice and the Red Queen, the developed region must keep running to stay in the same place'.

The technology gap and product-cycle theories have been a source of inspiration for later theoretical and applied work ever since (for surveys of empirical work, see Deardorff, 1984 and Leamer, 1994). One strand of research analyses technology gaps in the international economy from an evolutionary or Schumpeterian perspective (Dosi, Pavitt and Soete, 1990). Another, based on so-called 'new trade theory', focuses on the role of economies of scale (another classical idea, generally attributed to Adam Smith) and externalities as a source of technology gaps and specialization (Krugman, 1990). More recently, growth theorists have extended this perspective by suggesting models in which the creation of technology gaps has been endogenized (so-called 'new growth theory', see Grossman and Helpman, 1991).

In this book, the four empirical chapters evaluating the role of technology for competitiveness and trade all basically have the Ricardian, or technology gap, approach as the point of departure. While Fagerberg (Chapter 3) uses an input measure – R&D expenditure – of investments in new technology, Wolff (Chapter 1) and Gustavsson, Hansson and Lundberg (Chapter 2) focus on the output from these investments, as reflected in the 'total factor productivity' (TFP). Verspagen and Wakelin (Chapter 4) use both R&D and patents (another output measure). In spite of these differences in data and methods a common (and central) result is that technological innovation, whether measured by R&D, patents or TFP, significantly increases competitiveness and influences specialization patterns. Furthermore, both Fagerberg, and Verspagen and Wakelin find that although the estimated impact of R&D is larger in typical 'high-tech' industries, innovation matters in many 'low-tech' industries as well. Thus, according to these studies, technological competition is not an exclusively high-tech affair.

The findings do not preclude that national resource endowments may have an impact on industrial localization. While some factors of production may have become increasingly internationally mobile, others, such as natural resources and human capital, still have a low degree of international mobility. Gustavsson, Hansson and Lundberg report that current specialization patterns are influenced by cross-country differences in the supply of various natural resources whereas human capital accumulation together with productivity growth determines changes in specialization.

In a 'Ricardian' model analysed by Drud Hansen (Chapter 6), in which technical progress is a function of learning, history matters for competitiveness, and original comparative advantages of countries tend to be reinforced over time. This is consistent with the fact that the specialization patterns of developed countries tend to be rather stable over time (see Wolff). Drud Hansen demonstrates that when allowing for differences in (a) technological capability, or productivity, across countries and (b) technological dynamism across sectors, trade may increase the lead of the country that initially has the upper hand in the dynamic sectors. Hence, lagging countries may have some reason for concern, if trade leads to specialization in stagnant sectors.

Theories that focus on economies of scale as a source of competitive advantage generally predict that with trading costs, large countries will have an advantage in industries where economies of scale are important. Melchior (Chapter 5) shows that in such a model the competitive advantage of a large home market will increase with the degree of product differentiation. This provides a theoretical underpinning to the 'standard goods hypothesis' suggested by Dreze (1961), that is, that small countries will specialize in homogeneous goods for which international demand is relatively standardized. Melchior's empirical results give some support for this hypothesis.

Recently, the interest in technology as a source of trade and growth has been stimulated by the advent of the so-called 'new growth theory', combining the assumptions of economies of scale and imperfect competition with an explicit role for the firm in generating new technology (Romer, 1990; Grossman and Helpman, 1991). The traditional theory in this area only allowed for small and temporary effects on growth of increased trade. As pointed out by Dowrick (Chapter 7) in his survey, the new growth theories challenge this view. Following these theories, increased openness may have permanent effects on growth. Of particular interest for this book is the case when trade may act as a direct transmission mechanism for the international dissemination of knowledge.

The process of diffusion of new knowledge, as well as the notion of technological spillovers and their geographical reach, are important for recent theorizing on the impact of technology on growth and trade. If new technology is a global public good, it cannot induce trade; the argument is analogous to the case of perfectly mobile factors of production. However, little is known about the geographical reach of spillovers. Two of the chapters in this book throw some light on this issue. Fagerberg shows that new knowledge acquired indirectly through purchases of inputs – capital goods and intermediates – has a much higher impact on competitiveness and exports when inputs come from domestic sources than when they are imported. Sjöholm (Chapter 8) examines the impact of geographical proximity and contacts through trade on the dissemination of knowledge, using patent citations data as a measure of knowledge flows. He finds that both trade flows and proximity have a strong positive impact on knowledge flows.

New growth theory emphasizes the importance of business-sector R&D and its determinants for trade and growth. Countries that devote a large share of their resources to R&D will, other things being equal, gain the upper hand in 'high-tech' industry. However, if spillovers are national rather than global in nature, the social returns to investments in R&D will be higher in large countries. Hence, a large country may outperform a small one in 'high-tech' industry even if the latter initially spent more of its income on R&D (Grossman and Helpman, 1991). Fagerberg tests for the impact of R&D investment on export performance across countries of different sizes. Consistent with the theoretical predictions, the results suggest that the impact of R&D on exports is stronger in large countries.

The results reported here support the view that there is a strong geographical component to spillovers and knowledge flows in general. An important vehicle for overcoming such an obstacle is, of course, the multinational enterprise (MNE). If centres of technological excellence are widely dispersed, and proximity is important for being able to share in the progress that is generated, MNEs might find it useful to decentralize their R&D activities. Globerman (Chapter 9) considers the R&D strategies of multinational enterprises and the extent to which these have changed recently. He finds that some decentralization has occurred, though not for all MNEs and host countries. However, this seems to be mainly a response to increasing internationalization and the need to adapt products to foreign markets.

Sørensen (Chapter 10) and Honkatukia (Chapter 11) focus on the factors affecting innovation in open economies. Both chapters extend the models of the new growth literature by introducing a richer set of assumptions. Sørensen adds an educational sector and discusses the trade-off between devoting skilled labour to education or R&D in the private business sector. He points out that draining the educational sector for qualified personnel may have detrimental consequences for the long-run performance of the economy. Honkatukia introduces a monetary sector. He finds that in such a model an expansionary monetary policy may slow down the rate of innovation.

One of the reasons for the public interest in the technology-competitiveness issue is the possible link with employment. Verspagen and Wakelin consider this link in some detail for the mutual trade between three large European countries in the 1980s. They find that although the partial effect of differences in technological activity, capital accumulation and costs on employment might be quite important, they tend to cancel out, so that the total effect of trade on employment is negligible. However, if trade induces structural changes in the economy that change the demand for workers with different kinds of skills, a skill mismatch may occur. This may lead to reduced compensation for certain skill groups as well as unemployment. Hansson (Chapter 12) finds that the increase of the average skill level of the Swedish industrial labour force reflects increased use of skilled labour within firms, rather than a structural shift towards high-skill sectors. Although increased internationalization (trade exposure) may have had a say in this, Hansson points out that skill-biased technical change seems to have been the most important factor.

Competitiveness in the global market place is continuously shifting. New producers will emerge on the world market, in particular from Asia and the formerly planned economies in Europe. A basic conclusion from the work reported in this book is that technology plays a central role for competitiveness, and that its importance may very well be increasing, since many other factors, such as physical capital, will probably become increasingly mobile. To some extent, technology may have become more internationally mobile, for example, through the operations of multinational firms. Nevertheless, the results in this book indicate that domestic innovative activity is still a major determinant of competitiveness, and that geographical proximity seems to be important for knowledge flows. In comparison to technology, most other factors often linked to competitiveness seem to be of secondary importance.

The results presented in this book may give some guidance for policy. First, the results suggest that a sufficiently high level of domestic R&D is a necessary condition for international competitiveness. This holds for both large and small countries, although some of the results indicate that very large countries may get more out of their R&D than other countries. It also holds for a whole range of industries, not only the very 'high-tech' industries that increasingly have come to be dominated by the USA and Japan. Second, specialization in technologically stagnant sectors may present a problem for future economic growth. Third, the competitive advantages of large and small countries differ. Hence, it would be a mistake for the small countries to use the specialization pattern of the large ones as a kind of yardstick of success.

REFERENCES

Deardorff, A.V. (1984), 'Testing Trade Theories', in R.W. Jones and P.B. Kennen (eds), *Handbook of International Economics*, Volume I, Amsterdam: North-Holland, pp. 467–518.

Dosi, G., K. Pavitt and L. Soete (1990), *The Economics of Technical Change and International Trade*, London: Harvester Wheatsheaf.

Dreze, J. (1961), 'The Standard Goods Hypothesis'. Reprinted in A. Jaquemin and A. Sapir (eds) (1989), *The European Internal Market: Trade and Competition. Selected Readings*, Oxford: Oxford University Press, pp. 13–32.

Grossman, G.M. and E. Helpman (1991), *Innovation and Growth in the Global Economy*, Cambridge, MA: MIT Press.

Gruber, W., D. Metha and R. Vernon (1967), 'The R&D Factor in International Trade', *Journal of Political Economy*, **75**, 20–37.

Hirsch, S. (1967), *Location of Industry and International Competitiveness*, Oxford: Clarendon Press.

Johnson, H.G. (1959), 'Economic Development and International Trade', *Nationaløkonomisk Tidskrift*, **97**, 253–72.

Jones, R.W. (1965), 'The Structure of Simple General Equilibrium Models', *Journal of Political Economy*, **73**, 557–72.

Krugman, P. (1990), *Rethinking International Trade*, Cambridge, MA: MIT Press.

Leamer, E.E. (1994), 'Testing Trade Theory', in D. Greenaway and L.A. Winters, *Surveys in International Trade*, Oxford: Blackwell, pp. 66–106.

Posner, M.V. (1961), 'International Trade and Technical Change', *Oxford Economic Papers*, **13**, 323–41.

Romer, P. (1990), 'Endogeneous Technological Change', *Journal of Political Economy*, **98**, S71–102.

Vernon, R. (1966), 'International Investment and International Trade in the Product Cycle', *Quarterly Journal of Economics*, **80**, 190–207.

1. Productivity growth and shifting comparative advantage on the industry level

Edward N. Wolff[*]

Dollar and Wolff (1993) analysed changes in both productivity levels, resource abundance, and export patterns for a sample of nine OECD countries covering the period from 1970 to 1986. We found strong evidence of convergence on the economy-wide level in GDP per worker, the capital–labour ratio, aggregate total factor productivity (TFP), and average real wages. We also examined the same variables for nine manufacturing sectors and found that, except for real wages, convergence at the industry level was generally not as strong as that for the economy as a whole. In fact, aggregate convergence in labour productivity, for example, was to some extent attributable to the modest labour-productivity leads that different countries enjoyed in different industries. The results are similar for TFP and capital intensity.

A further result of this development is that the export patterns of the industrial countries were not converging or becoming more similar. This result is consistent with our conclusion that specialization has continued at the industry level in the advanced industrial countries. Moreover, at least in the case of Japan and the USA, a clear relationship is evident between TFP growth at the industry level and changing comparative advantage. The industries in Japan with growing comparative advantage over this period tended to be those in which its TFP relative to the USA increased especially rapidly. We argued that TFP captures some influence that contributes to comparative advantage, and this factor is likely to be technology as disembodied knowledge, as embodied in machinery, or as reflected in skilled labour.

The present chapter will extend the time period to 1992 and the country coverage to 14 OECD countries. Moreover, it will employ regression analysis to examine the relationship between comparative advantage and relative technology levels to the full set of countries, rather than to bilateral comparisons as we did in our previous work. It will make use of the 1994 version of the OECD International Sectoral Database (ISDB). The focus will be on both revealed comparative advantage in terms of export shares and on total production shares by industry. The advantage of the ISDB is that it contains capital stock data, which allows computation of total factor productivity.

The results show that TFP is a powerful predictor of a country's share of total industry output (for the countries in the sample). It is also significantly related to industry export performance for the 1982–92 period but generally not for the 1970–82 period. The results also show that relative labour cost is generally negatively related to a country's export advantage and its relative share of total industry output for the 1970–82 period but is not significant for the 1982–92 period. Capital intensity does not appear to play an important role in either export performance or production shares.

The remainder of the chapter is organized in four parts. The next (Section 1) will consider guidance from trade theory and review previous research on this issue. Section 2 presents descriptive statistics on trade performance of OECD countries over the time period. In Section 3, I present regression results on the relation between export performance and technology indicators. Concluding remarks are made in the last part.

1   THEORETICAL CONSIDERATIONS

There appear to be four principal approaches used to explain why different countries will specialize in different industries with regard to trade patterns. The first is the Heckscher–Ohlin (HO) model with factor-price equalization theorem (or FPET). In this model, trade specialization is seen to depend on relative differences in factor abundance. The second is the technology gap model, whose central argument is that technical change originating in one country will induce trade during the period for which it takes other countries to imitate the new technology and catch up. The third emphasizes the role of increasing internal returns to scale, geographical externalities and history. In this approach, fortuitous circumstances combined with learning by doing are seen to play a major role in industrial specialization. The fourth is the product life-cycle model. The focus is on technology 'leap-frogging' and standard product life-cycle forces, in which new technology is eventually standardized and passes on to low-wage countries.

1.1   The Heckscher–Ohlin Model

In general, classical trade theory does not provide any clear predictions about the relationship between productivity and trade patterns in a world with many countries and many goods. The one exception to this statement is the HO model with factor-price equalization. That model makes very sharp predictions about cross-country patterns in labour and total factor productivity at the industry level: namely, that productivity should be the same in all countries. The results presented in Dollar and Wolff (1993, Chapter 3), however, demonstrate clearly that this unambiguous prediction is not borne out at all in data for developed countries in the post-war period. In general there is more variation in both labour and total factor productivity at the industry level than at aggregate levels, which conflicts with the predictions of factor-price equalization construct.

Leamer's classic (1984) empirical study of trade patterns for more than 100 economies found that actual patterns could be explained fairly well by an endowment-based model with ten factors, including capital, several types of natural resources and land, and three skill classes of labour. It should be noted, though, that in that study manufacturing was disaggregated into only four industry classifications. Furthermore, the model was considerably more successful at explaining trade in primary products than trade in manufactures. Those results are consistent with the argument that the broad pattern of exports – primary versus secondary goods, heavy versus light manufactures – can be explained by general factor endowments, but the *specific pattern of exports of manufactures at a more disaggregated level* depends on industry-specific factors captured in the TFP measure.

Other trade models, such as the HO model without factor-price equalization or the Ricardo–Viner (specific factors) model, generally do not yield clear testable implications about productivity or the other pertinent variables.[1] Nevertheless, they do provide a framework within which a number of general propositions can be explored. As noted, there has been a marked convergence of labour productivity, capital–labour ratios and TFP in the aggregate for developed economies in the postwar period. There has been a similar convergence at the industry level, though it is weaker for capital intensity than for labour productivity or TFP. An HO-type of model suggests that convergence in aggregate capital–labour ratios should be accompanied by a convergence in the trade patterns of these countries. On the other hand, our research on convergence of aggregate TFP suggests that this convergence may be the result of different countries developing relatively high levels of TFP in different industries. In that case there may be a growing *divergence* of trade patterns as different countries increasingly concentrate production and exports in different industries. In the next section, I examine the changing trade patterns among OECD countries to see whether there is any trend towards convergence or divergence.

In Section 3, I consider whether changing comparative advantage is related to the growth of TFP at the industry level. The theoretical justification for this examination is the idea that growth of TFP may be capturing an increase in some industry-specific factor, which should lead to a shift in production and exports towards that industry. Actually, it is growth of TFP in one country relative to other countries that is important here. If TFP in a particular industry is growing rapidly throughout the world, then this should have no effect on any one country's comparative advantage. On the other hand, if in that industry one country's TFP is growing rapidly relative to other countries, then we would expect that country's industry to become increasingly competitive and to expand its share of the world market.

It should also be noted that the convergence of factor prices at the industry level, found in Dollar and Wolff (1993), greatly strengthens the notion that TFP growth should be an important determinant of changing comparative advantage. Those results imply that among OECD countries differences in the cost of labour (and, to some extent, capital) were not important determinants of differences in unit costs by the 1980s. Given the similarity in factor prices, trends in relative TFP then become crucial determinants of cost competitiveness. In particular, increased relative TFP in a particular industry and country should translate into increased competitiveness and exports.[2]

It is also possible that converging factor prices, particularly in conjunction with decreasing barriers to trade, could lead to constant or even increasing specialization in an HO model. This would be the case if relative factor endowments remained different among countries. However, if relative factor endowments also converge over time, which has been the case with the aggregate capital–labour ratio among these countries, then we would also expect that trade patterns would become likewise more similar.[3]

1.2   The Technology Gap Model

The 'technology gap', or neo-Ricardian literature, provides another view of the source of trade specialization. The central notion is that technology gaps between countries will be a major source of trade flows. As originally articulated by Posner (1961), the argument is that technical change originating in one country will induce trade during the period for which it takes other countries to imitate the new technology and catch up.[4] As later argued by Fagerberg (1988b) and Dosi, Pavitt and Soete (1990), this type of approach emphasizes country differences in innovativeness as the basis for international trade flows. The former emphasizes both technological competitiveness and the 'ability to deliver' as measured by productive capacity, as the basis of both export and import flows. The latter argue that a dynamic relationship exists between 'early innovative leads, economies of scale, learning by doing, oligopolistic exploitation of these advantages, and international competitiveness' (p. 34).

Regression analysis conducted by Dosi, Pavitt and Soete (1990) on the industry level also strongly confirms the positive relation between export performance and innovative activity. In particular, a country's export share (of total OECD exports) for each industry was regressed on that country's share of total OECD patents in that industry over the 1963–77 period, as well as several other explanatory variables, for 40 manufacturing industries. With the exception of several resource-based industries and several in which patents are not a reliable indicator of innovative activity, the patenting variable proved to be a significant determinant of export share. Other variables that also proved generally significant are labour productivity (the ratio of output to employment) and capital intensity (the ratio of capital to employment), which Dosi, Pavitt and Soete interpret as a measure of the degree of mechanization of an industry.[5]

In later work, Verspagen and Wakelin (1993) investigated the relation between the trade balance by industry (industry exports less imports) and industry R&D intensity (the ratio of industry R&D expenditures to industry output) among a sample of nine OECD countries over the periods 1970–78 and 1980–88 for 22 manufacturing industries. They found a significant effect of R&D intensity on the industry trade balance in 11 of the 22 industries. Amable and Verspagen (1995), in a follow-up study of 18 manufacturing industries for five countries covering the period 1970 to 1991, reported that patents proved to be a significant determinant of export share in a majority of the sectors. Wage costs were significant in a third of the sectors, while investment played a role in only a few sectors.

In related work, Blomstrom, Lipsey and Ohlsson (1990) investigated bilateral trade patterns between Sweden and the USA between 1970 and 1986. They found that the US exports to Sweden generally came from high-tech, R&D-intensive industries, while Swedish exports to the USA were concentrated in machinery and transport equipment, which relied heavily on the expertise of Swedish engineers and the skilled manual workers available in the Swedish trades.

Other trade economists emphasize the role of relative unit labour costs in international competitiveness. If unit labour costs increase less in one country than a second, this will reduce the relative cost of its exports and increase the relative cost of the other's imports, thus causing the trade balance to move in its favour (see Fagerberg, 1988b, for further discussion). Fagerberg (1988b) finds that a country's relative unit labour costs are statistically significant as a determinant of a country's trade balance but that the effect is much weaker than that from technological variables. Dosi, Pavitt and Soete (1990) also find a much stronger effect of labour productivity than unit labour costs on exports of total manufacturing.

1.3 Increasing Internal Returns to Scale

A fourth group of models emphasizes the role of increasing internal returns to scale (IIRS) and learning by doing in the formation of comparative advantage. As developed by Krugman (1979, 1980), Helpman and Krugman (1985) and Grossman and Helpman (1991), this type of analysis suggests that it is the presence of economies of scale and/or high startup costs that allows different countries to achieve specialization in different products. The country that enters a new field or new product line first may be able to dominate that line by increasing production to the point at which its costs are so low that potential new competitors are unable to enter the field successfully (at least, without sufficient subsidies from their governments). Even more important is the accumulation of specialized knowledge that is acquired only by being in the industry. This may include knowledge of the details of production steps, as well as specialized skills that are mainly acquired on the job, knowledge of marketing channels, and a knowledgeable sales force that is known to customers. This process is also referred to as 'learning by doing', since the firm or country that first establishes an industry may be able to descend the cost curve by acquiring the expertise that comes through experience in making the product (see Arrow, 1962).

Which industries a country may specialize in may depend on history, and a variety of influences, some of them perhaps fortuitous (for an illuminating discussion of the process, see Krugman, 1991). Moreover, an important role can be played by the availability or unavailability of ancillary industries that can substantially facilitate a country's success in the production of some particular product or type of products. Geographical externalities may also play an important role, since once an industry is established in a country or place, there is a greater likelihood of suppliers and customers also specializing there. This approach suggests that leadership positions may persist for long periods of time, thus ensuring relatively stable industry comparative advantage over time.

1.4　The Product Life-Cycle Model

This model emphasizes standard product life-cycle forces and technology 'leap-frogging' as a source of comparative advantage. The argument, as originally formulated by Vernon (1966, 1979) and later developed by Nelson and Norman (1977), is that as a new technique becomes well established, it is often easily transferred to countries with lower labour costs. The creation of an industry usually entails high startup costs, the development of specialized processes, the training of labour for new skills, and so on. But once this technology is in place, there is constant pressure to routinize the technology so that it becomes cheaper to use. If it becomes routinized, then it may not have to rely on expensive, highly trained labour, or on special production processes to supply its inputs. As such, the costs of production gradually diminish over time. Once this stage is reached, the technology becomes relatively easy to transfer to countries where both skills and wages are lower. Since the imitator does not have to duplicate the original startup costs, the entry costs into the industry are much lower.

In this approach, relative labour costs play a key role in the determination of comparative advantage. Moreover, one would expect that revealed comparative advantage will change on a continuing basis over time as the high-cost countries shift their production into new technologies over time. On the surface, at least, it would seem that this model is more appropriate for explaining changing trade patterns *between* more- and less-developed countries than trade among developed countries alone.

2   CONVERGENCE OF TRADE PATTERNS?

In this section I investigate whether trade patterns of developed countries have tended towards convergence over the last two decades. I use the 1994 OECD International Sectoral Database (ISDB), available on diskettes. This source provides statistics on GDP, which is measured in 1985 US dollars; gross capital stock, also in 1985 US dollars; total employment; employee compensation; and exports and imports, expressed in current US dollars. Data on each of these variables are provided on the industry level – a total of 13 manufacturing industries. The ISDB data cover 14 OECD countries – Australia, Belgium, Canada, Denmark, Finland, France, Germany (West), Italy, Japan, the Netherlands, Norway, Sweden, the United Kingdom and the United States. The time period covered is 1970 to 1992.

In examining changes in trade patterns, I use Balassa's Revealed Comparative Advantage (RCA) measure (Balassa, 1965), which is given by

$$RCA_i^h = [X_i^h / \sum_h X_i^h] / [(\sum_i X_i^h) / (\sum_i \sum_h X_i^h)] \tag{1.1}$$

where X_i^h is country h's exports of good i.

The aggregation over h covers the 14 countries in the ISDB, and the aggregation over i covers the 13 manufacturing industries. Hence this measure takes as its benchmark (denominator) country h's share of total manufacturing exports for these 14 countries. The numerator is country h's share of product i exports for the 14 countries. An RCA above (below) 1 indicates that country h's share of the group's product i exports is higher (lower) than its share of total manufactured exports. By construction, some RCAs for a country will be greater than 1, while others will be less than 1 (unless the country has exactly the same share of every export market). This index indicates in which product lines a country's exports are concentrated, which is taken as a measure of revealed comparative advantage.

There is no ideal measure of comparative advantage. Net exports (exports less imports) are often employed; however, net exports change as a result not only of alterations in the pattern of trade, but also of fluctuations in the overall trade balance, which is basically a macroeconomic phenomenon and not indicative of comparative advantage. Hence I prefer the Balassa RCA measure, even though it focuses only on exports.

I calculated RCAs for the 14 countries and 13 industries and investigated what has happened to the cross-country dispersion in these measures. Table 1.1 shows the coefficient of variation among countries for each industry in 1970, 1976, 1982, 1988 and 1992. Industries are grouped on the basis of a somewhat arbitrary classification into 'low-tech' and 'high-tech' industries, on the basis of US R&D intensity by industry.

Table 1.1   Coefficients of variation in revealed comparative advantage (RCA) measures for 14 OECD countries and 14 manufacturing industries, 1970–1992[a]

	Coefficient of Variation Across 14 Countries				
Industry	1970	1976	1982	1988	1992
A. *Low-tech industries*					
1. Food, beverages, and tobacco	1.14	1.12	0.94	0.98	0.88
2. Textiles	0.61	0.60	0.67	0.76	0.79
3. Wood and wood products	1.33	1.02	0.95	0.91	0.85
4. Paper, printing and publishing	1.36	1.31	1.23	1.23	1.19
5. Other manufactured products	0.71	0.84	1.07	1.11	1.05
B. *High-tech industries*					
6. Chemicals	0.41	0.44	0.41	0.37	0.31
7. Non-metal mineral products	0.57	0.58	0.55	0.58	0.52
8. Basic metal products	0.61	0.56	0.65	0.75	0.69
9. Fabricated metal products, machinery, and equipment	0.35	0.33	0.36	0.35	0.31
a. Metal products, excluding machinery and equipment	0.24	0.24	0.23	0.27	0.29
b. Agricultural and industrial machinery	0.52	0.44	0.43	0.40	0.36
c. Office and data processing equipment, precision and optical equipment	0.64	0.56	0.57	0.54	0.47
d. Electrical goods	0.50	0.49	0.54	0.57	0.48
e. Transport equipment	0.46	0.48	0.53	0.52	0.47

Note: a.   The coefficient of variation is defined as the ratio of the standard deviation to the (unweighted) mean.

There is no clear trend over this period: between 1970 and 1992 dispersion increased in five industries and decreased in eight industries (excluding Industry 9, which is a conglomerate of 5 sub-industries). Furthermore, there is no important difference between low-tech and high-tech industries. Among the former, for instance, variation in RCAs declined in food and wood products but increased in textiles. Among the latter, dispersion increased in basic metal products and metal products but decreased in chemicals and office and data-processing equipment.

This result is somewhat surprising in the light of the evidence that aggregate measures of factor endowments (such as the capital–labour ratio for the whole economy) have become more similar in these advanced economies. On the other hand, the result is consistent with the finding that dispersion of TFP at the industry level remains high, and that there has been no strong trend towards cross-country convergence of industry-level TFP since the mid-1970s. It appears that countries are developing specializations in different industries; in this way convergence of aggregate TFP can be consistent with continuing divergence of industry-level TFP and a continuing high dispersion in export patterns.

Table 1.2   Revealed comparative advantage in manufacturing industries by country, 1992

	Highest RCAs	Lowest RCAs
Australia	Food, beverages and tobacco 4.45	Wood and wood products 0.13
Belgium	Other manufacturing 4.03 Basic metal products 1.80	Agricult. and indust. mach. 0.41
Canada	Wood and wood products 4.08	Textiles 0.22
Denmark	Food, beverages and tobacco 3.71	Other manufacturing 0.33 Transport equipment 0.37
Finland	Paper, printing and publishing 8.02	Food, beverages and tobacco 0.30
France	Food, beverages and tobacco 1.61	Wood and wood products 0.67
Germany	Metal products, exc. equip. l.26	Food, beverages and tobacco 0.69
Italy	Textiles 3.42	Office and precision equip. 0.56
Japan	Electrical goods 1.92	Food, beverages and tobacco 0.07
Netherlands	Food, beverages and tobacco 2.74	Transport equipment 0.35
Norway	Basic metal products 3.60	Other manufacturing 0.24 Textiles 0.28
Sweden	Paper, printing and publishing 3.79	Food, beverages and tobacco 0.25
United Kingdom	Other manufacturing 1.75 Chemicals 1.27	Wood and wood products 0.33
United States	Office and precision equipment 1.33	Basic metal products 0.48

To examine this latter idea, Table 1.2 lists for each country in 1992 the industries with the highest and lowest RCAs. By construction, if the RCA for industry i is high in one country, it has to be low somewhere else. But there is no algebraic constraint on two or three countries having similar RCAs. Inspection of this table indicates that these countries have exports that are generally concentrated in different industries and that the countries also differ in industries which have low values for RCA.

The absolute size of the RCAs is also of interest; small differences in trade patterns would be indicated by RCAs that deviate little from 1. In Table 1.2, however, there are quite a few in the 2–8 range, indicating very substantial specialization. The smaller economies, in particular, appear to be highly specialized in their exports. The high degree of specialization for the relatively small economies suggests that economies of scale may be important, either in direct production, or, more likely, in development of the specific capabilities such as knowledge and skilled labour needed to produce particular manufactures. It is also noteworthy that among the smaller economies, the industries of chief specialization tend to be resource based – particularly, wood products, paper and food products.

It is also striking that most countries retain their trade specialization over time. Table 1.3 shows correlation coefficients of RCAs by industry between 1970 and 1982, and between 1970 and 1992. With only a few exceptions, these correlations remain very high over time. Between 1970 and 1982, the correlation coefficients are 0.90, or greater for 11 of the 14 countries; and between 1970 and 1992, they exceed 0.80 for 11 of the 14 countries. The three exceptions are Germany, Japan and Belgium (though even among them, the correlations exceed 0.60).

Perhaps a better indicator of specialization is the share of the total production of a given commodity made in an individual country. We can define a measure of 'Revealed Production Advantage' (RPA), in analogous fashion to RCA, as:

$$RPA_i^h = [Y_i^h / \sum_h Y_i^h] [(\sum_i Y_i^h) / (\sum_i \sum_h Y_i^h)] \qquad (1.2)$$

where Y_i^h is country h's output (in 1985 US dollars) of good i. The numerator of RPA indicates country h's share of the total production of industry i, while the denominator measures country h's share of total manufacturing output for these 14 countries. As for RCA, an RPA above 1 indicates that country h's share of output i is higher than its share of total manufacturing output, and conversely. This index indicates in which manufacturing industries a country's output is concentrated.

Correlations over time in RPA by industry within country are also shown in Table 1.3. The stability in industries of specialization by country is again striking. Between 1970 and 1982, the correlation coefficients are 0.89 or greater for 11 of the 12 countries (all except Belgium); and between 1970 and 1992, they exceed 0.80 for 10 of the 12 countries (all except Belgium and the UK). For Belgium, the correlations exceed 0.70 in both years. The major outlier is the United Kingdom, for which the correlation coefficient for 1970 and 1992 RCAs is only 0.48. It is also interesting that for Germany and Japan, their RPAs are more stable over time than their RCAs.[6] For the UK, the opposite is the case for the 1970–92 period (and also for the 1980–92 period alone), suggesting a major restructuring of UK manufactures over the 1980s.

Table 1.3 *Correlation over time in revealed comparative advantage (RCA) and revealed production advantage (RPA) in manufacturing industries by country, 1970–1982 and 1970–1992*[a]

Country	Revealed Comparative Advantage (RCA)		Revealed Production Advantage (RPA)	
	1970–1982	1970–1992	1970–1982	1970–1992
Australia	0.90	0.83	NA	NA
Belgium	0.68	0.70	0.76	0.74
Canada	0.99	0.98	0.98[b]	0.92[b]
Denmark	0.95	0.88	0.90	0.79
Finland	0.98	0.90	0.97[b]	0.91[b]
France	0.95	0.90	0.91	0.84
Germany	0.79	0.74	0.89	0.83
Italy	0.90	0.88	0.99[b]	0.98[b]
Japan	0.79	0.64	0.98[c]	0.95[c]
Netherlands	0.94	0.94	NA	NA
Norway	0.98	0.86	0.96[b]	0.86[b]
Sweden	1.00	0.98	0.97[b]	0.95[b]
United Kingdom	0.94	0.89	0.91[d]	0.48[d]
United States	0.90	0.86	0.97	0.92

Notes
a. Correlations are based on 13 industries unless otherwise indicated.
b. Correlations are based on 9 industries: (1) wood, beverages and tobacco; (2) textiles; (3) wood and wood products; (4) paper, printing and publishing; (5) other manufactured products; (6) chemicals; (7) non-metal mineral products; (8) basic metal products; and (9) fabricated metal products, machinery and equipment.
c. Correlations are based on 8 industries: all industries listed in note b except wood and wood products.
d. All industries except wood and wood products.

The general stability in industries of specialization over time would tend to support both the IIRS and technology gap models and contradict the FPET and life-cycle models. The IIRS model stresses the advantages of initial leadership in an industry and the consequent cost reduction emanating from increased production volume. The technology gap model also emphasizes the role of early technological leadership in an industry and the consequent advantages this gives the industry in keeping on the technological frontier.

In contrast, the FPET would predict that specialization among the advanced countries would become less marked over time as their relative factor abundance converged. The coefficient of variation in the overall capital–labour ratio among these 14 countries fell from 0.28 in 1970 to 0.19 in 1982 and 0.17 in 1992. Despite the growing similarity in relative factor abundance, these countries tended to maintain specialization in the same industries in 1992 as in 1970. The life-cycle model, moreover, would suggest that as technologies matured over time, the more advanced countries would switch their industries of specialization away from those with matured product lines to those characterized by startup technologies. The results of Table 1.3 indicate very little switching of specialization, though it should be noted that the 13-industry classification is still highly aggregated.

3 CHANGES IN COMPARATIVE ADVANTAGE AND RELATIVE PRODUCTIVITY GROWTH

The last question to address is whether changes in comparative advantage can be linked to productivity growth at the industry level. This is not an easy question to formalize, in that the productivity growth of a particular industry in a particular country should be considered relative to the same industry in other countries and to other industries within the same country. In other words, rapid TFP growth may have no effect on comparative advantage if it is occurring in the same industry in every country. At the same time, rapid TFP growth in every industry of one country should also have little effect on comparative advantage, since it would not enhance the competitiveness of any industry relative to other industries in the economy.

We now turn to regression analysis to provide a formal analysis of these relations. Let us first define TFP (π) as:

$$\mathrm{Ln}\pi_i^h = \mathrm{Ln}Y_i^h - \bar{\alpha}_i\,\mathrm{Ln}L_i^h - (1 - \bar{\alpha}_i)\mathrm{Ln}K_i^h \qquad (1.3)$$

where Y_i^h is the total output of industry i in country h, L_i^h is labour input, K_i^h is capital input, and $\bar{\alpha}_i$ is the international average wage share for industry i. Two estimating forms are used. The first is:

$$DLNRCA_i^h = b_0 + b_1 \cdot DTFPAVE_i^h + b_2 \cdot DWAGAVE_i^h$$
$$+ b_3 \cdot DKLAVE_i^h + \epsilon_i^h. \qquad (1.4)$$

$DLNRCA_i^h$ is the change in the natural logarithm of industry i's revealed comparative advantage in country h. $DTFPAVE_i^h = \Delta(Ln\pi_i^h) - \Delta(Ln\bar{\pi}_i)$ is the log change (percentage growth) in industry i's TFP in country h relative to the log change in the average TFP in industry i of the 14 OECD countries in the sample. Likewise, $DWAGAVE_i^h = \Delta(Lnw_i^h) - \Delta(Ln\bar{w}_i)$, where w_i^h is the average wage (in 1985 US dollars) in industry i in country h and $\bar{w}_i$ is the average wage in industry i among the 14 countries, and $DKLAVE_i^h = \Delta(Lnk_i^h) - \Delta(Ln\bar{k}_i)$, where $k_i^h \equiv K_i^h/L_i^h$, the ratio of the capital stock to labour in industry i in country h, and $\bar{k}_i$ is the average capital to labour ratio in industry i among the 14 countries. The term ϵ_i^h is a stochastic error term, which is assumed to be independently and identically distributed.[7]

The coefficient b_1 is predicted to have a positive sign. The coefficient b_2 is predicted to have a negative sign, since higher labour costs in a country should reduce that country's competitiveness and hence export share. The coefficient of DKLAVE is predicted to have a positive sign, since increasing capital intensity should be associated with a greater degree of mechanization of an industry, and therefore with lower costs and greater competitiveness.

The second form is:

$$DLNRCA_i^h = b_0 + b_1 \cdot DRELTFP_i^h + b_2 \cdot DRELWAG_i^h$$
$$+ b_3 \, DRELKL_i^h + \epsilon_i^h. \qquad (1.5)$$

$DRELTFP_i^h = DTFPAVE_i^h - (DTFPMFG^h - DTFPMAVE)$, where $DTFPMFG^h - DTFPMAVE$ is the log change in TFP in total manufacturing in country h ($DTFPMFG^h$) relative to the log change in the average TFP of total manufacturing in the 14 countries in the sample (DTFPMAVE). $DRELTFP_i^h$ thus shows how an industry's productivity performance in a given country relative to the average productivity performance of that industry compares to the country's overall productivity performance in total manufacturing relative to the average performance in total manufacturing. The variables $DRELWAG_i^h$ and $DRELKL_i^h$ are defined in like fashion. The second form is the preferred specification since it accords more closely to the underlying theory. The predictions for the coefficients b_1, b_2 and b_3 are the same as for the first specification. In addition to export performance, I also use the RPA_i^h, which measures country h's output share of industry i relative to country h's share of total manufacturing output, as a dependent variable in the two specifications.

I use the first difference form for two reasons. First, the technology gap model, as well as our previous work (Dollar and Wolff, 1993), suggests that changes

Table 1.4 Regressions of the change in RCA and RPA on the growth in TFP, wages and capital intensity relative to the industry average[a]

Dependent Variable	Constant	DTFPAVE	DWAGAVE	DKLAVE	R^2	Adj. R^2	Std Error	Sample Size
A. 1970–1982 Period								
DLNRCA	0.050	0.41*	−0.64**		0.09	0.07	0.28	102
	(1.73)	(2.30)	(2.94)					
DLNRCA	0.050	0.26	−0.49*	−0.22	0.11	0.08	0.28	102
	(1.87)	(1.32)	(2.13)	(1.64)				
DLNRPA	−0.012	0.62**	−0.51**		0.33	0.32	0.14	102
	(0.83)	(6.87)	(4.68)					
DLNRPA	−0.011	0.61**	−0.50**	−0.02	0.33	0.31	0.14	102
	(0.80)	(5.96)	(4.20)	(0.28)				
B. 1982–1992 Period								
DLNRCA	0.011	0.24*	−0.13		0.06	0.04	0.17	102
	(0.66)	(2.58)	(0.71)					
DLNRCA	0.011	0.23*	−0.11	−0.02	0.06	0.04	0.17	102
	(0.62)	(2.39)	(0.50)	(0.20)				
DLNRPA	0.049**	0.60**	−0.11		0.39	0.37	0.14	102
	(3.51)	(7.92)	(0.74)					
DLNRPA	0.048**	0.58**	−0.06	−0.05	0.39	0.37	0.14	102
	(3.40)	(7.38)	(0.34)	(0.58)				

Note: a. *t*-ratios are shown in parentheses below the coefficient estimate. All variables are computed from the OECD ISDB, 1994 version.

Key

$DLNRCA_i^h$ change in the logarithm of RCA of industry i in country h.

$DLNRPA_i^h$ change in the logarithm of RPA of industry i in country h.

$DTFPAVE_i^h$ change in the logarithm of TFP of industry i in country h minus the change in the logarithm of the 14-nation average TFP in industry i.

$DWAGAVE_i^h$ change in the logarithm of wages of industry i in country h minus the change in the logarithm of the 14-nation average wages in industry i.

$DKLAVE_i^h$ change in the logarithm of K/L of industry i in country h minus the change in the logarithm of the 14-nation average K/L in industry i.

*   Significant at the 5 per cent level (2-tailed test).

**   Significant at the 1 per cent level (2-tailed test).

in export performance may be more directly related to changes in relative technology indicators than levels of export performance are to technology levels. Second, there is strong reason to believe that export performance is highly dependent on historical developments in a country, as well as its resource base. The levels equation can thus be interpreted as a fixed effect model, and first differencing allows us to remove the unobservables from the equation.[8] The logarithmic form is used for the two dependent variables, RCA and RPA,

Table 1.5   *Regressions of the change in RCA and RPA on the growth in TFP,*
              wages and capital intensity relative to industry and country averages[a]

Dependent Variable	Constant	DRELTFP	DRELWAG	DRELKL	R^2	Adj. R^2	Std Error	Sample Size
A. 1970–1982 Period								
DLNRCA	0.043	0.27	−0.32		0.02	0.00	0.29	102
	(1.34)	(1.26)	(0.89)					
DLNRCA	0.042	0.28	−0.33	−0.03	0.02	0.00	0.29	102
	(1.28)	(1.25)	(0.89)	(0.14)				
DLNRPA	−0.022	0.91**	−0.49**		0.53	0.52	0.12	102
	(1.71)	(10.47)	(3.30)					
DLNRPA	−0.015	0.84**	−0.48**	−0.22*	0.57	0.56	0.11	102
	(1.14)	(9.77)	(3.41)	(2.19)				
B. 1982–1992 Period								
DLNRCA	0.014	0.31**	−0.12		0.09	0.07	0.17	102
	(0.80)	(3.15)	(0.40)					
DLNRCA	0.013	0.32**	−0.18	0.05	0.09	0.07	0.17	102
	(0.78)	(3.12)	(0.54)	(0.42)				
DLNRPA	0.056**	0.78**	−0.18		0.60	0.59	0.11	102
	(4.81)	(11.88)	(0.93)					
DLNRPA	0.056**	0.77**	−0.15	−0.03	0.60	0.58	0.14	102
	(4.81)	(11.19)	(0.69)	(0.34)				

Note: a.   *t*-ratios are shown in parentheses below the coefficient estimate. All variables are computed from the OECD ISDB, 1994 version.

Key
$DLNRCA_i^h$ change in the logarithm of RCA of industry i in country h.
$DLNRPA_i^h$ change in the logarithm of RPA of industry i in country h.
$DRELTFP_i^h$ $DTFPAVE_i^h$ relative to the log change of manufacturing TFP in country h minus the log change of the 14-nation average manufacturing TFP.
$DRELWAG_i^h$ $DWAGAVE_i^h$ relative to the log change of manufacturing wages in country h minus the log change of the 14-nation average manufacturing wages.
$DRELKL_i^h$ $DKLAVE_i^h$ relative to the log change of manufacturing K/L in country h minus the log change of the 14-nation average manufacturing K/L.
*   Significant at the 5 per cent level (2-tailed test),
**   Significant at the 1 per cent level (2-tailed test).

because the variables, by construction, are highly skewed, with a range from zero to infinity. The logarithm form, on the other hand, is more normally distributed.[9]

Regressions are run separately for the 1970–82 period and the 1982–92 period. Results for equation (1.4) are shown in Table 1.4 and those for equation (1.5) in Table 1.5. The relation between the change in industry RCA (DLNRCA) and the relative growth in industry TFP is positive but statistically significant in only one of the four cases for the 1970–82 period but positive and significant in all four cases for the 1982–92 period. For the latter period, the estimated coefficient of DTFPAVE (industry TFP growth relative to the international industry average) is significant at the 5 per cent level while the estimated coefficient of DRELTFP (DTFPAVE relative to the difference between the TFP performance of total manufacturing in the country and the average of all countries) is significant at the 1 per cent level.

Relative wage growth has the predicted negative sign in all cases. For the 1970–82 period, DWAGAVE is statistically significant (at the 5 per cent level in one case and at the 1 per cent level in the others), whereas DRELWAG is not significant. For the 1982–92 period, none of the wage variables is significant. The relative change in capital intensity is not significant in any case.

The results are more powerful for the change in RPA, the relative share of total production by industry. The estimated coefficients of the relative growth in TFP are all positive and significant at the one per cent level. The estimated coefficients of the relative change in industry wages are negative in all cases, significant at the one per cent level in all four cases for the 1970–82 period but not significant in any case for the 1982–92 period. Relative growth in the capital–labour ratio is significant in only one case (at the 5 per cent level) but its estimated coefficient is negative, not positive as predicted.

In the DLNRCA regressions for the 1970–82 period, the goodness of fit, as measured by the adjusted-R^2 statistic, is of the order of 0.08 for equation (1.4) (based on relative industry performance alone) and 0.0 for equation (1.5) (based on relative industry performance relative to total manufacturing performance). For those covering the 1982–92 period, the adjusted R^2 is 0.04 for equation (1.4) and 0.07 for equation (1.5). The relative industry performance variables provide more explanatory power for the earlier period while the variables measuring industry performance relative to both average industry and total manufacturing performance provide a somewhat better fit for the later one.

In contrast, for the DLNRPA regressions, the fit is uniformly superior for the forms using equation (1.5) than those using equation (1.4). The adjusted-R^2 statistic ranges from 0.52 to 0.60 for the former and from 0.31 to 0.37 for the latter.

It is also of note that the explanatory power of the model is substantially higher for relative production shares than relative export performance. This might be expected since, as is evident from Table 1.3, the former are generally more stable over time than the latter (with the notable exception of the UK). There are three likely explanations for the greater volatility of RCA over time than RPA. First, changes in tariffs and other trade barriers will affect movements in exports much more than in total production. Second, exchange-rate fluctuations will likewise have a much larger impact on changes in RCA than in RPA. Third, macroeconomic conditions, particularly business cycles, will exert more influence on imports than GDP and affect RCA more than RPA. As a result, it is likely that RPA is more closely associated with long-term comparative advantage as reflected in TFP than is RCA. Since regressions are in first differences, the goodness of fit should be markedly better for DLNRPA than for DLNRCA.

4   CONCLUDING REMARKS

The regression results generally support the central thesis of the chapter that there is a positive and significant relation between both export performance and relative industry production on the one hand and relative TFP performance on the other. The results are much stronger for production shares. Changes in industry production shares, as measured by RPA, are strongly related to the industry's relative TFP growth. Relative TFP performance is also significantly associated with the industry's change in RCA for the 1982–92 period but generally not for the 1970–82 period. The overall fit of these regressions is relatively low (less than 10 per cent). In previous work of mine (Wolff, 1995), I found much stronger relations between export performance and productivity at the aggregate level (R^2 ranging from 0.5 to 0.9), suggesting that TFP performance may have more to do with the general success of a country's exports than changes in *comparative advantage* at the industry level.

The results also show that relative labour costs are generally negatively related to a country's export advantage and its relative share of total industry output for the 1970–82 period but is not significant for the 1982–92 period. These results are consistent with those reported in Dollar and Wolff (1993), which found very strong convergence in industry wages among OECD countries by the early 1980s. Those results imply that among these countries differences in labour costs were not important determinants of differences in unit costs by the 1980s. Capital intensity does not appear to play an important role in either export performance or production shares. Amable and Verspagen (1995) report similar findings for industry investment.

The fact that TFP changes are generally significantly related to changes in specialization does support the view that TFP growth encapsulates the expansion of industry-specific productive factors that contribute, at least to some degree, to comparative advantage. Moreover, this analysis redirects attention to the determinants of high levels of TFP. To the extent that it reflects technology-related assets owned by the firm or embodied in technical labour, clearly investment in research and development and training of skilled labour are important ingredients for promoting rapid TFP growth. Furthermore, if many of these assets really are industry specific, then it is likely that past history, as well as past and current government policy, will have a major effect on the kinds of assets developed, and consequently on the industries that emerge as major exporters.

For instance, US concentration of R&D on military-related industries clearly is a major explanation of US comparative advantage in aircraft, large-scale computers, and advanced telecommunications. Japanese industrial policy, on the other hand, has targeted R&D at advanced consumer products, such as automobiles and consumer electronics. Past history is also important in certain industries: large German and US firms that got into the chemical industry early on continue to devote substantial resources to R&D in this industry and to maintain relatively high TFP.

NOTES

*   The author is professor of economics at New York University. I would like to thank the C.V. Starr Center for Applied Economics at NYU and the Alfred P. Sloan Foundation for their support of the research reported herein. An earlier draft was presented at the Conference on 'Technology and International Trade', Leangkollen, Norway, in October 1995. I would like to thank those present for their comments, particularly Tor Jakob Klette.

1.   See, for example, Leamer (1984) for a discussion of these models.

2.   Nakamura's (1989) study of Japan, Germany, and the US also found that by the late 1970s input prices were quite similar among these three countries, so that the 'relative TFP level has become the principal determinant of sectoral cost advantage and disadvantage among the three countries' (p. 713).

3.   I thank Pär Hansson and Lars Lundberg for this point.

4.   Freeman (1963) and Hufbauer (1966) also make similar arguments to this effect.

5.   Also, see Fagerberg (1988a) for related empirical analysis.

6.   However, in the case of Japan it should be noted that the RPA calculation is based on only eight industries, whereas the RCA calculation is based on 13. A smaller number of industries would tend to lead to more stability in the measure.

7.   I also assumed that the ϵ_{jt} are independently distributed but may not be identically distributed. For the regressions reported in tables 1.4 and 1.5 below, I also re-estimated them using the White procedure for a heteroscedasticity-consistent covariance matrix, with very similar results (results not shown).

8.   Relative TFP growth rates may provide a superior indicator of changing comparative advantage than relative TFP levels for two additional reasons. First, comparing TFP levels across countries is sensitive to the choice of price deflators and PPP exchange rates and the assumptions of service lives used to construct the capital stock estimates. If there are biases in the TFP-level estimates, there is a good chance that these biases are relatively stable over time, so that relative TFP growth rates are more likely to be accurately measured than relative TFP levels. A second reason is that other factors, such as trade restrictions, clearly influence the composition of trade. Again, if these factors are relatively stable over time, there may be a stronger relationship between relative TFP growth and changing RCAs than between relative levels at a point in time.

9.   I would like to thank Tor Jakob Klette for pointing this out to me.

REFERENCES

Amable, B. and B. Verspagen (1995), 'The Role of Technology in Market Share Dynamics', *Applied Economics*, **27**, 197–204.

Arrow, K. (1962), 'The Economic Implications of Learning by Doing', *Review of Economic Studies*, **29** (2), 155–73.

Balassa, B.(1965), 'Trade Liberalization and "Revealed" Comparative Advantage', *The Manchester School*, **33**, May, 99–123.

Blomstrom, M., R. Lipsey and L. Ohlsson (1990), 'What do Rich Countries Trade with Each Other? R&D and the Composition of U.S. and Swedish Trade', *Banco Nazionale del Lavoro Quarterly Review*, **173**, June, 215–35.

Dollar, D. and E.N. Wolff (1993), *Competitiveness Convergence and International Specialization*, Cambridge, MA: MIT Press.

Dosi, G., K. Pavitt and L. Soete (1990), *The Economics of Technical Change and International Trade*, London: Harvester Wheatsheaf.

Fagerberg, J.E. (1988a), 'Technology, Growth and Trade: Schumpeterian Perspectives', D.Phil. Thesis, University of Sussex, UK.

Fagerberg, J.E. (1988b), 'International Competitiveness', *Economic Journal*, **98**, June, 355–74.

Freeman, C. (1963), 'The Plastics Industry: A Comparative Study of Research and Innovation', *National Institute Economic Review*, No. 26.

Grossman, G.M. and E. Helpman (1991), *Innovation and Growth in the Global Economy*, Cambridge, MA: MIT Press.

Helpman, E. and P.R. Krugman (1985), *Market Structure and Foreign Trade*, Cambridge, MA: MIT Press.

Hufbauer, G.C. (1966), *Synthetic Materials and International Trade*, London: Duckworth.

Krugman, P.R. (1979), 'Increasing Returns, Monopolistic Competition, and International Trade', *Journal of International Economics*, **9**, 469–79.

Krugman, P.R. (1980), 'Scale Economies, Product Differentiation, and the Patterns of Trade', *American Economic Review*, **70** (5), December, 950–59.

Krugman, P.R. (1991), 'History Versus Expectations', *Quarterly Journal of Economics*, **106**, May, 651–67.

Leamer, E. (1984), *Sources of International Comparative Advantage*, Cambridge, MA: MIT Press.

Nakamura, S. (1989), 'Productivity and Factor Prices as Sources of Differences in Production Costs between Germany, Japan, and the U.S.', *Economic Studies Quarterly*, **40**, March 701–15.

Nelson, R.R. and V.D. Norman (1977), 'Technological Change and Factor Mix over the Product Cycle: A Model of Dynamic Comparative Advantage', *Journal of Development Economics*, **4**, 3–24.

Posner, M. (1961), 'International Trade and Technical Change', *Oxford Economic Papers*, **13** (3), October, 323–41.

Vernon, R. (1966), 'International Investment and International Trade in the Product Cycle', *Quarterly Journal of Economics*, **80**, 190–207.

Vernon, R. (1979), 'The Product-Cycle Hypothesis in a New International Environment', *Oxford Bulletin of Economics and Statistics*, **41**.

Verspagen, B. and K. Wakelin (1993), 'International Competitiveness and its Determinants', MERIT Working Paper 93–008, Maastricht, Netherlands.

Wolff, E.N. (1995), 'Technological Change, Capital Accumulation, and Changing Trade Patterns Over the Long Term', *Structural Change and Economic Dynamics*, **6** (1), March, 43–70.

2. Technical progress, capital accumulation and changing international competitiveness*

Patrik Gustavsson, Pär Hansson and Lars Lundberg

1 INTRODUCTION

This chapter attempts to evaluate the role of differences in rates of resource accumulation between countries and different rates of technical progress as determinants of changes in the industrial patterns of comparative advantage, international competitiveness and specialization within manufacturing among OECD countries. Thus we attempt to combine two paradigms from trade theory, namely the technology or Ricardian view, and the factor proportions or Heckscher–Ohlin[1] explanations of changes in trade patterns.

Within the large empirical literature on the determinants of patterns of comparative advantage and specialization (for surveys, see Deardorff, 1984 and Leamer, 1994), the main part analyses only the role of factor endowments. The factor proportion paradigm clearly cannot give a satisfactory explanation of *all* trade. In particular, it is not well suited for explaining intra-industry trade. Opinions on the value of factor endowments for explaining trade patterns are far from unanimous. While some authors argue that a generalized factor proportions model 'seems to have stood up remarkably well to empirical scrutiny' (Deardorff, 1984) and that it gives 'a surprisingly good explanation of the main features of the trade data in terms of a relatively brief list of resource endowments' (Leamer, 1984), others maintain that 'the empirical validity of the endowment based theory of trade remains ... very much subject to debate' (Dosi, Pavitt and Soete, 1990).

The technology factor has been introduced into the empirical analysis of comparative advantage in various ways. Early studies used relative labour productivity data (MacDougall, 1951, 1952) to explain countries' specialization according to the Ricardian model. Other studies found R&D intensity, in addition to a set of factor-proportion variables, to be positively related to US export performance (Gruber, Metha and Vernon, 1967; Stern and Maskus,

1981). Variables such as product age or income elasticity have also been used (Wells, 1969; Hufbauer, 1970; Finger, 1975) as a proxy for various aspects of technology.

Introducing R&D intensity as a product or industry characteristic implies that R&D capacity is treated as just another resource (Dosi, Pavitt and Soete, 1990). A different approach is to express competitiveness in terms of *relative* R&D intensity (Hughes, 1986; Lundberg, 1988). While R&D measures the input of resources in the production of new knowledge, patents may be a proxy for the output. Dosi, Pavitt and Soete (1990) found that countries' share of the number of patents in a product group was positively related to export shares. In a study by Amable and Verspagen (1995) changes in bilateral market shares among OECD countries were found to be positively related to relative (bilateral) R&D as well as to the relative number of patents.

According to Deardorff (1984), the technology paradigm has 'identified an important set of variables that can help to explain trade'. A reasonable point of departure for an empirical study would be that *both* technology and factor proportions are likely to be important determinants of trade patterns, and therefore that both should be included in the set of explanatory variables. In this chapter we will focus on total factor productivity as a measure of technology. Before proceeding to the empirical tests, however, we believe that it is necessary to specify exactly how these concepts are related to competitiveness and how they should be measured. In Section 2 we develop a simple model that leads to a set of testable hypotheses and regressions formulated in Section 3, which also contains a presentation of the data. The results are reported in Section 4, and Section 5 concludes.

2 PRODUCTIVITY, FACTOR PROPORTIONS AND INTERNATIONAL SPECIALIZATION: THE BASIC MODEL

2.1 Factor Prices, Costs and Goods Prices

Assume n traded goods, $i = 1, ..., n$, each produced by N_{ij} firms, $h = 1, ..., N_{ij}$, in each of M countries, $j = 1, ..., M$, with m factors of production, $k = 1, ..., m$, which are perfectly mobile between sectors but immobile between countries. For the case of Cobb–Douglas technology, the production function of firm h in industry i and country j may be written as

$$q_{hij} = A_{ij} \prod_{k=1}^{m} x_{khij}^{\alpha_{ki}} \qquad (2.1a)$$

where constant returns to scale implies that

$$\sum_{k=1}^{m}\alpha_{ki}=1$$

If all firms in industry i, country j are assumed to be identical, we may write the aggregate production function for the i'th industry in country j as

$$q_{ij}=A_{ij}\prod_{k=1}^{m}x_{kij}^{\alpha_{ki}} \qquad (2.1b)$$

where q_{ij} is the output, and x_{kij} the amount of factor k used in the i'th industry in country j. Technology in a particular industry is the same for all firms in a certain country and differs across countries only with a shift factor A_{ij} that corresponds to Hicks-neutral technical change. Factor shares α_{ki} are the same.

For the case of constant returns to scale and perfectly competitive factor markets, we derive the cost function dual of the Cobb–Douglas function by cost minimization:[2]

$$Z_{ij}(w,q)=A_{ij}^{-1}\prod_{k=1}^{m}\alpha_{ki}^{-\alpha_{ki}}w_{kj}^{\alpha_{ki}}q_{ij} \qquad (2.2a)$$

where w_{kj} is the price of factor k in country j.

Let us now introduce economies of scale at the firm level and abandon the assumption of perfect competition. If the production function is assumed to be homothetic, we may write the unit cost function[3] as

$$c(w,q_{hij})=A_{ij}^{-1}q_{hij}^{-\varepsilon_i}\prod_{k=1}^{m}\alpha_{ki}^{-\alpha_{ki}}w_{kj}^{\alpha_{ki}} \qquad (2.2b)$$

where ε_i is a measure of scale economies in the i'th industry (we assume $\varepsilon_i > 0$).

Perfect competition in the product market ensures that prices equal unit costs. However, this result will also hold for the case of monopolistic competition with free entry:

$$p_{ij}=c_{ij}(w,q_{hij})=G_iA_{ij}^{-1}q_{hij}^{-\varepsilon_i}w_{mj}\prod_{k=1}^{m-1}\left(\frac{w_{kj}}{w_{mj}}\right)^{\alpha_{ki}}=G_iA_{ij}^{-1}q_{hij}^{-\varepsilon_i}w_{mj}\prod_{k=1}^{m-1}\omega_{kj}^{\alpha_{ki}} \qquad (2.3)$$

where

$$G_i = \prod_{k=1}^{m} \alpha_{ki}^{-\alpha_{ki}}$$

and ω_{kj} is the relative price of factor k in terms of factor m.

Consider now a particular country j versus the rest of the world w. Assume that factor prices are not equalized and that there are no transport costs. The unit cost, and thus the price in all markets, for the i'th good produced in j, relative to the cost and price of the same good produced in the rest of the world, will then be

$$\frac{p_{ij}}{p_{iw}} = \frac{w_{mj}}{w_{mw}} \frac{A_{iw}}{A_{ij}} \frac{q_{hiw}^{-\varepsilon_i}}{q_{hij}^{-\varepsilon_i}} \prod_{k=1}^{m-1} \left(\frac{\omega_{kj}}{\omega_{kw}} \right)^{\alpha_{ki}} \tag{2.4}$$

Let us choose the average world market unit cost and price for the i'th product, average world technology, average firm size and the average world factor price ratios as standards of reference. We define

$$\xi_{ij} = \frac{p_{ij}}{p_{iw}} \qquad T_{ij} = \frac{A_{ij}}{A_{iw}} \qquad W_{kj} = \frac{\omega_{kj}}{\omega_{kw}} \qquad \phi_{ij} = \frac{q_{hij}}{q_{hiw}}$$

as the relative price of the i'th good produced in country j, the productivity advantage (disadvantage) of country j in the i'th industry, the relative price of factor k in country j and the relative firm size in the i'th industry in country j. The price of the products of all firms in the i'th industry in country j, relative to the price charged by foreign firms in the same industry, is then

$$\xi_{ij} = B_j T_{ij}^{-1} \phi_{ij}^{\varepsilon_i} \prod_{k=1}^{m-1} W_{kj}^{\alpha_{ki}} \tag{2.5}$$

where $B_j = w_{mj} / w_{mw}$ (a country constant). Thus, if factor k is relatively expensive in country j ($W_{kj} > 1$) then the unit cost of good i in j relative to the cost in the rest of the world will be higher the more intensive the production of i in the use of factor k, that is, the larger α_{ki}.[4] In addition, the unit cost will be lower the greater the productivity advantage of country j in the i'th industry ($A_{ij} > A_{iw}$) and the larger the firms of country j in industry i relative to the rest of the world.

2.2 Demand

Consumer demand is assumed to be determined by a Spence–Dixit–Stiglitz (S–D–S) utility function, identical for all consumers and all countries. Let products of firms in the i'th industry be differentiated in such a way that the elasticity of substitution for any pair of firms – domestic or foreign – is the same. Since all firms in the i'th industry in a particular country are identical, and thus charge the same price, we may aggregate the demand for the output of all firms in each country in a particular industry. The analysis may then proceed as if products were differentiated only with respect to country of origin ($j = 1, ..., N$).[5] If the products of all firms in the i'th industry in country j are treated as an aggregate, the S–D–S function gives the utility of the representative consumer as

$$U = \prod_{i=1}^{n} \left(\sum_{j=1}^{M} C_{ij}^{b_i} \right)^{\frac{a_i}{b_i}} \qquad \sum_{i=1}^{n} a_i = 1 \tag{2.6}$$

where C_{ij} denotes consumption of the 'aggregate product' in the i'th industry produced in country j.

From (2.6) we can derive the demand for the i'th good produced in country j in any market g, and thus the imports of good i from j to g.[6] Its demand will depend only on its relative price and total income in g:

$$C_{ijg} = \left[\frac{p_{ij}}{p_{iw}} \right]^{-\sigma_i} a_i Y_g = \xi_{ij}^{-\sigma_i} a_i Y_g \tag{2.7}$$

where $\sigma_i = 1/(1 - b_i)$ is the elasticity of substitution, Y_g is aggregate income in g and p_{iw} is an aggregate price index for all products in the i'th industry.[7]

2.3 The Coefficient of Specialization

Consider now a particular country's trade with the rest of the world. A measure of international competitiveness, specialization and net exports in the i'th industry in country j is given by the coefficient of specialization, defined as the ratio of domestic production in the i'th industry to domestic consumption of the i'th good, including imports:

$$r_{ij} = \frac{Q_{ij}}{C_{ij}} = \frac{C_{ij} + X_{ijw} - X_{iwj}}{C_{ij}} \qquad (2.8)$$

where X_{ijw} is the exports of good i from country j, X_{iwj} is imports and Q_{ij} is gross production.[8]

By inserting (2.7) into (2.8) we obtain

$$r_{ij} = 1 + \frac{\left[\xi_{ij}^{-\sigma_i} Y_w - \left\{Y_j - \xi_{ij}^{-\sigma_i} Y_j\right\}\right]}{Y_j} = \xi_{ij}^{-\sigma_i}\left[\left(Y_w / Y_j\right) + 1\right] \qquad (2.9)$$

Inserting the expression for the relative unit cost and price from (2.5) finally gives

$$r_{ij} = \left[B_j T_{ij}^{-1} \phi_{ij}^{\varepsilon_i} \prod_{k=1}^{m-1} W_{kj}^{\alpha_{ik}}\right]^{-\sigma_i} F_j \qquad (2.10)$$

where B_j and F_j are country-specific constants. Re-writing (2.10) in logarithms we have

$$\ln r_{ij} = \left(-\sigma_i \ln B_j + \ln F_j\right) + \sigma_i \ln T_{ij} + \sigma_i \varepsilon_i \ln \phi_{ij} - \sum_{k=1}^{m-1} \sigma_i \alpha_{ki} \ln W_{kj} \qquad (2.11)$$

where the first term is a country-specific constant. Thus the value of the specialization coefficient for a given country in any good/industry is low for goods intensively using the country's expensive (and scarce) factors (that is, factor intensity α_{ki} and relative factor cost W_{kj} are both high), where the country has a productivity disadvantage (T_{ij} is low) and where firms are relatively small. These mechanisms work through the relative unit cost and price. Moreover, the effect of a given cost difference is larger the higher the elasticity of substitution among products σ_i in the i'th industry.[9]

By differentiating (2.11) we obtain an equation for the rates of change:

$$\hat{r}_{ij} = \sigma_i \hat{T}_{ij} + \sigma_i \varepsilon_i \hat{\phi}_{ij} - \sum_{k=1}^{m-1} \sigma_i \alpha_{ki} \hat{W}_{kj} \qquad (2.12)$$

where $\hat{r}_{ij} = dr_{ij} / r_{ij} dt$ and correspondingly for $\hat{T}_{ij}$, $\hat{W}_{kj}$ and $\hat{\phi}_{ij}$.

3 DATA AND ECONOMETRIC MODELS

The hypotheses emerging from the model discussion can be briefly summarized as follows.

The specialization coefficient of the i'th industry in country j will be determined, first, by a combination of industries' resource requirements and countries' resource endowments. Countries will specialize on industries intensively using their cheap resources. This effect is represented in a log-linear equation by an interaction term $\sigma_i \alpha_{ki} \ln W_{kj}$, where α_{ki} is the share of k of total factor costs in the i'th industry, and W_{kj} is the relative price of factor k in country j compared to the rest of the world. The effect of a given cost difference on market shares and specialization is determined by σ_i, the elasticity of substitution among products from different firms within the i'th industry.

Surveys of empirical work (for example, Leamer, 1994 and Deardorff, 1984) conclude that natural resources affect industrial localization, not only of extractive industries but also of processing industries. In addition, both human and physical capital have been found to be important. In principle, one should include resources which are internationally immobile, where endowments differ among countries, and requirements differ among industries. In this study, we have included interaction variables measuring country endowments, in combination with industry requirements, of

- forest land per worker/cost share of roundwood
- arable land per capita/food industry (a dummy)
- electrical energy[10]
- physical capital
- human capital or skilled labour, measured by formal education.

In the standard Heckscher–Ohlin multi-sector and multi-factor model, it can be shown (Ethier, 1984) that factor prices in autarky are negatively correlated with factor abundance, so that abundant factors, as well as goods intensively using these factors, tend to be cheap; thus, such goods will be exported. Formally this requires homothetic and identical consumer demand, perfect competition and that goods outnumber factors. In this chapter we use this equivalence of factor endowments and factor prices.

We measure countries' resource endowments in physical terms (that is, aggregate capital stock per worker, proportion of labour force with higher education, and so on) rather than resource prices, since comparable data for prices are not available. Moreover, the variables measuring industries' factor intensities are also in physical terms, that is, capital intensity is measured by the stock of machinery and equipment per worker, rather than cost shares. One reason for this choice is that factor rewards, especially profits, are probably more affected by spurious short-term variability than quantities. All industry characteristics, that is, capital, energy and roundwood intensities, are measured using Swedish data and thus are assumed to be the same across countries.

Thus the hypothesis may be reformulated as follows: countries will, on average, specialize in industries intensively using their abundant factor. The term $\sigma_i \alpha_{ki} \ln W_{kj}$ is replaced in (2.11) by $\sigma_i v_{ki} \ln V_{kj}$, where V_{kj} is the relative endowment of resource k (for example, total stock of physical capital per worker), proportion of skilled workers of the labour force or forest (arable) land per worker in country j, and v_{ki} is the factor k intensity (for example, machinery and equipment per worker) in the i'th industry.

Second, specialization will also be determined by the level of productivity or efficiency in an industry relative to its competitors (T_{ijt}). According to the model the relevant concept here is total factor productivity, TFP, defined as the ratio of output to a weighted sum of the inputs used. For the case of a Cobb–Douglas production function, the relevant input weights are the cost shares, which corresponds to the output elasticities α_{ki} in (2.1a).

Third, specialization is affected by relative firm size ϕ_{ij}: the larger the firms, the lower will be costs and prices. The effect on costs of a given size difference depends on the extent of scale economies in the industry ε_i. Finally, the effect of a given cost and price difference, caused by factor proportions, technology or firm size, on specialization is larger the higher is σ_i, the elasticity of substitution among products of different firms in the i'th industry. The Appendix describes the definitions, sources and calculations used to obtain T_{ijt}, $\hat{T}_{ij}$, ϕ_{ij}, ε_i and σ_i in detail.[11]

For nine industries[12] in nine OECD countries we have estimated two basic equations, one for 1987–89 *levels* of r_{ij}:

$$\ln r_{ijt} = \beta_0 + \sum_{j=1}^{N-1}\beta_{0j}D_j + \sum_{i=1}^{n-1}\beta_{0i}D_i + \beta_1 \ln T_{ijt} + \sum_{k=1}^{m-1}\beta_{2k}v_{ki} \ln V_{kjt} + \beta_3\varepsilon_i \ln \phi_{ij} + \mu_{ijt}$$

(2.13)

the other for *changes* from 1970–72 to 1987–89:

$$\hat{r}_{ij} = \beta_0 + \sum_{j=1}^{N-1}\beta_{0j}D_j + \sum_{i=1}^{n-1}\beta_{0i}D_i + \beta_1\hat{T}_{ij} + \sum_{k=1}^{m-1}\beta_{2k}v_{ki}\hat{V}_{jk} + \mu_{ij}$$

(2.14)

where μ_{ij} and μ_{ijt} are error terms. Since endowments of forest and arable land do not change they are excluded from (2.14); so, too, is the plant size variable ϕ_{ij}, since data for changes are not available. In addition, we have attempted to allow for industry differences in the degree of substitution between firms' products by estimating a version of (2.13) and (2.14) where all of the independent variables (except the dummy variables) have been multiplied by a measure of σ_i, the elasticity of substitution among differentiated products within the i'th industry (compare (2.11) and (2.12); see Appendix).

The coefficients β_1 for relative TFP level T_{ijt} and relative TFP growth rate $\hat{T}_{ij}$ are expected to be positive: other things being equal, the higher the level (rate of growth) of TFP in the i'th industry in country j relative to the rest of the world, the lower the (increase of the) unit cost, and the higher the (increase of the) coefficient of specialization. The factor endowments coefficients β_{2k} will be positive; specialization coefficients will be higher in industries intensive in abundant factors, and increase in industries intensive in factors with a high rate of growth of domestic supply. Finally, by utilizing economies of scale larger firms will be more competitive ($\beta_3 > 0$).

The regression equations contain a number of country and industry intercept dummy variables, D_j and D_i. The country dummies can be motivated by the variation in trade balance in manufactures, surplus countries having a tendency to higher specialization coefficients in all industries. Since the countries in the analysis are all 'rich' by global standards, all tend to have surpluses (deficits) with 'poor' countries in the same type of goods (compare computers versus textiles). The same argument holds for the second equation where dummies represent common trends.

The sources, measurement and definition of the variables are presented in detail in the Appendix.

4   EMPIRICAL RESULTS

4.1   Factor Endowments and Specialization

The results in Table 2.1 indicate that natural resources, represented by forest land and arable land, as well as domestic supplies of electrical energy, influence countries' specialization patterns. The coefficients of the corresponding interaction variables are mostly positive and significant. This holds also for human capital, but only in robust regressions; thus this result is somewhat sensitive to the treatment of extreme observations. Physical capital does not seem to have any link whatsoever to specialization.

The inclusion of country and industry dummy variables in columns (iii) and (iv) results in a highly significant addition to the explanatory value of the regression. Countries with export surplus in manufactures, such as Japan and Germany, tend to show positive coefficients, while for deficit countries such as Norway coefficients are mostly negative.

Table 2.1   Determinants of the pattern of specialization ,1987–1989, in OECD countries

Variable	(i)	(ii)	(iii)	(iv)
Total factor productivity	0.144	0.114	−0.039	0.006
	(1.97)*	(1.55)	(−0.53)	(0.13)
	/2.29/**	/2.15/**	/−0.98/	/0.19/
	[1.13]	[1.02]	[0.51]	[0.80]
Physical capital		−9.16 × 10^{-8}	1.67 × 10^{-6}	1.18 × 10^{-6}
		(−0.76)	(0.43)	(0.71)
		/−1.08/	/0.60/	/0.92/
		[−1.12]	[0.69]	[0.89]
Human capital		0.649	8.750	6.646
		(1.21)	(0.92)	(1.54)
		/1.60/	/1.02/	/1.91/*
		[1.35]	[3.08]***	[2.29]***
Energy		0.001	0.019	0.006
		(2.28)**	(2.72)***	(1.87)*
		/3.69/***	/3.58/***	/2.30/**
		[3.44]***	[3.11]***	[1.95]*
Forest land		2.78 × 10^{-5}	2.11 × 10^{-5}	1.79 × 10^{-5}
		(1.75)*	(1.31)	(1.85)*
		/1.70/*	/1.64/	/2.38/**
		[3.94]***	[4.89]***	[5.54]***
Arable land		−0.063	0.101	0.053
		(−1.09)	(1.58)	(1.55)
		/−1.97/*	/2.05/**	/2.13/**
		[−0.99]	[2.02]**	[2.22]**
Plant size		0.180	0.198	0.094
		(2.41)**	(2.48)**	(2.50)**
		/2.98/***	/2.86/***	/2.77/***
		[2.73]***	[2.28]***	[2.22]**
Constant	−0.059	−0.180	−8.220	−1.085
Country dummies			yes	yes
			0.000	0.000
Industry dummies			yes	yes
			0.000	0.000
$\bar{R}^2$	0.036	0.161	0.559	0.558
Observations	78	70	70	70

Notes: The table shows the estimated regression coefficients and their t values. Numbers in parentheses ( ) give t-values in OLS regressions, slashes / / White's (1980) t-statistics corrected for heteroscedasticity by computing Huber standard errors, and square brackets [ ] t-values in robust regressions, where extreme observations are given lower weights. The parameter estimates in robust regressions differ somewhat from those in OLS regressions but are not presented. The symbol * indicates that the estimated coefficient is significant at the 10 % level, ** at the 5% level, and *** at the 1% level. For the dummy variables we report the probability that all coefficients for the group equal zero. In equation (iv) all dependent variables have been multiplied by a measure of the intra-industry elasticity of substitution (σ_i in 2.11).

Table 2.2   Determinants of changes in the pattern of specialization, 1970–1972 to 1987–1989, in OECD countries

Variable	(i)	(ii)	(iii)	(iv)
Total factor productivity growth	0.156	0.093	0.127	0.070
	$(1.90)^*$	(1.18)	$(1.96)^*$	$(2.07)^{**}$
	$/2.32/^{**}$	$/1.68/^*$	$/2.17/^{**}$	$/2.41/^{**}$
	$[1.75]^*$	$[1.10]$	$[3.85]^{***}$	$[4.42]^{***}$
Physical capital growth		9.56×10^{-7}	-1.14×10^{-6}	-8.40×10^{-7}
		$(1.73)^*$	(-0.89)	$(-1.85)^*$
		$/1.87/^*$	$/-0.88/$	$/-2.29/^{**}$
		$[1.50]$	$[-1.78]^*$	$[-3.06]^{***}$
Human capital growth		-0.129	0.865	0.315
		(-1.47)	$(2.93)^{***}$	$(3.54)^{***}$
		$/-1.47/$	$/2.32/^{**}$	$/3.35/^{***}$
		$[-1.09]$	$[0.84]$	$[4.18]^{***}$
Growth of energy supply		0.006	-0.005	-0.002
		$(2.33)^{**}$	(-1.06)	(-1.18)
		$/3.17/^{***}$	$/-1.40/$	$/-1.56/$
		$[2.34]^{**}$	$[-0.82]$	$[-1.46]$
Constant	-0.030	-0.076	-0.441	-0.055
Country dummies			yes	yes
			0.001	0.000
Industry dummies			yes	yes
			0.000	0.000
$\bar{R}^2$	0.033	0.170	0.590	0.615
Observations	78	78	78	78

Notes: See Table 2.1. For forest land, arable land and plant size no time series data were available: thus these variables are not included here. Column (iv) gives the estimated coefficients when all variables are multiplied by the elasticity of substitution variable.

Table 2.2 shows that countries where the domestic supply of skilled labour did increase at a high rate have increased their specialization in skill-intensive goods.[13] Thus the results indicate that the stock of human capital and its rate of increase are important determinants of levels and changes of international competitiveness. The growth of the stock of machinery and equipment and the increase in the capacity for energy production do not seem to be important in this respect; in fact, the physical capital variable turns out to have the wrong sign.[14]

Furthermore, as shown by Table 2.1, specialization coefficients seem to increase with relative plant size in industries where economies of scale of various types are common. This is indicated by the strongly significant positive coefficient for the variable ϕ_{ij}.[15]

Finally, column (iv) shows the results of an attempt to take account of the degree of intra-industry product differentiation, by adjusting the independent variables for differences in the elasticity of substitution among products. This seems to improve the performance of the model somewhat, especially in the equation for changes in Table 2.2, in the sense that the significance of certain variables tends to increase.

4.2 The Role of Total Factor Productivity for International Competitiveness

On the issue of the importance of technology for competitiveness and specialization, Tables 2.1 and 2.2 seem to lead to radically different conclusions. According to Table 2.1, column (i), the relative TFP *level* seems to have a positive effect on specialization, which disappears when we allow for country and industry fixed effects (columns (iii) and (iv)). The poor performance of the technology variable could be explained by measurement errors. Since the TFP indices have to be deflated to a common currency, the choice of deflator – here PPP-adjusted exchange rates in 1985 – is bound to have a substantial effect on the results; other ways of transforming the indices would probably give widely different results.[16]

That the data for TFP *levels* might be less reliable than those for *changes* in 1970–89 (which are calculated from volume changes in fixed prices in domestic currency) is indicated by the results in Table 2.2.[17] In particular, column (iv) shows that the technology effect becomes strongly significant after taking account of varying elasticities of substitution. This result is not affected by adjustment for heteroscedasticity or the treatment of extreme observations.[18]

Our results show that international competitiveness has improved in industries and countries where the rate of increase of total factor productivity was high relative to the OECD average. Thus the hypothesis about the central role of technical progress for competitiveness is confirmed. However, the results also point to the role of changing endowments of human capital. Countries where the average level of education (mean years of schooling) did increase tended to increase their specialization on human-capital-intensive goods.

5 CONCLUDING COMMENTS

In this chapter we attempt to evaluate two central paradigms in international trade theory concerning the determinants of comparative advantage and specialization, namely technology versus factor proportions. Our main conclusion is that *both* sets of variables seem to be important. Factor endowments of countries, in combination with factor requirements of industries, seem to be significant determinants of trade and specialization. Different rates of factor accumulation

– in particular of human capital – contribute to the explanation of changing specialization patterns. But so do differences in rates of technical progress.

In an empirical study covering nine OECD countries and nine industry groups we find that countries tended to increase their specialization in the period 1970–89 in industries where total factor productivity had been growing at a high rate compared to competitors. We also found that specialization increased in human-capital-intensive goods in countries with a high rate of growth of the national supply of skilled labour. These results are reinforced by allowing for country- and industry-specific fixed effects and different degrees of homogeneity among products within industries. For specialization levels, however, the technology variable performed poorly, whereas factor proportions – especially natural resources – were significant. This result may be due to measurement problems.

This chapter cannot, of course, give a definite answer to the question of whether technology or factor proportions is the single most important explanation for competitiveness and trade patterns. One reason for this is that our analysis is likely to omit some of the effects of improved technology. In principle, an innovation resulting in a new and better product, which will command a higher price, should be reflected in an increase in TFP. In practice, however, this effect is often likely to be deflated away, to the extent that price indices are not properly adjusted for quality changes. We may, however, conclude that both explanations are important, and that our results indicate that analyses of changing patterns of international competitiveness and specialization which focus only on one of the paradigms, omitting the other, may be seriously misleading.

NOTES

*   We are grateful to Steven Globerman and other participants at the conference at Leangkollen for comments, and to the Swedish Council for Research in the Humanities and Social Sciences for financial support.
1. There is, of course, not necessarily an unambiguous distinction between the two paradigms, either in theory, or in empirical studies. Knowledge or technology may be treated either as a variable in the production function, or as embodied in the parameters of the function.
2. See, for example, Berndt (1991), pp. 68–9.
3. Helpman and Krugman (1985), p. 143; the particular form of equation (2.2b) is obtained if we introduce increasing returns to the production function in (2.1a) by raising the right-hand side (excluding the A_{ij} term) to the power of $\varepsilon_i > 0$.
4. From the first-order condition of profit maximization we know that the value of the m'th factor's marginal product equals the factor price of m. With Cobb–Douglas production technology this implies that

$$\frac{\alpha_{ki} x_{mij}}{\alpha_{mi} x_{kij}} = \frac{w_{kj}}{w_{mj}}$$

which means that the k intensity in the i'th sector in country j is

$$f_{kij} = (x_{kij} / x_{mij}) = \alpha_{mi}^{-1} \alpha_{ki} \, \omega_{kj}^{-1}.$$

Hence, the k intensity – units of k per unit of m – in country j is a function of the cost share of k in industry i (equal internationally) and the national relative factor price (same in all industries).

5. Armington (1969).
6. See, for example, Helpman and Krugman (1985), pp. 118–19.
7. The utility function in (2.6) implies that the dual aggregate price index for all products produced in the i'th industry is (Varian, 1992, p. 112)

$$p_{iw} = \left[\sum_{j=1}^{N} p_{ij}^{1-\sigma_i} \right]^{\frac{1}{1-\sigma_i}}$$

8. The r measure is thus equivalent to the net export ratio.
9. The model assumes that trading costs equal zero. Otherwise, the r_{ij}:s will approach one when tariffs or transport costs increase.
10. A country's production of electrical energy may be treated as a 'natural' resource to the extent that it is based on, for example, hydroelectric power. However, energy-intensive production, while historically based on cost advantages of abundant and cheap hydroelectric capacity, may over time acquire a technological advantage that creates the base for future competitiveness. This may lead to investment in 'non-natural' energy production capacity such as nuclear power. Thus the causal interpretation of a correlation between energy production and the size of the energy-intensive industry sector may be ambiguous.
11. The value of r would also be affected by transport costs, tariffs and other barriers to trade: the higher and more restrictive these are the more r will approach one. However, no comprehensive measure of trading costs was available for the econometric analysis.
12. In principle one would prefer to do the analysis at a rather disaggregated industry level. In practice, however, the aggregation level is given by the availability of capital stock data.
13. The measure of skilled labour is not the same in Tables 2.1 and 2.2. In Table 2.1 the human capital interaction variable is based on the proportion of employees with a university degree in scientific, mathematical, computing or engineering subjects in employment in the i'th industry, respectively of the age group 25–35 years in the population of the j'th country. Since these data are not available over time we have used an interaction variable in Table 2.2 calculated as mean years of schooling of employees in the i'th industry, multiplied by the *increase* in mean years of schooling of the total labour force of the j'th country.
14. The variables measuring human and physical capital, as well as energy and plant size, are positively correlated; thus the estimates for each of these are affected by exclusion of the others.
15. The fact that countries' national industrial statistics use different size criteria for inclusion will produce some measurement errors; this, however, will not affect industries with large economies of scale where there are no small plants. The plant size coefficient might be biased if competitiveness leads to larger plants, that is, if there is simultaneity. A Hausman test indicates that plant size is uncorrelated with the error term in equation (iv) Table 2.1.
16. However, in a study of bilateral intra-Nordic trade Torstensson (1996) finds a positive effect of technology advantages measured as relative levels of labour productivity.
17. The same result – that the relationship between TFP *growth* and *changes* in comparative advantage was much stronger than that between *levels* of relative TFP and export patterns – was found by Dollar and Wolff (1993).
18. Since the dummy variables can be motivated both by statistical (F-tests) and economic (as proxies for trade deficits/surpluses) criteria we chose equation (iv) as the preferred one.

REFERENCES

Amable, B. and B. Verspagen (1995), 'The Role of Technology in Market Share Dynamics', *Applied Economics*, **27**, 197–204.

Armington, P. (1969), 'A Theory of Demand for Products Distinguished by Place of Production', *IMF Staff Papers*, **16**, 159–78.

Batra, R.N. (1973), *Studies in the Pure Theory of International Trade*, London: Macmillan.

Berndt, E.R. (1991), *The Practice of Econometrics. Classic and Contemporary*, New York: Addison-Wesley.

Deardorff, A.V. (1984), 'Testing Trade Theories and Predicting Trade Flows', in R.V. Jones and P.B. Kenen (eds), *Handbook of International Economics*, Volume I, Amsterdam: North-Holland, pp. 467–517.

Dollar, D. and E.N. Wolff (1993), *Competitiveness, Convergence, and International Specialization*, Cambridge, MA: MIT Press.

Dosi, G., K. Pavitt, and L. Soete (1990), *The Economics of Technical Change and International Trade*, London: Harvester/Wheatsheaf.

Ethier, W. (1984), 'Higher Dimensional Issues in Trade Theory', in R.W. Jones and P. Kenen (eds), *Handbook of International Economics*, Volume I, Amsterdam: North Holland, pp. 131–84.

Finger, J.M. (1975), 'A New View of the Product Cycle Theory', *Weltwirtschaftliches Archiv*, **111**, 79–99.

Gruber, W., D. Metha and R. Vernon (1967), 'The R&D Factor in International Trade and International Investment of United States Industries', *Journal of Political Economy*, **75**, 20–37.

Helpman, E. and P.R. Krugman (1985), *Market Structure and Foreign Trade*, Cambridge, MA: MIT Press.

Hufbauer, G.C. (1970), 'The Impact of National Characteristics and Technology on the Commodity Composition of Trade in Manufactured Goods', in R. Vernon (ed.), *The Technology Factor in International Trade*, New York: Columbia University Press, pp. 145–231.

Hughes, K. (1986), *Exports and Technology*, Cambridge: Cambridge University Press.

Leamer, E.E. (1984), *Sources of International Comparative Advantage. Theory and Evidence*, Cambridge, MA: MIT Press.

Leamer, E.E. (1994), 'Testing Trade Theories', in D. Greenaway and L.A. Winters (eds), *Surveys in International Trade*, Oxford: Blackwell, pp. 66–106.

Lundberg, L. (1988), 'Technology, Factor Proportions and Competitiveness', *Scandinavian Journal of Economics*, **90**, 173–88.

MacDougall, G.D.A. (1951), 'British and American Exports: A Study Suggested by the Theory of Comparative Costs. Part I', *Economic Journal*, **61**, 697–724.

MacDougall, G.D.A. (1952), 'British and American Exports: A Study Suggested by the Theory of Comparative Costs. Part II', *Economic Journal*, **62**, 487–521.

Stern, R.M. and K.E. Maskus (1981), 'Determinants of the Structure of US Foreign Trade 1958–76', *Journal of International Economics*, **11**, 207–24.

Torstensson, J. (1996), 'Technical Differences and Inter-Industry Trade in the Nordic Countries', *Scandinavian Journal of Economics*, **98**, 93–110.

Varian, H. (1992), *Microeconomic Analysis*, Third Edition, London: W.W. Norton.

Wells, L.T., Jr (1969), 'Test of a Product Cycle Model of International Trade: US Exports of Consumer Durables', *Quarterly Journal of Economics*, **82**, 152–62.

White, H. (1980), 'A Heteroskedasticity-Consistent Covariance Matrix Estimator and a Direct Test for Heteroskedasticity', *Econometrica*, **48**, 817–38.

APPENDIX   VARIABLES: DEFINITIONS, MEASURE-MENT AND SOURCES

Coefficient of specialization: r_{ijt}

$$r_{ijt} = \frac{Q_{ijt}}{C_{ijt}} = \frac{Q_{ijt}}{Q_{ijt} + X_{iwjt} - X_{ijwt}}$$

Q_{ijt} production (gross output), industry i, country j, time t
C_{ijt} consumption, industry i, country j, time t
X_{iwjt} import, industry i, from the whole world w to country j, time t
X_{ijwt} export, industry i, from country j to the whole world w, time t
$t = 1, 2$; 1 = average 1970–72 and 2 = average 1987–89

Source: OECD (1994a).

Total factor productivity variables: $T_{ijt} = \ln(A_{ijt} / A_{iwt})$ and $\hat{T}_{ij} = \hat{A}_{ij} - \hat{A}_{iw}$

$$\ln A_{ijt} = \ln q^{*}_{ijt} - \alpha_i \ln L_{ijt} - (1 - \alpha_i) \ln K^{*}_{ijt}$$

A_{ijt} total factor productivity, industry i, country j, time t
q^{*}_{ijt} value added, industry i, country j, time t, US dollar 1985 PPP, 1985 prices
K^{*}_{ijt} capital stock, industry i, country j, time t, US dollar 1985 PPP, 1985 prices
L_{ijt} employment, industry i, country j, time t
α_i output elasticity of labour, industry i; measured as wages' share of value added
A_{ijt} / A_{iwt} relative productivity
A_{iwt} average total factor productivity in the studied countries
$\hat{A}_{ij} - \hat{A}_{iw}$ relative productivity growth
$\hat{A}_{ij} = \ln A_{ij2} - \ln A_{ij1}$
$\hat{A}_{iw} = \ln A_{iw2} - \ln A_{iw1}$

Source: OECD (1993).

Economies of scale and firm size variable: $\varepsilon_i \phi_{ij} = \varepsilon_i (\ln s_{ij} - \ln s_{iw})$

ε_i dummy variable for industries with large economies of scale, according to a ranking made by Pratten (1988), Table 5.3b
s_{ij} average number of employees per establishment 1988, country j, industry i

s_{iw} average number of employees per establishment 1988, all countries, industry i

Source: OECD (1992).

Physical capital interaction variables: $k_i \ln k_{j2}$ and $k_i \hat{k}_j$

k_i capital stock per employee, industry i, USA 1988
k_{j2} capital stock per employee in manufacturing, country j, average 1987–89
$\hat{k}_j$ $\ln k_{j2} - \ln k_{j1}$

Source: OECD (1993).

Human capital interaction variables: $h_i \ln h_j$ and $h_i^* \hat{h}_j^*$

h_i proportion of employees in industry i with a university degree in engineering (3 years or more), Sweden, 1990. *Source*: SCB, 'Regional Labor Statistics'
h_j number of graduates in science and engineering per 100,000 of population aged 25–35, country j, 1991. *Source*: OECD (1994b)
h_i^* average number of years of schooling in industry i, Sweden, 1990. *Source*: SCB, 'Regional Labor Statistics'
$\hat{h}_j^*$ $\ln h_{j85}^* - \ln h_{j70}^*$ increase in average number of years of schooling of labour force in country j from 1970 to 1985. *Source*: Barro and Lee (1993)

Interaction variable for forest land: $t_i \ln t_j$

t_i input of roundwood SEK per 10,000 SEK output, industry i, Sweden, 1985. *Source*: SCB, *Input–Output Table for Sweden 1985*
t_j forest land per worker, country j, 1990. *Source*: SCB (1993)

Energy interaction variable: $e_i \ln e_j$

e_i cost of electrical power per employee, industry i, Sweden, 1987. *Source*: SCB, *SOS Manufacturing 1987*
e_j production of electrical power per capita 1991, country j. *Source*: SCB (1994)

Interaction for arable land: $a_i \ln a_j$

a_i dummy variable for industry 31 (food)
a_j hectare arable land per capita 1991. *Source*: SCB (1994)

Elasticity of substitution: σ_i

In the theoretical model in Section 2, the elasticity of substitution between products in an industry equals the elasticity of demand in the case of a large number of products. Such elasticities have been estimated for industries at the 6-digit level of Swedish Standard Industrial Classification (SNI) in Sweden 1983 (Hansson, 1989). From those estimates we have constructed consumption weighted elasticities of substitution at the International Standard Industrial Classification (ISIC) 2-digit level.

Table 2A.1   Industries and countries in the study

ISIC	Industry	Country
31	Food	United States
32	Textile	Canada
33	Wood	Japan
34	Paper	Germany
35	Chemical	France
36	Non-Metallic	United Kingdom
37	Basic metal	Denmark
38	Machinery	Norway
39	Other	Sweden

Data Sources

Barro, R.J. and J.-W. Lee (1993), 'Appendix Tables to International Comparisons of Educational Attainment', Mimeo.

Hansson, P. (1989), 'Intra-Industry Trade: Measurement, Determinants and Growth. A Study of Swedish Foreign Trade', *Umeå Economic Studies,* No. 205.

OECD (1992), *Industrial Structure Statistics 1989/90*, Paris: OECD.

OECD (1993), *International Sectoral Database (ISDB)*, Paris: OECD.

OECD (1994a), *The STAN Database 1970–91*, April, Paris: OECD.

OECD (1994b), *Education at a Glance*, Paris: OECD.

OECD (1994c), *The STAN Database 1970-93*, December, Paris: OECD.

Pratten, C. (1988), 'A Survey of the Economies of Scale', in Commission of the European Communities, *Research on the 'Cost of Non-Europe'. Basic Findings.* Volume 2, Luxembourg: Office for Official Publications of the European Communities.

SCB (1993), *Statistical Yearbook of Sweden 1994*, Örebro: SCB förlag.

SCB (1994), *Statistical Yearbook of Sweden 1995*, Örebro: SCB förlag.

SCB, *SOS Manufacturing Part I. 1987*, Örebro: SCB förlag.

SCB, *Input–Output Table for Sweden 1985*, Örebro: SCB förlag.

SCB, 'Regional Labour Statistics', Unpublished data on employees by industry and level of education.

3. Competitiveness, scale and R&D

Jan Fagerberg

1 INTRODUCTION

Recent theorizing on growth and trade points to the importance of R&D and spillovers from this to other firms, industries and countries. According to this literature, the geographical boundaries of such spillovers are of prime importance for trade patterns. Country size may also play an important role. However, until recently, applied work in this area has had relatively little to say about these issues. This chapter begins with a short review of the theoretical and applied literature in this area. Based on the lessons learned, an eclectic model is formulated and applied to data for ten OECD countries and 20 industries in 1985. The data set includes, among other things, data for direct R&D and R&D acquired indirectly through purchase of capital goods and intermediary products. The results give some support to theories that focus on the importance of R&D investments and spillovers for exports.

2 THE AGENDA

The interest in the relationship between technology and competitiveness dates back to the so-called neo-technological trade theories of the 1960s (technology gap, product cycle and so on; for an overview see Dosi and Soete, 1988). These may be seen as attempts to overcome the rigidity of the standard neoclassical approach to international trade, which had become apparent for many observers. Most of these attempts were, explicitly or implicitly, based on Schumpeter's analysis of innovation and diffusion as the driving forces behind the competitiveness of firms (and economic growth in general).[1] Writers in this tradition pointed to the importance of R&D and innovation for trade flows and possible differences across industries and countries in this respect.

Since this issue was first introduced by Posner (1961), Vernon (1966) and others, economic theory has changed considerably. Trade theorists started to apply the insights from models of imperfectly competitive markets to the analysis of international trade and worldwide competitiveness (the so-called 'new trade theory'; see Helpman, 1984 for an overview). In this literature the existence of fixed costs, such as, for instance, investment in R&D, plays an important role (since they give rise to economies of scale). Thus, following this approach, R&D investment may be an important competitive factor. The size of the domestic market also plays an important role in such models. One possible outcome[2] in a world characterized by imperfect competition, economies of scale and trading costs (that are neither too small, nor prohibitive) is, other things being equal, that countries specialize in products for which there is a relatively large domestic market – the so-called 'home-market effect' (Krugman, 1990). Furthermore, if some industries are characterized by economies of scale while others are not, one might expect the large countries to specialize in the former and the small countries in the latter.

More recently, growth theorists started to introduce the Schumpeterian insight of the importance of innovation-diffusion into formal growth models based on the assumption of imperfectly competitive markets (the so-called 'new growth theory'; for an overview see Grossman and Helpman, 1995). These models also point to the importance of R&D for growth of GDP and exports. While much of the earlier literature in this area emphasized the direct impact of the R&D effort of a firm, industry or country, the new growth literature focuses more sharply on the impact of diffusion or 'technological spillovers'. Following this approach, it matters a lot what the actual boundaries of these spillovers are. If technological spillovers are (mainly) national in scope, a large country will benefit more from investments in new technology (R&D) than a small one. Hence, on this assumption, a large country should be considered more likely to gain a competitive advantage in R&D-intensive activities than a small country.

Differences across countries in the efficiency of R&D and other technological activities have also been emphasized by the recent literature on 'national systems of innovation' (Lundvall (ed.), 1992; Nelson (ed.), 1993). This literature stresses the systemic aspects of innovation, the importance of interaction across firms, industries and sectors and the advantage of a coherent national system in this area. A related perspective is that of Porter (1990), who also emphasizes the potential benefits of close links and interaction between producers and their (domestic) customers and suppliers, often referred to as 'clustering' or 'agglomeration'.[3] This phenomenon is also consistent with a perspective that focuses on scale economics, for instance among domestic suppliers of goods and services, see Venables (1994). What is of interest here is that all these approaches suggest that a high reliance of domestic sources of technology may imply a competitive advantage.

3   THE EVIDENCE

Empirically, analysts have tried to highlight the relationship between competitiveness and technology by regressing a measure of export performance on a technology variable, usually based on R&D or patent statistics, and – in some cases – other variables that were deemed relevant for the analysis. Generally, the relationship is the following:

$$X = f(T, O), \tag{3.1}$$

where X is a measure of export performance, T is a technology proxy and O is a set of other variables.

A distinction may be made between cross-sectional work, using data for a number of industries and countries at one point in time (the static case), and applications on time-series data (the dynamic case). Among the former, Lacroix and Scheuer (1976), Walker (1979), Soete (1981, 1987), Dosi and Soete (1983), Dosi, Pavitt and Soete (1990) and Fagerberg (1995a) may be mentioned. Generally, the results of these studies support the hypothesis of a positive relationship between competitiveness and technological activity for a large number of industries, not only those that are commonly regarded as 'high tech'. However, tests that use R&D instead of a patent-based technology indicator tend to come up with a narrower list of industries for which technology matters. Some of these studies also included a variable assumed to reflect scale factors (population). Fagerberg (1995a), in a cross-sectional study of 19 OECD countries and 40 industries, found scale factors to be important in only a few industries, covering about one-fifth of total OECD trade.

A dynamic version of equation 3.1 was suggested by Fagerberg (1988) and applied to pooled cross-sectional time-series macro data for a number of industrialized countries. Time-series estimates for the macro level have also been presented by Amendola et al. (1993). Magnier and Toujas-Bernate (1994) and Amable and Verspagen (1995) both analysed pooled time-series and cross-sectional data for five large OECD countries in the 1970s and 1980s. Generally, the results from these studies confirm much of the previous evidence from cross-sectional samples, but the role of scale factors was largely ignored.

4   DATA AND METHOD

The applied literature surveyed above has generated a lot of insights and knowledge on the impact of R&D and innovation (and other factors) on trade performance across countries and industries. However, many questions remain open, in particular those related to the possible impact of technology flows across firms, industries and countries. The purpose of this chapter is to add to the existing literature in this area by exploring the relationship between competitiveness, scale and R&D with the help of the OECD STAN and ANBERD Data Bases and the recent work by the OECD on embodied technology flows. The ensuing data set is unique in the sense that it provides data for a number of variables – including direct R&D and R&D acquired through purchase of capital goods and intermediates – at the level of the industry (mostly in current prices).

Ten countries, 22 industries[4] and (roughly) two decades are included. We excluded two industries on the grounds that they were ill defined (two residual categories). For some of the technology variables data were available for selected years only (in some cases only one year). This made a regular time series difficult. What will be presented here is a cross-sectional analysis for 1985, the only year for which the technology variables are available for all ten countries (even then about 5 per cent of the observations are missing because of a lack of data for certain variables, industries and countries).

International competitiveness at the industry level may be defined as the ability to sell products in international markets in competition with suppliers from other countries. Exports seem to be a natural indicator for that, and most of the applied literature on competitiveness also uses an export-based indicator.[5] The model we wish to apply is an eclectic one in which the international competitiveness of a country at the industry level is explained by technological factors (direct R&D efforts and its ability to profit from R&D acquired indirectly through purchase of inputs, whether of domestic or foreign origin), cost competitiveness (wage level), the rate of investment and the size of the domestic market. More formally, we have:

$$X = f(RD, DIF, FOR, INV, WAGE, HOME), \qquad (3.2)$$

where:

 X is exports,
 RD (direct R&D) is business enterprise R&D,
 DIF (indirect R&D) is R&D acquired indirectly through purchases of capital
  goods and intermediate goods from domestic and foreign suppliers,
 FOR (foreign share) is indirect R&D acquired through purchases of capital
  goods and intermediate goods from foreign suppliers as a percentage of
  total indirect R&D (both foreign and domestic),
 $WAGE$ is labour costs per worker,
 INV is gross fixed capital formation,
 $HOME$ is domestic demand (measured as production + imports – exports).

All variables are measured in current prices in a common currency (US dollars) and are country and industry specific. The data for R&D acquired through purchases of capital goods and intermediates were calculated by the OECD and supplied as shares of production (these data were then scaled up by using data for production in 1985). In their calculation of indirect R&D acquired through domestic sources the OECD applied an input–output methodology, based on the so-called Leontief inverse (Papaconstantinou et al., 1996). This means that the indirect R&D from domestic sources for a particular industry in a particular country reflects not only the direct R&D carried out by its domestic suppliers but also the R&D acquired by these suppliers through their use of domestically produced capital goods and intermediates. For various reasons, indirect R&D acquired from foreign sources was calculated using a less sophisticated methodology, weighting direct R&D in the supplying (foreign) industries with actual import shares for the industry and country in question. As noted by the OECD, this implies an underestimation of the total amount of foreign R&D. Probably this does not constitute a serious problem in the present context, since the impact on the variables used here is likely to be small.[6]

Consistent with most theoretical perspectives in this area we expect a positive impact of both R&D and investment in physical capital (*INV*) on exports. Which of them is the most efficient way to enhance competitiveness is a matter of controversy. Some theories predict that the impact of investment in R&D (Romer, 1990; Grossman and Helpman, 1991) or physical capital (Romer, 1986) is more prominent in large countries; we will be able to test for that as well. If there are important positive externalities stemming from the use of product-embodied R&D, we might expect a large positive impact of indirect R&D (*DIF*). An unresolved issue is, as mentioned, to what extent national boundaries matter for the impact of technology flows; the *FOR* variable was designed to throw some light on that. If the estimated impact is deemed to be not different from zero, this implies that the source (domestic or foreign) does not really matter. If, on the other hand, the estimated impact is negative, this means that indirect R&D from domestic sources is valued more highly, consistent with the suggestion from some theories in this area. Cost competition figures prominently in the public debate on competitiveness and in some theories as well (the product-cycle theory, for example). To take this possibility into account, we included the *WAGE* variable. We also included the *HOME* variable to allow for an impact of market size on competitiveness, consistent with some of the suggestions of 'new trade theory' (the 'home-market effect'). Finally we test for the widely held view, often associated with the product-cycle theory (Vernon, 1966), that the impact of R&D and other factors vary systematically across broad classes of industry ('high tech' versus 'medium' or 'low tech'). Following this theory R&D and market size should be of prime importance for competitiveness in innovative, high-tech industries; while in mature, low-tech industries investments in physical capital and low wages should be assumed to matter most.

5   A PREVIEW OF THE DATA

Table 3.1 gives summary statistics (total manufacturing) for the ten OECD countries included in the investigation for the year 1985.[7] There is a large spread in direct R&D efforts (as a percentage of production), with the USA far ahead of the others (3.5 per cent). The remaining nine countries divide neatly into two groups, five in the area 2–2.5 per cent, and four between 0.7 and 1 per cent. In the former we find the Netherlands, Japan, France, the UK and Germany, in the latter Italy, Australia, Canada and Denmark. As could be expected there is also a marked difference between large and small countries with respect to the importance of domestic versus foreign indirect R&D, with the large ones benefiting almost exclusively from the former and the small countries mostly geared towards the latter. This is clearly reflected in the share of foreign indirect R&D in total indirect R&D: column four in Table 3.1 (the 'foreign share').

Table 3.1   Summary statistics -10 OECD countries, 1985

	Direct R&D	Domestic indirect R&D	Foreign indirect R&D	Foreign share	Relative wage level	Market size	Investment share
USA	3.5	0.8	0.1	11.1	146.5	39.8	3.9
Netherlands	2.0	0.2	0.7	77.8	107.1	1.7	5.8
Japan	2.0	0.7	0.1	12.5	73.3	20.2	6.3
Italy	0.7	0.2	0.2	50.0	87.7	7.4	5.5
UK	2.2	0.3	0.4	57.1	94.2	7.4	4.1
France	2.0	0.4	0.3	42.9	106.9	7.1	5.0
Denmark	1.0	0.1	0.4	80.0	74.5	0.6	5.6
Germany	2.5	0.6	0.2	25.0	102.7	11.0	4.1
Canada	1.0	0.2	0.6	75.0	117.3	3.3	4.5
Australia	0.9	0.3	0.3	50.0	89.8	1.6	5.2

Table 3.2 ranks the 22 industries in our sample after their direct R&D intensity (calculated as direct business R&D divided by production). More information about the definition of each of these industries is given in the Appendix. If one adopts the criterion that an industry with R&D efforts of 1.5 times the average or higher is 'high tech', and one with efforts between 0.5 and 1.5 times the average 'medium tech', we end up with five high-tech industries (aerospace, computers, drugs, telecommunication/semiconductors and instruments) and five medium-tech industries (electrical machinery, other transport, cars, industrial chemicals and non-electrical machinery). The remaining 12 industries, many of which are related to the use of natural resources in one way or another, are all 'low tech' by this definition.

Table 3.2 R&D intensity, production, 1985 (per cent)

High		Medium		Low	
Aerospace	20.08	Electrical machinery	3.26	Stone, glass	1.10
Computers	10.41	Other transport	3.03	Plastics	1.01
Drugs	9.01	Cars	2.83	Non-ferrous metals	0.89
Telecommunications	7.88	Industrial chemicals	2.76	Petroleum refining	0.78
Instruments	6.10	Non-electrical machinery	1.68	Fabricated metal products	0.64
				Other manufacturing	0.64
				Ferrous metals	0.61
				Ships	0.36
				Food, drinks	0.29
				Paper	0.23
				Textiles	0.19
				Wood, furniture	0.16

Notes
High: R&D intensity 1.5 times the mean R&D intensity or higher.
Low: R&D intensity 0.5 times the mean R&D intensity or lower.
Medium: R&D intensity between 0.5 and 1.5 times the mean R&D intensity.

6. RESULTS

The small sample (8–10 observations per industry, 17–20 observations per country) does not allow for very extensive testing of differences across industries and countries on the impact of the variables included in our investigation. What we do is to pool all the data and then test for the sensitivity of allowing the coefficients to vary across high-, medium- and low-tech sectors and, where appropriate, also across countries of different sizes. All equations are estimated in logs by OLS. As part of the estimation procedure, tests for heteroscedasticity were conducted and heteroscedastic consistent standard errors (HCSEs) calculated (White, 1980). The results indicate that heteroscedasticity is not an important problem in this case, that is, the HCSEs did not differ much from standard errors as calculated by OLS. Hence, we report the latter.

It is common in analyses of this type to adjust for differences in size across countries and sectors. We do this by including a full set of country and industry dummies. What these do is to adjust for factors that affect competitiveness in the same way for each country (independent of industry) and industry (independent of country). These include size but also a host of other factors that impact on the propensity to export, such as distance and transport costs. Thus, even if we had divided all variables by a measure of size such as, say, the labour force or GDP of the country, we would still have had to include dummies and, except for the dummies, the estimates thus obtained would have been identical to the ones reported here.[8]

Table 3.3 contains the main results from the estimations. Four different models are presented. The first (3.3.1) is our basic model (see equation 3.2). The three others extend the basic model by allowing for differences in the impact of variables across technology classes and country groups. In Table 3.4 we test the different models against each other. Finally, we test for the sensitivity of changes in the specification and the way data are handled. Some of the more interesting results from these tests are included in Table 3.5.

Generally, the results (3.3.1) confirm many of our priors. Both direct R&D, indirect R&D and investment are positively correlated with competitiveness at the 1 per cent level of significance. It is noteworthy that the estimated impact of indirect R&D is about twice as high as that of direct R&D. The foreign share had a significant negative impact, as suggested by several theories in this area. Contrary to popular belief, wage levels were found to be uncorrelated with competitiveness.[9] This confirms the finding from Wolff in this volume (Chapter 1) that low wages do not seem to be an important competitive factor among OECD countries. The size of the domestic market (*HOME*) has a significant negative impact, in contrast to the predictions of some theories emphasizing economies of scale.

Table 3.3   Factors affecting exports, 1985

Equation	3.3.1	3.3.2			3.3.3	3.3.4		
		High tech.	Medium tech.	Low tech.		High tech.	Medium tech.	Low tech.
Direct R&D	0.18 (2.76) *	0.52 (3.22) *	0.15 (1.00)	0.18 (2.45) **	0.12 (1.63) ***	0.47 (2.52) **	0.14 (0.87)	0.17 (1.87) ***
Indirect R&D	0.37 (3.24) *	0.32 (1.81) ***	0.59 (2.05) **	0.52 (2.99) *	0.44 (3.79) *	0.33 (1.87) ***	0.69 (2.32) **	0.53 (2.93) *
Foreign share	−0.25 (2.14) **	−0.56 (2.25) **	−0.24 (1.11)	−0.26 (1.96) ***	−0.34 (2.86) *	−0.45 (1.70) ***	−0.10 (0.44)	−0.32 (2.34) **
Investment	0.69 (6.63) *	0.34 (1.43) ****	0.51 (2.04) **	0.68 (5.28) *	0.67 (5.54) *	0.36 (1.41) ****	0.48 (1.83) ***	0.73 (4.76) *
Wage	0.06 (0.18)	−0.09 (0.42)	0.47 (0.89)	−0.05 (0.16)	−0.00 (0.01)	−0.20 (0.46)	0.24 (0.45)	0.32 (0.08)
Home market	−0.51 (2.87) *	−0.51 (1.79) ***	−0.41 (1.35) ****	−0.85 (3.77) *	−0.64 (3.66) *	−0.56 (1.91) ***	−0.46 (1.46) ****	−0.93 (3.97) *
R&D – large	—	—			0.44 (3.90) *	0.24 (1.37) ****		
R&D – medium	—	—			0.09 (1.42) ****	−0.01 (0.15)		
Investment – large	—	—			−0.21 (1.28)	−0.06 (0.30)		
Investment – medium	—	—			−0.15 (1.26)	−0.09 (0.69)		
Country dummies	yes	yes			yes	yes		
Product dummies	yes	yes			yes	yes		
$R^2(\bar{R}^2)$	0.86 (0.83)	0.89 (0.85)			0.88 (0.85)	0.89 (0.85)		

Notes

Estimated in log-form. For definition of variables, see text. $N = 192$. Absolute t-statistics in brackets. * = Significant, 1% level. ** = Significant, 5% level. *** = Significant, 10% level. **** = Significant, 20 % level.

Table 3.4   Testing for inclusion of additional variables

Country and product dummies	3.3.1 (against $3.3.0^1$)$F_{(28,157)}$ = 10.03^*
High, medium and low R&D sectors	3.3.2 (against 3.3.1) $F_{(12,145)}$ = 2.59^*
	3.3.3 (against 3.3.1) $F_{(4,153)}$ = 4.86^*
Large-country advantages (R&D and investment)	3.3.4 (against 3.3.2) $F_{(4,141)}$ = 1.28
	3.3.4 (against 3.3.3) $F_{(12,141)}$ = 1.37

Notes
1. 3.3.1 without country and product dummies (a common constant term), $R^2 = 0.61$, not reported.
*   Significance of test, 1% level.

When the impact of the variables was allowed to vary across high-, medium- and low-tech sectors (3.3.2), the explanatory power of the model increased somewhat. The test (Table 3.4) suggests that this is a real improvement, indicating that there are important differences across sectors in the way variables work. The impact of direct R&D, for example, is about twice as large in high-tech as in low-tech industries. Indirect R&D and investment in physical capital, on the other hand, appear to matter more in low-tech industries. To some extent these results resemble the kind of 'stylized' facts that led Vernon (1966) to formulate the product-cycle theory. However, low wages do not seem to matter, not even in low tech, where cost-competition – following Vernon – should be expected to have a sizeable impact. Following Vernon one might also have expected market size to be positively correlated with competitiveness in high-tech industries. The results suggest that competitiveness is negatively correlated with market size in all three sectors, but less so in high-tech than in the other sectors.

A division of countries into large, medium-sized and small can be made along the same lines as for the technology classes. If this methodology is adopted, two countries appear as large: the USA and Japan. The medium-sized countries are Italy, the UK, France and Germany. According to new growth theory, the rewards from investments in R&D and/or physical capital should be larger in large countries. We test for this by allowing the estimated impact of R&D and investment in large and medium-sized countries to deviate from the rest of the sample, that is, the small countries (3.3.3). For physical capital there is little evidence of large-country advantages. If anything it is the other way around. However, there is strong support for the hypothesis that direct R&D has a higher impact on exports in large countries. Furthermore, the test in Table 3.4 also suggests that the version allowing for large-country advantages (3.3.3) should be preferred when tested against the basic model (3.3.1).

Table 3.5   Testing for changes in specification

Equation	3.5.1	3.5.2	3.5.3[1]	3.5.4[1]	3.5.5	3.5.6
Dependent variable	Export–import ratio	Export–import ratio	Exports per worker	Exports per worker	Exports	Exports
Direct R&D	0.22 (2.62) *	0.14 (1.55) ***	0.20 (2.92) *	0.12 (1.60) ****	0.17 (2.54) *	0.19 (1.48) ****
Indirect R&D	0.37 (2.59) *	0.48 (3.35) *	0.29 (2.44) **	0.32 (2.66) *	0.25 (2.33) **	0.37 (2.45) **
Foreign share	−0.62 (4.16) *	−0.70 (4.85) *	−0.18 (1.52) ****	−0.25 (2.03) **	−0.23 (1.93) ***	−0.32 (2.31) **
Investment	0.85 (6.49) *	0.79 (5.33) *	0.50 (4.01) *	0.65 (4.16) *	0.59 (5.88) *	0.74 (5.25) *
Wage	0.33 (0.80)	0.27 (0.69)	0.29 (0.82)	0.26 (0.74)	0.02 (0.06)	0.02 (0.06)
Home market	−0.84 (3.77) *	−1.07 (4.96) *	−0.43 (3.01) *	−0.31 (2.02) **	—	−0.70 (3.11) *
RSE (human capital)	—	—	—	—	—	−0.00 (0.03)
R&D – large	—	0.56 (4.09) *	—	0.38 (3.35) *	—	—
R&D – medium	—	0.11 (1.39) ****	—	0.09 (1.31) ****	—	—
Investment – large	—	−0.07 (0.34)	—	−0.66 (2.87) *	—	—
Investment – medium	—	−0.17 (1.15)	—	−0.37 (2.06) **	—	—
Country dummies	yes	yes	yes	yes	yes	yes
Product dummies	yes	yes	yes	yes	yes	yes
$R^2(\bar{R}^2)$	0.62 (0.53)	0.68 (0.60)	0.80 (0.76)	0.82 (0.77)	0.86 (0.82)	0.86 (0.82)
N	192	192	192	192	192	152

Notes
1.   In this equation, all variables except 'foreign share' are divided by the number of workers in the industry and country in question.
Estimated in log-form. For definition of variables, see text. Absolute t-statistics in brackets.
* = Significant, 1% level. ** = Significant, 5% level. *** = Significant, 10% level. **** = Significant, 20 % level.

What is the interpretation of this? That large countries specialize in high-tech industries is no secret. Apparently they also get more out of their investments in R&D. However, do they specialize in high tech because they gain higher rewards to R&D, or do they enjoy higher rewards because they specialize in high tech? Unfortunately we are unable to tell. As is evident from Tables 3.3–4, if we start out with one of these assumptions (sector or size differences), then adding the other does not increase the explanatory power of the model in a significant way. This might perhaps have been different for a larger sample of countries including, for instance, some small high-tech countries such as Sweden and Switzerland. For the present sample, however, sector and size differences go hand in hand.

Some of the implications of these results might be clearer by way of an example. Assume that we want to know the impact on exports of reallocating a part, say 1 per cent, of a country's investments in physical capital to direct R&D. Since on average the OECD countries invest twice as much in physical capital as in R&D, this means that an average country would have to increase direct R&D by 2 per cent. Our basic model (3.3.1), which we use here, estimates that a 1 per cent reduction in investment in physical capital reduces exports by 0.69 per cent, while a 2 per cent increase in direct R&D increases it by 0.36 per cent, indicating a net loss in exports of 0.33 per cent from this operation. For the economy as a whole, however, this may be different, because a general increase in direct R&D also implies a rise in the R&D content of the goods and services that firms acquire from their domestic suppliers. For simplicity we abstract from any change that might occur in the demand or price level of domestic inputs as a result of the reallocation from investment in physical capital to R&D. Furthermore, let us assume – as seems reasonable – that the ratio between direct and indirect R&D is constant, so that a 2 per cent increase in direct R&D implies a 2 per cent increase in the domestic part of the total indirect R&D. On these assumptions (and based on the estimates in 3.3.1) the impact on exports of increased domestic indirect R&D, caused by a 2 per cent increase in direct R&D, can be calculated to be 0.87 per cent.[10] This indirect gain more than outweighs the direct loss, indicating a net gain of 0.54 per cent for the country as a whole. Thus, for the average country, R&D appears to be a more potent competitive factor than investments in physical capital. For the individual firm, however, this may not be so clear, because the lion's share of this effect accrues to other domestic firms. This resembles the familiar case from the literature, where a large gap between social and private returns to R&D justifies an R&D subsidy.

This example may also be applied to countries of different sizes. It then becomes clear that the basic model generates some unwarranted results. Since small countries do much less R&D compared to what they invest than large countries, an increase in R&D equivalent to 1 per cent of investment translates itself into a much larger percentage increase in direct R&D in a small country than in a large one. If, as in the basic model, the impact of direct R&D on exports is assumed to be the same across industries and countries, this implies that this effect is much larger in small countries than in large ones. If this was the case, then firms in small countries should face a stronger (private) incentive to invest in R&D than firms in large countries. This is, of course, contrary to what we observe. Allowing for a differential impact of investment in R&D and physical capital across technology classes or countries of different size adjusts for this. For instance, when large-country advantages are allowed (3.3.3), an increase in direct R&D equivalent to 1 per cent of investment yields a 0.59 per cent increase in exports in a small country compared to 0.92 per cent for a large one, consistent with the observation that firms in small countries devote much less resources to R&D than firms in large countries. The total (combined direct and indirect) effect is also stronger in large countries than in small ones if large-country advantages are allowed. However, the conclusion of the previous paragraph, that is, that the total impact on exports of an investment of given size is larger for R&D than for physical capital, still holds for all countries (independent of size).

We are not aware of any study that may be directly compared to this one. There are, however, some attempts to quantify the impacts of direct and indirect R&D on productivity, see in particular the recent study by Coe and Helpman (1995). Arguably, for a sample of high-income countries, competitive advantages and superior productivity should be expected to go hand in hand,[11] so perhaps something may be learned by comparing their results to ours. What they find, based on evidence for OECD countries in the last decades, is that the returns to R&D investments are high, especially in the larger and medium-sized countries. This is consistent with the findings reported here. Furthermore, they report that for the larger countries, domestic R&D matters most, while for the small countries R&D acquired indirectly through imports is the most important source of technological advance. To see how this latter finding compares to the results of this study, assume a 1 per cent increase in R&D world-wide that leads to a similar increase in indirect R&D (this leaves the ratio between foreign and domestic indirect R&D unaffected). Using the estimates in 3.3.3 (allowing for large-country advantages) the combined direct and indirect impact on exports from domestic sources can be shown to be 0.21 per cent for the small, 0.39 per cent for the medium-sized and 0.85 per cent for the large countries. Similar estimates for the foreign contribution are 0.29 per cent for the small, 0.14 per cent for the medium-sized and 0.04 per cent for the large countries. Hence, for the largest countries, inflows of technology through trade are of negligible importance compared to technology from domestic sources, while for the small countries the foreign contribution is what matters most. Thus, our results, although based on different data and methods, are consistent with those reported by Coe and Helpman.

How sensitive are the results reported here for changes in specification? We tested this extensively, and the results appear reasonably robust. The first two columns in Table 3.5 (3.5.1–2) report the result from substituting the dependent variable (log exports) with the log of the export–import ratio, a measure of export specialization. The results were only marginally different from those reported in Table 3.3 apart from, perhaps, that the detrimental impact of relying heavily on technology import (the foreign share) was even more pronounced. In the two next columns (3.5.3–4) we report the result of deflating all level variables (all variables except 'foreign share') with the number of workers in the industry and country in question. This implies a slight change in the meaning of the test, since this way of doing things excludes that part of the total variance which refers to cross-country differences in the employment structure, that is, patterns of specialization. Still, the results were not qualitatively different, although the numerical values of the estimates were lower in most cases. We also checked for the impact of excluding the HOME variable, since the estimated impact of this variable, although highly significant, was contrary to expectations. Again, the numerical estimates were lower, but not qualitatively different. Finally we made an attempt to include a variable reflecting 'human capital' (*RSE*), defined as (the log of) the share of researchers, scientists and engineers in the labour force of the industry and country in question (*source*: OECD), even if this implied a marked reduction in the size of the sample (3.5.5). However, the *RSE* variable turned out to be uncorrelated with competitiveness.[12]

7   CONCLUDING REMARKS

The purpose of this study has been to explore the relationship between competitiveness, scale and R&D with the help of OECD data bases and the ongoing work in the OECD on embodied technology flows. The results suggest that both direct and indirect R&D have a significant, positive impact on competitiveness. Indirect R&D from domestic sources appear to be more conducive to competitiveness than indirect R&D from abroad. On average the total (direct and indirect) impact of a given investment in R&D on exports is about twice as large as the impact of an investment of similar size in physical capital. The impact of R&D investment appears to be especially high in large countries and R&D-intensive industries.

However, the preliminary and exploratory character of the study should be stressed. What is presented here is a pure cross-sectional analysis. As is well known, this does not allow for testing of causality. The most we can do is to use our theoretical knowledge as a guide for presenting and analysing the structure (and relationships) of the data and compare the findings thus obtained with the theoretical predictions. Furthermore, the number of countries included is small, and this may bias the results, in particular since many of the omitted countries are small. Finally, although these data go much further than most other data sets in quantifying knowledge flows, disembodied knowledge flows are clearly not accounted for. Further research and more extensive data are necessary to validate these results and dig deeper into the question of how scale, R&D and other factors interact in the competitive process.

NOTES

*   This chapter is based on data supplied by the OECD Directorate for Science, Technology and Industry (DSTI) as part of a project there. I am grateful to the DSTI for allowing me to use them for this chapter. An earlier version was presented at the conference on 'Technology and International Trade' in Oslo, 6–8 October 1995. I wish to thank the participants, in particular the commentator and my fellow editors, for comments and suggestions, retaining sole responsibility for the final version.

1. See Dosi, Pavitt and Soete (1990) for an elaboration and empirical application of this perspective.
2. As shown by Melchior (Chapter 5 in this volume), in general the predictions for trade patterns in such models depend very much on the specific assumptions made in each case.
3. See Fagerberg (1995b) for an empirical test of the relationship between export performance and the strength of advanced domestic users.
4. See the Appendix for a complete listing of products/industries.
5. There may be different ways to handle the data (such as deflation); see the section on results for how this is done.
6. To see this, recall that on average the share of domestic indirect R&D in total domestic R&D (direct and indirect) varies between one-tenth and one-quarter across OECD countries (Table 3.1). For the OECD as a whole this share is 20 per cent. Similarly, for the OECD as a whole, the share of foreign indirect R&D in total indirect R&D (*DIF*) is 23 per cent. This means that on average the underestimation of *DIF* is (100*0.23*0.20) per cent = 4.6 per cent, not a very large number. Note also that in the case of the *FOR*-variable, foreign indirect R&D enters both in the numerator and the denominator, reducing the problem even further.
7. For the sake of exposition the variables in this table have been deflated. Market size (domestic demand) is deflated by total OECD demand, wages by average OECD wages, the others are presented as share of production in the country in question. All variables in per cent
8. An additional reason for including dummies in this case would be that the relationship between the propensity to trade and country size is clearly non-linear. For instance, large countries export much less compared to their size than small countries do.
9. The wage level is sometimes used as a proxy for skills; thus one might perhaps have expected a high correlation with direct R&D efforts. However, the result that *WAGE* is uncorrelated with exports holds even when direct R&D is excluded (not reported).
10. The formula used for calculating the total indirect effect (including the decrease in the foreign share) is $b(1 - f)(0.37) + (-b(1 - f)(-0.25))$ where b is the increase in direct R&D (0.02) and f the foreign share (0.23).
11. See the discussion and empirical evidence in Wolff (Chapter 1) and Gustavsson et al. (Chapter 2) in this volume.
12. This might be due to multicollinearity with the direct R&D and/or wage variables. However, even when these variables were excluded (not reported), the *RSE* variable failed to make a significant impact.

REFERENCES

Amable, B. and B. Verspagen (1995), 'The role of technology in market shares dynamics', *Applied Economics*, **27**, 197–204.

Amendola G., G. Dosi and E. Papagni (1993), 'The Dynamics of International Competitiveness', *Weltwirtschaftliches Archiv*, **129**, 451–71.

Coe, D.T. and E. Helpman (1995), 'International R&D Spillovers', *European Economic Review*, **39**, 859–87.

Dosi, G., K. Pavitt and L. Soete (1990), *The Economics of Technical Change and International Trade*, London: Harvester Wheatsheaf.

Dosi, G. and L. Soete (1983), 'Technology Gaps and Cost-based Adjustment: Some Explorations of the Determinants of International Competitiveness', *Metroeconomica*, **35**, 357–82.

Dosi, G. and L. Soete (1988), 'Technical change and international trade', in G. Dosi, C. Freeman, R. Nelson, G. Silverberg and L. Soete (eds), *Technical Change and Economic Theory*, London: Pinter, pp. 401–43,

Fagerberg, J. (1988), 'International Competitiveness', *Economic Journal*, **98**, 355–74.

Fagerberg, J. (1995a), *Is there a large-country advantage in high-tech?*, Working Paper, No. 526, January, Oslo: Norwegian Institute of International Affairs.

Fagerberg, J. (1995b), 'User–Producer Interaction, Learning and Comparative Advantage', *Cambridge Journal of Economics*, **19**, 243–56.

Grossman, G.M. and E. Helpman (1991), *Innovation and Growth in the Global Economy*, Cambridge, Ma: MIT Press.

Grossman, G.M. and E. Helpman (1995), *Technology and Trade*, Discussion Paper Series, No. 1134, February, London: CEPR.

Helpman, E. (1984), 'Increasing Returns, Imperfect Markets and Trade Theory', in R.W. Jones and P.B. Kenen, *Handbook of International Economics*, Volume l, Amsterdam: North Holland, pp. 325–65.

Krugman, P. (1990), *Rethinking International Trade*, Cambridge, MA: MIT Press.

Lacroix, R. and P. Scheuer (1976), 'L'Effort de R&D, l'Innovation et le Commerce International', *Revue Economique*, No. 6, 1008–29.

Lundvall, B.Å. (1985), *Product Innovation and User-Producer Interaction*, Aalborg: Aalborg University Press.

Lundvall, B.Å. (1988), 'Innovation as an Interactive Process – from User-Producer Interaction to the National System of Innovation', in G. Dosi, C. Freeman, R. Nelson, G. Silverberg and L. Soete (eds), *Technical Change and Economic Theory*, London: Pinter, pp. 349–69.

Lundvall, B.Å. (ed.) (1992), *National Systems of Innovation – Towards a Theory of Innovation and Interactive Learning*, London: Pinter.

Magnier, A. and J. Toujas-Bernate (1994), 'Technology and Trade: Empirical Evidence from Five Industrialized Countries', *Weltwirtschaftliches Archiv*, **130**, 494–520.

Nelson, R. (ed.) (1993), *National Innovation Systems, A Comparative Study*, Oxford: Oxford University Press.

Papaconstantinou, G., N. Sakurai and A. Wyckoff (1996), 'Embodied Technology Diffusion: An Empirical Analysis for 10 OECD Countries', *OECD Working Paper*, **4** (8).

Porter, M.E. (1990), *The Competitive Advantage of Nations*, London: Macmillan.

Posner, M.V. (1961), 'International Trade and Technical Change', *Oxford Economic Papers*, **13**, 323–41.

Romer, P.M. (1986), 'Increasing Returns and Long-Run Growth', *Journal of Political Economy*, **94**, 1002–37.
Romer, P.M. (1990), 'Endogenous Technological Change', *Journal of Political Economy*, **98**, S71–102.
Soete, L. (1981), 'A General Test of Technological Gap Trade Theory', *Weltwirtschaftliches Archiv*, **117**, 638–60.
Soete, L.(1987), 'The Impact of Technological Innovation on International Trade Patterns: The Evidence Reconsidered', *Research Policy*, **16**, 101–30.
Venables, A. (1994), 'Economic Integration and Industrial Agglomeration', *Economic and Social Review*, **26**, 1–17.
Vernon, R. (1966), 'International Investment and International Trade in the Product Cycle', *Quarterly Journal of Economics*, **80**, 190–207.
Walker, W.B. (1979), *Industrial Innovation and International Trading Performance*, Greenwich, CT: JAI Press.
White, H. (1980), 'A heteroskedastic-consistent covariance matrix estimator and a direct test for heteroskedasticity', *Econometrica*, **48**, 817–38.

APPENDIX   STAN CLASSIFICATION

ISIC codes	STAN names	Our names
3100	Food, drink and tobacco	Food, drinks
3200	Textiles, footwear and leather	Textiles
3300	Wood, cork and furniture	Wood, furniture
3400	Paper and printing	Paper
351+352 −3522	Industrial chemicals	Industrial chemicals
3522	Pharmaceuticals	Drugs
353+354	Petroleum refining	Petroleum refining
355+356	Rubber and plastics products	Plastics
3600	Stone, clay and glass	Stone, glass
3710	Ferrous metals	Ferrous metals
3720	Non-ferrous metals	Non-ferrous metals
3810	Fabricated metal products	Fabricated metal products
382–3825	Non-electrical machinery	Non-electrical machinery
3825	Office machinery and computers	Computers
383–3832	Electrical machinery	Electrical machinery
3832	Electronic equipment and components	Telecommunications, semiconductors
3841	Shipbuilding	Ships
3842+3844 +3849	Other transport equipment	Other transport
3843	Motor vehicles	Cars
3845	Aerospace	Aerospace
3850	Instruments	Instruments
3900	Other manufacturing	Other manufacturing
30000	Total manufacturing	

4. Technology, employment and trade: perspectives on European integration*

Bart Verspagen and Katharine Wakelin

1 INTRODUCTION

This chapter contributes to the debate on European integration by looking at the employment effects of differences in 'competitiveness' between EU member states. At the aggregate level, the complex links between employment, trade and competitiveness have more often than not been assumed away: the labour content of imports and exports is generally considered to be the same (the exception being imports from the South and their 'unskilled labour' content, the size of which has been an issue of some debate, Wood, 1994). Conventional wisdom argues that trade will adjust through exchange rates, so that any kind of long-term unemployment emerging from the loss of employment in import-competing sectors, will be due only to inefficiencies or other bottlenecks in labour adjustments from import to export sectors. Thus there is, by assumption no direct relationship between trade and employment, but at best an indirect one: the increased openness of most European economies calls for more flexible, adjustable labour markets.[1]

In contrast to this popular line of argument, the present chapter starts from the idea that the relationship between competitiveness, trade, economic growth and employment is not necessarily characterized by equilibrium tendencies. In doing so, we present an empirically oriented approach which tries to assess the ('impulse') employment effects related to changes in international market shares due to differences in competitiveness between nations. We do this by drawing rather loosely on ideas emerging out of the non-mainstream thinking on trade and economic growth, such as Kaldor (1966), Fagerberg (1988) and Cornwall (1977), as well as the recent, more theoretical, literature on 'evolutionary growth theory' (for example, Dosi et al., 1994; Metcalfe, 1988; Silverberg and Verspagen, 1995; Verspagen, 1993). As argued in Fagerberg (1994), this rather heterogeneous set of non-mainstream approaches cannot easily be summarized by means of a simple formal model, but there are a few central conclusions which come out of this literature. First, it is argued that one of the 'real' factors of greatest influence on a country's competitiveness is innovation. Second, differences in innovation levels, and in the commitment of resources to innovation, remain a fundamental source of divergence in the world economy, as well as an explanation for variations in trade performance between countries.

This relationship between trade and innovation is the starting point of our analysis, and we therefore start the chapter with a brief overview of this literature in Section 2. Section 3 puts forward a model which analyses the (partial) employment effects of trade effects related to differences in relative innovation, investment and labour costs, using the insights of the literature summarized in Section 2. The model is applied to bilateral market shares between Germany, Italy and the UK. Section 4 concludes, and provides a discussion of the broader implications of our analysis for European convergence and integration.

2   INNOVATION AND INTERNATIONAL COMPETITIVENESS

Interest in differences in technology as a basis for trade grew partly in response to the Leontief paradox. Superior technology was turned to as a potential explanation for the pattern of US trade. The first theoretical contribution was the technology gap model of Posner (1961), who observed that the production of new products and processes conveyed a temporary monopoly advantage on the producing country and could provide a basis for trade not founded on differences in natural endowments. The diffusion of the innovation over national boundaries would undermine the monopoly advantage, however. Only by continually producing new innovations, could a country maintain a comparative advantage in new products over time.

This theory emphasizes the ability to appropriate the benefits from new innovations, and the monopoly advantages they confer on the innovator. The product-cycle approach considers a similar dynamic framework for the international location of production based on the characteristics of goods as they mature. Maturity brings standardization over time, and leads to the diffusion of production from the advanced innovating country, which has an advantage in the production of non-standardized products, to less technologically advanced countries.

These theoretical perspectives on trade and technology are distinct from attempts to incorporate differences in technology into the Heckscher–Ohlin framework, by the way they treat technology as a concept. These have expanded the two-factor endowment model (labour and capital) to include an additional endowment of 'knowledge' or intellectual capital. This so-called neo-endowment approach also frequently involves the sub-division of labour into endowments of skilled and unskilled labour, the former of which is clearly related to technological superiority. The outcome is that a country with a relatively large endowment of knowledge will have a comparative advantage in producing knowledge-intensive goods, a prediction consistent with that from the technology gap approach. However, in the neo-endowment approach, knowledge is perceived as a static endowment to the economy, not as a dynamic process involving innovation followed by diffusion as in the technology gap or product-cycle models.

While the technology gap and product-cycle models included some relevant features of innovation, such as monopoly advantage, they also lack a more complete treatment of the innovation process. In the technology gap model the benefits of innovation are appropriable in the short run and lead to monopoly power, but the dynamic implications of such benefits are not addressed. In what they term a 'neo-Schumpeterian' approach, Dosi, Pavitt and Soete (1990) observed that the cumulative benefits of innovation, because of its firm specific nature and the ability to partially exclude others from its benefits, can lead to the firm-, sector- and country-specific technological advantage accumulating over time, causing 'virtuous' and 'vicious' cycles of development. Technology is characterized as embodying specific, local, often tacit, and only partly appropriable knowledge which can explain the geographical concentration of innovation over time (Dosi et al., 1990).

Dosi et al. (1990) consider the outcome, in terms of divergence or convergence, as depending on the balance between factors favouring the accumulation of technological advantage over time, and opportunities for countries to catch up to the technology frontier. The latter include imitation, and technology transfer through the diffusion of innovation. Dosi et al. (1990) frequently refer to the 'disequilibrium' nature of this process in general terms. The recent literature on evolutionary growth and trade theory (for example, Dosi et al., 1994; Verspagen, 1993; see Silverberg and Verspagen, 1996, for an overview) provides a more detailed insight on the nature and consequences of such a view. Rather than the traditional point of view that the (international) economy can be usefully characterized by a steady state, or at least the *transitory dynamics* towards it, this literature argues that technology dynamics are a constant source for differential trade and growth performance between countries. It thus proposes a modelling framework in which disequilibrium is the starting point, and in which international growth regimes are characterized by *stochastic distributions* of growth rates rather than well-identified steady states. The most commonly used modelling tool in this literature is taken from the biological literature on Darwinian selection, and is called a replicator equation:

$$\dot{x}_i = x_i\big(f_i(x) - \bar{f}(x)\big), \quad i = 1, n, \quad \text{with } \bar{f}(x) = \sum_{i=1}^{n} x_i f_i(x),$$

where x_i is the market share of country i, and f is a 'competitiveness' (or 'fitness') function (see Hofbauer and Sigmund, 1988, for an overview of replicator dynamics). The economic intuition is simple: countries with above-average competitiveness will expand in relative importance, those with below-average competitiveness will contract, while the average competitiveness $\bar{f}(x)$ in turn changes with the relative population weights.

Note that such a perspective implies important differences with regard to the common 'equilibrium' approach in economics (see, for example, Boggio, 1996, for a more elaborate discussion). The standard approach is (implicitly) based on the idea that the economy is on (or close to) its equilibrium path, implying that the market share of each trading partner corresponds to the underlying cost and quality conditions. Market shares will thus only change if these underlying conditions change, which means there is a relation between market share *changes* and *changes in relative prices*. The replicator logic differs because it does not make the implicit assumption of the economy being on its equilibrium path. Instead, it argues that the economy can usefully be modelled as an adjustment process, where differences in cost and quality (that is competitiveness) are the source for changes of market shares, without equilibrium actually being reached.[2]

The 'new' trade theory or 'new' growth theory, by incorporating endogenous technical change into neoclassical models of trade, not only differs fundamentally from such a 'neo-Schumpeterian' or 'evolutionary' perspective by its equilibrium nature, but also by its conceptualization of technological change. In this approach, technology is frequently conceptualized as consisting of 'blueprints' or inventions, the benefits of which can be partially appropriated by the innovating firm, but which also contribute to a pool of collective knowledge. The role of spillovers of knowledge between countries is emphasized along with the public-good aspects of innovation. This separates it from the neo-Schumpeterian approach outlined above, which places more emphasis on the cumulative nature of technological change.

While these different theoretical approaches to trade and technology all stress different aspects of the innovation process, the actual empirical differences between them have not come out so clearly in the literature so far. Partly because of a lack of precise technology indicators, many of the empirical papers have focused on issues in the technology–trade relationship which are too general to be identified with one of the specific theoretical frameworks mentioned above, such as the importance of innovation in influencing non-price competitiveness. One empirical framework is to include innovation in an export demand model (for instance, Greenhalgh, 1990, for the UK, and Magnier and Toujas-Bernate, 1994, for a number of OECD countries), as a proxy for the quality of goods, along with price and income factors. Growth in market shares relies not just on the ability to compete in terms of price (or unit labour costs) but also to compete in terms of technology, or product quality and in the creation of new products and markets. The results from these models of competitiveness indicate an important role for non-price factors in positively influencing trade performance. For the UK, Greenhalgh (1990), found that this relationship varied considerably according to the sector; while the trade performance of more than half the sectors considered benefited from innovation, either their own or from other sectors, some important innovating sectors did not. Likewise, Magnier and Toujas-Bernate (1994) for five OECD countries, found innovation (proxied by R&D expenditure) to be an important factor in affecting market shares in the long run, again with 'significant national and sectoral disparities' emphasizing the importance of considering the relationship at the sector level. Amable and Verspagen (1995) confirmed these results using patents as the proxy for innovation and allowing country- and sector-specific effects. Amendola et al. (1993), in a country-level model of the dynamic determinants of international competitiveness, confirmed that differences in innovation have important long-run consequences for trade performance.

The link to employment is another issue that has not been elaborated very extensively. It is only recently that the topic has become fashionable. Given the lack of existing literature in the field, we proceed by a rather simple approach, which aims at estimating the (partial) impact of differences in competitiveness on trade performance. In doing so, we choose the explicit evolutionary, disequilibrium framework as it has been discussed above. In order to estimate the impacts of differences in competitiveness on employment, we integrate our model of the relationship between trade and competitiveness with an input–output model that estimates the 'impulse' effects of changes in market shares on employment. Our approach concentrates on demand-side effects only (that is, export demand and import leakage), and does not pretend to be able to provide a complete picture of the relationship between employment, trade and technology. We do not, for example, consider the effects of changes in labour productivity, or ('general equilibrium') effects on the wage rate due to changes in the demand for labour.

3   AN 'EVOLUTIONARY' APPROACH TO TRADE AND EMPLOYMENT

3.1   A Bilateral Model of Competitiveness and Employment

We begin our analysis by formulating a model that captures the 'evolutionary' ideas on the interaction between competitiveness and innovation, as formalized in a broad way in the replicator equation in the previous section. Note that the specific functional form is not an exact replicator, but is based upon earlier empirical models, such as Amendola et al. (1993) and Amable and Verspagen (1995).[3]

The starting point of this approach is that the relationship between competitiveness variables and changes in market shares is sector and country specific, because of different national systems of innovation (Nelson, 1993; Lundvall, 1993), and sectoral differences in technology and production structure. The following linear specification is proposed:

$$\hat{z}_{pqs} = c_p + c_s + \sum_v \left(\kappa_{pv} + \kappa_{sv} \right) \vartheta_{pqsv},$$

$$\text{with } \vartheta_{pqsv} \equiv \ln\left(\left[\vartheta_{psv} / \vartheta_{qsv} \right]_T \right), \tag{4.1}$$

where z denotes a market share, p and q are countries (p is the domestic country, q is the exporter) and s is a sector. Thus, z_{pqs} is the market share of exports from country q in sector s on the domestic market of country p. The hat denotes a proportionate growth rate. ϑ_v is the value scored on competitiveness indicator v (v will denote wages, investment in fixed capital and technology, see below), the κ's are parameters, the c's are constants, and $[\ ]_T$ indicates an unweighted average over time for the division inside the square brackets. The equation thus states that changes in market shares are a function of absolute differences in competitiveness between domestic producers and foreign producers. The slope and intercepts of the additive components of this function have sector- and market-specific components, as indicated by the constants c and parameters κ.

This model is estimated for a data set of 15 manufacturing sectors and ten countries (that is, ten home countries whose market shares on each other's markets are estimated).[4] The sectors are documented in Insert 4.1. There are four different competitiveness indicators which have been used (indicated by v in equation 4.1). The first two are related to technological differences between countries: R&D expenditures as a percentage of output, and patents (issued in the United States) per employee.[5] The third indicator measures the application of (new) capital equipment in the production process, and is defined as the share of investment in output. Finally, a wage indicator is used to show relative labour costs, which is defined as the wage rate in current dollars. All these variables are expressed (on a yearly basis) relative to the importing country and in natural logs, as in equation (4.1) above, and then averages are taken over 1980–85 (average annual growth rate of z, and period averages for the competitiveness variables), so that only one observation remains for a combination of partner country, domestic country and sector. The variables are set up in such a way that if a high value has a positive (negative) influence on competitiveness, the associated parameter is positive (negative). Thus, positive coefficients would be expected for investment, R&D and patents, and a negative sign would be expected for wages.

Insert 4.1   The manufacturing sectors used in the regression and their definition in ISIC and NACE/CLIO terms

Num	Description	ISIC, rev. 2	NACE/CLIO
4.	Basic metal	37	151+152+211+212+221+222+223
5.	Glass, stone, clay	36	23+24
6.	Chemicals	351+352	252 thru 260
7.	Metal products	381	311 thru 316
8.	Machinery	382–3825	321 thru 328
9.	Computers, instruments	3825+385	330+371 thru 374
10.	Electrical goods	383	341 thru 347
11.	Motor vehicles	3843	351 thru 353
12.	Other transport equipment	384–3843	361 thru 365
13.	Food products	31	41+42
14.	Textiles	32	41 thru 43
15.	Wood	33	46
16.	Paper and printing	34	47
17.	Rubber and plastic	355+356	48
18.	Other manufacturing	39	49

Note that ores are included in the NACE/CLIO definition of basic metals, but not in the ISIC definition. This makes the input–output material and data taken from OECD slightly incompatible for this sector, a problem that is necessarily disregarded in any calculations in this chapter. As the sample countries produce few ores this is unlikely to be a serious problem.

From equation (4.1), it is easily seen that for each combination of sector and home country, the sectoral elasticity of a specific competitiveness indicator is equal to the sum of κ_{pv} and κ_{sv}. The t-value for this elasticity can readily be computed from the covariance matrix of the estimated parameters, so statistical estimation of the model (OLS) yields an indication of the significance and size of the effects involved. Two different models are estimated, one for each of the two indicators of technology (R&D and patents). The two other indicators, wages and investment, are included in each of these regressions. These models are denoted equations I and II in Table 4.1.

As will become evident below, the primary interest of this chapter is not to evaluate the estimation results for this specific model.[6] We therefore confine ourselves only to a few remarks with regard to the results documented in Table 4.1. This table gives the results of the estimation for the three countries (Germany, Italy, and the United Kingdom) that will be used in Section 3.2, where the relationship between trade and employment will be analysed. The last four columns in the table will be discussed further below. The estimated coefficients in the other columns of Table 4.1 generally have the expected sign, and a great number of them are significant at reasonable confidence levels. With regard to the technology variables, these are significant (at the 10 per cent level) with the expected (positive) sign in 22 cases (out of 45) for R&D, and in 16 (out of 36) for patents. The sectors in which these variables are generally significant are metal products (7, only R&D); computers and instruments (9); electrical goods (10, only patents); motor vehicles (11, only patents), other transport equipment (12); textiles (14); wood and products (15, only R&D); and other manufacturing (18, only R&D). This list of sectors includes all of the sectors that would normally be classified as high- or medium-tech sectors, except chemicals (6). The list is, however, broader than just these sectors: typically low-tech sectors, such as food, wood and textiles also have significantly positive technology variables. This indicates that the importance of technology for competitiveness goes further than just a few so-called high-tech sectors (see also Dosi et al., 1990, for similar findings). It is true, however, that the estimated parameters for the technology variables are smaller in the case of sectors such as food and textiles than they are in computers, or electrical goods (with the exception of the patenting variable in textiles, which is rather high in comparison with other sectors).

The investment variable is significant with the expected sign in 29 (out of 45) in equation I, and 16 cases (out of 33) in equation II. The sectors for which this variable is generally significant are basic metals (4); glass, stone and clay (5); chemicals (6); metal products (7); computers (9); food products (13); textiles (14); wood and products (15); and other manufacturing (18). This list of sectors includes the common 'scale-intensive' sectors, such as basic metals, textiles and chemicals. The wage variable is significant with the expected sign in 20 cases in both equations. The sectors for which the wage-variable is generally significant are basic metals (4); computers and instruments (9); and textiles (14). There are quite a few sectors for which the wage-rate variable is only significant in one of the two equations estimated: wood (15); paper and printing (16), where it is significant only in equation I, and electrical goods (10); motor vehicles (11); other transport equipment (12); and food products (13), where it is significant only in equation II.

The next step in the analysis is to set up a framework that enables us to relate the impact of competitiveness differences on international market shares to

Table 4.1 Estimations results for equation (4.1)

	Estimated equation I								Estimated equation II				Results used in simulations			
	R&D		Invest.		Wages		Patents		Invest.		Wages					
Sec Cou	Est.	t	Est.	t	Est.	t	Est.	t	Est.	t	Est.	t	Patents	R&D	Invest.	Wages
4 DEU	-0.005	0.33	0.079	3.73	-0.095	2.91	-0.006	0.34	0.054	1.98	-0.122	2.69	0.000	0.000	0.067	-0.109
GBR	0.002	0.12	0.103	4.92	-0.139	5.07	0.001	0.04	0.088	3.16	-0.173	4.06	0.000	0.000	0.095	-0.156
ITA	0.005	0.35	0.088	3.93	-0.167	5.03	-0.004	0.26	0.066	2.32	-0.161	3.75	0.000	0.000	0.077	-0.164
5 DEU	0.008	0.90	0.072	3.37	0.026	0.69	0.019	1.26	0.068	2.66	-0.033	0.67	0.000	0.000	0.070	0.000
GBR	0.015	1.59	0.096	4.41	-0.019	0.55	0.025	1.63	0.102	3.88	-0.085	1.70	0.025	0.000	0.099	-0.052
ITA	0.018	2.25	0.081	3.62	-0.046	1.21	0.020	1.37	0.080	3.02	-0.072	1.52	0.000	0.018	0.081	0.000
6 DEU	-0.007	0.38	0.053	1.82	0.024	0.68	-0.003	0.20	0.030	1.10	0.002	0.03	0.000	0.000	0.041	0.000
GBR	-0.001	0.04	0.076	2.60	-0.020	0.62	0.003	0.17	0.064	2.26	-0.050	1.02	0.000	0.000	0.070	0.000
ITA	0.003	0.14	0.061	2.04	-0.047	1.33	-0.002	0.13	0.042	1.47	-0.037	0.81	0.000	0.000	0.052	0.000
7 DEU	0.034	1.91	0.032	1.96	-0.009	0.23	-0.005	0.23	0.024	1.09	0.015	0.22	0.000	0.034	0.028	0.000
GBR	0.040	2.24	0.055	3.41	-0.053	1.52	0.001	0.04	0.058	2.52	-0.036	0.51	0.000	0.040	0.056	0.000
ITA	0.044	2.45	0.040	2.46	-0.081	2.08	-0.004	0.17	0.036	1.57	-0.023	0.34	0.000	0.044	0.038	-0.052
8 DEU	0.009	0.69	0.011	0.54	-0.004	0.10	0.001	0.04	0.003	0.14	-0.022	0.34	0.000	0.000	0.000	0.000
GBR	0.016	1.15	0.034	1.66	-0.049	1.22	0.007	0.34	0.037	1.64	-0.073	1.13	0.000	0.000	0.035	0.000
ITA	0.019	1.44	0.019	0.92	-0.076	1.76	0.002	0.10	0.015	0.65	-0.061	0.97	0.000	0.000	0.000	-0.068
9 DEU	0.040	1.55	0.002	0.14	-0.108	1.84	0.050	2.92	0.004	0.26	-0.171	3.10	0.050	0.000	0.000	-0.140
GBR	0.046	1.78	0.026	1.58	-0.152	2.66	0.056	3.23	0.038	2.16	-0.222	4.11	0.056	0.046	0.032	-0.187
ITA	0.049	1.91	0.011	0.64	-0.180	3.08	0.051	2.95	0.016	0.88	-0.210	3.95	0.051	0.049	0.000	-0.195
10 DEU	-0.028	1.44	-0.040	1.83	0.018	0.42	0.030	1.84	-0.021	1.00	-0.092	1.79	0.030	0.000	**-0.029**	-0.037
GBR	-0.022	1.13	-0.010	0.65	-0.027	0.70	0.036	2.17	0.013	0.59	-0.143	2.79	0.036	0.000	0.000	-0.085
ITA	-0.018	0.94	-0.030	1.33	-0.054	1.30	0.031	1.87	-0.009	0.41	-0.131	2.66	0.031	0.000	0.000	-0.092
11 DEU	-0.005	0.28	0.008	0.34	0.056	1.49	0.045	2.05	-0.012	0.66	-0.067	1.14	0.045	0.000	0.000	0.000
GBR	0.001	0.07	0.032	1.25	0.012	0.36	0.051	2.32	0.022	1.14	-0.119	2.02	0.051	0.000	0.000	-0.053
ITA	0.005	0.26	0.017	0.67	-0.015	0.40	0.046	2.04	0.000	0.00	-0.106	1.81	0.046	0.000	0.000	-0.061

12 DEU	0.046	4.40	-0.050	1.94	0.014	0.37	0.087	4.37	-0.037	1.51	-0.155	2.47	0.087	0.046	**-0.041**	-0.071
GBR	0.053	5.16	-0.020	0.93	-0.030	0.87	0.093	4.37	-0.003	0.12	-0.207	3.41	0.093	0.053	0.000	-0.118
ITA	0.056	5.71	-0.040	1.49	-0.057	1.44	0.088	4.11	-0.025	0.97	-0.194	3.19	0.088	0.056	0.000	-0.126
13 DEU	0.010	0.91	0.049	2.39	-0.001	0.04	0.014	0.94	0.044	1.93	-0.063	1.26	0.000	0.000	0.046	0.000
GBR	0.016	1.51	0.073	3.48	-0.046	1.34	0.020	1.32	0.078	3.31	-0.114	2.27	0.000	0.000	0.075	-0.080
ITA	0.020	1.95	0.058	2.70	-0.073	1.90	0.015	0.99	0.056	2.33	-0.102	2.13	0.000	0.020	0.057	-0.087
14 DEU	0.023	2.58	0.144	5.84	-0.165	3.96	0.046	3.24	0.133	5.47	-0.212	4.02	0.046	0.023	0.139	-0.189
GBR	0.029	3.29	0.168	6.74	-0.210	5.49	0.052	3.45	0.167	6.65	-0.263	4.97	0.052	0.029	0.168	-0.236
ITA	0.033	4.58	0.153	6.04	-0.237	5.62	0.047	3.30	0.145	5.72	-0.251	4.87	0.047	0.033	0.149	-0.244
15 DEU	0.023	2.45	0.087	4.88	-0.167	4.14			-0.017	0.87	-0.003	0.06		0.023	0.044	-0.084
GBR	0.029	3.05	0.111	6.17	-0.211	5.66			0.017	0.81	-0.055	0.94		0.029	0.055	-0.106
ITA	0.033	3.88	0.096	5.10	-0.239	5.85			-0.005	0.25	-0.042	0.75		0.033	0.048	-0.119
16 DEU	0.005	0.60	0.063	2.81	-0.094	1.99			-0.017	0.87	-0.003	0.06		0.000	0.032	-0.047
GBR	0.012	1.31	0.087	3.82	-0.138	3.05			0.017	0.81	-0.055	0.94		0.000	0.043	-0.069
ITA	0.015	1.98	0.072	3.06	-0.165	3.44			-0.005	0.25	-0.042	0.75		0.015	0.036	-0.083
17 DEU	0.009	0.55	-0.010	0.51	0.048	1.28	0.012	0.75	-0.012	0.56	0.005	0.09	0.000	0.000	0.000	0.000
GBR	0.016	0.95	0.012	0.55	0.004	0.11	0.019	1.09	0.022	1.04	-0.047	-0.93	0.000	0.000	0.000	0.000
ITA	0.019	1.16	-0.000	0.10	-0.024	0.62	0.014	0.80	0.000	0.01	-0.034	-0.71	0.000	0.000	0.000	0.000
18 DEU	0.021	2.60	0.047	2.58	-0.051	1.68			-0.017	0.87	-0.003	-0.06		0.021	0.024	-0.025
GBR	0.028	3.36	0.071	3.82	-0.095	4.75			0.017	0.81	-0.055	-0.94		0.028	0.035	-0.047
ITA	0.031	4.71	0.056	2.88	-0.122	3.96			-0.005	0.25	-0.042	-0.75		0.031	0.028	-0.061

Note: Coefficients printed in bold were set to zero in the simulations below.

employment changes. In order to do so, we use a bilateral input–output model. Consider the following input–output structure.

$$
\begin{array}{ccccccc}
u_{11} & \cdots & u_{1n} & f_1 & b'_1 & b_1 & q_1 \\
\cdot & & \cdot & \cdot & \cdot & \cdot & \cdot \\
\cdot & & \cdot & \cdot & \cdot & \cdot & \cdot \\
\cdot & & \cdot & \cdot & \cdot & \cdot & \cdot \\
u_{n1} & \cdots & u_{nn} & f_n & b'_n & b_n & q_n \\
v_1 & \cdots & v_n & & & & \\
q_1 & \cdots & q_n & & & & \quad (4.2)
\end{array}
$$

Upper case denotes vectors or matrices, lower case elements of these. B' is the vector of sectoral trade balances with country $*$; B the counterpart of this for the rest of the world; U is the $n \times n$ square matrix of intermediate use u_{ij} of sector-i products by sector j $(i, j = 1, ..., n$, total use consists of imports and domestic origin); F is the vector of final demand, including investment, consumption and mutations in stocks, but not exports; V is the vector of value added; and Q the vector of production.

Defining the matrix of technical coefficients A in the usual manner $(a_{ij} = u_{ij} / q_j)$, one may write

$$ Q = AQ + F + B' + B. \quad (4.3) $$

Next, define the market shares for country $*$ on the domestic market z_i as $m_i / (q_i + m_i - x_i) = m_i / (q_i - b' - b)$, and z' (the counterpart for the rest of the world) accordingly (i denotes a sector, m imports, and x exports). Setting up the diagonal matrices Z' and Z, with elements z'_i and z_i on the diagonal, respectively, these definitions can be used to write the following expressions for the trade balances B' and B (X denotes exports):

$$ B' = Z'^*(Q^* - B'^* - B^*) - Z'(Q - B' - B), \quad B = X - Z(Q - B' - B). \quad (4.4) $$

Now, consider 'the rest of the world', as well as the market shares of the 'domestic country' and 'country $*$' on each other's markets as exogenous.[7] In that case, equations (4.3) and (4.4), together with their (symmetric) counterparts for country $*$, form a simultaneous system with endogenous variables Q, Q^*, B', B'^*, B and B^*. This means that for any value of the 'exogenous' variables in the system (that is, domestic final demand and the production structure in the two countries, market shares, as well as all variables in 'the rest of the world'), one can calculate the solution for Q and Q^* (which are the two variables of interest here), as well as the other endogenous variables (that is, the trade balances). Although the procedure of solving this model, and the resulting expressions, are somewhat tedious, it is, in principle, quite straightforward and only requires simple linear algebra. The outcome can be expressed as follows:

$$Q = [I - \alpha\gamma\alpha^*\gamma^*]^{-1} [\alpha\beta + \alpha\gamma\alpha^*\beta^*],$$
$$Q^* = [I - \alpha^*\gamma^*\alpha\gamma]^{-1} [\alpha^*\beta^* + \alpha^*\gamma^*\alpha\beta], \qquad (4.5)$$

subject to the following definitions (definitions for country * are not documented, but are symmetric):

$$\varphi \equiv [I - Z' - Z]^{-1}, \Psi = [I - Z]^{-1},$$
$$\Pi \equiv \Psi Z\varphi Z', W \equiv [I - \Pi] \Psi Z\varphi Z'^*,$$
$$E \equiv [I - WW^*]^{-1}[[I - \Pi]^{-1}\Psi X - W[I - \Pi^*]^{-1}\Psi^* X^*],$$
$$F \equiv [I - WW^*]^{-1} [[I - \Pi]^{-1} [\Pi + \Psi Z] + WW^*],$$
$$H \equiv [I - WW^*]^{-1}[W + W[I - \Pi^*]^{-1} [\Pi^* + \Psi^* Z^*]] \qquad (4.6)$$
$$\alpha \equiv [I - A + \varphi Z' + F + \varphi Z'F + \varphi Z'^* H^*]^{-1}$$
$$\beta \equiv F + E + \varphi Z'E - \varphi Z'^* E^*,$$
$$\gamma \equiv H + \varphi Z'H + \varphi Z'^* + \varphi Z'^* F^*.$$

Our procedure in the rest of the chapter is the following. We use the estimation results from equation (4.1) to calculate the predicted changes in market shares for each possible combination of two countries from the set which includes Germany, the United Kingdom and Italy. These predicted changes, together with the initial values for the market shares, are used to calculate two matrices Z and Z'^*, which are substituted into expressions (4.6) and (4.5), respectively. Using the other exogenous variables (such as the production structure, final demand and 'the rest of the world'), which are kept constant throughout the analysis, this procedure yields, for each combination of two countries, a vector of sectoral output values which is different from the actual input–output table used. This difference can be interpreted as the 'impulse' effect of competitiveness differences between the two countries on output. Using the assumption of a fixed vector of labour productivities, this can readily be 'translated' into the 'impulse' effect of competitiveness differences on employment in the two countries.

Let us say a few words on the meaning of this procedure. A by now quite common approach to calculating the employment effects of international trade, is to calculate the actual changes over some period in time in what is called here the Z matrices, and analyse the employment effects related to this according to formulas such as (4.5).[8] This procedure is commonly known as 'decomposing' output and employment changes into several, distinct, effects. There are several criticisms one may have about such a method. These mainly relate to the fact that the method does not provide any insight into the question of what causes the changes in the Z matrix (the factors into which employment changes are decomposed do not have a theoretical underpinning), and the fact that such a method does not include 'second-order', or 'general-equilibrium', effects of the calculated changes in employment. For example, one may argue that if a country loses market share on international markets, and this leads to a change in its employment level, wages will drop (given that the labour market is sufficiently flexible), and hence its market share will grow again.

The present chapter tries to respond to the first part of this criticism, while leaving the second part largely unaddressed. What the present model does is, by applying the 'evolutionary' reasoning implicit in equation (4.1), to provide some insight into what are the underlying forces for changes in international market shares. It thus attempts to take the analysis one step further, by estimating the impact of several factors upon the dynamics of Z, thereby attempting to open the black box of 'competitiveness'. The details of the empirical procedure by which this will be done are explained in more detail in the next section.

3.2   Putting Things Together: The Employment Effects of Competitiveness

What do the results in Table 4.1 imply for intra-European labour markets? In order to answer this question, the parameter values in the last four columns of Table 4.1 were used to calculate the predicted changes in bilateral market shares for three major European countries (Germany, Italy and the United Kingdom) according to equation (4.1).[9] These parameter values were set to zero for cases where a non-significant effect was found in the regressions (for investment and wages, zero was used when coefficients in both regressions were insignificant; the mean of the two coefficients was used otherwise).[10] The right-hand-side data in equation (4.1) used to calculate the market share changes refer to the period 1980–85, and can therefore be regarded as a reasonable proxy for predicting the effects over the 1980s (keeping in mind a time lag between cause and effect of several years). These predicted changes of bilateral market shares between the three countries were subsequently used to calculate the associated employment effects, using the method outlined above. For this purpose, input–output data from EUROSTAT for 1980 were used. This procedure yields one employment effect for each of the four variables, and for each of the two trading partners. The results are documented in Table 4.2.[11]

Note that because of the additive form of the regression equation (4.1), it is possible to calculate partial effects related to each of the four competitiveness indicators. These partial effects are defined as the employment effects of the predicted changes in market shares on the basis of differences in one competitiveness variable only, keeping the other differences equal to zero. (Thus, for example, the partial effect relating to wages is the effect of differences in wage levels, under the assumption that competitiveness levels of the two countries for the other variables are equal.) This procedure is repeated for each competitiveness variable, and the results are presented as the first four numbers in each of the cells in Table 4.2 ('partial effects'). The last two numbers in the cells are simple additions of the partial effects, where we have two additions, because we use each of the two innovation indicators separately. These totals can thus be seen as two separate estimations of the effect of differences in 'total' competitiveness between the two countries. The last column in the table sums up effects over the two trading partners and gives, again, partial as well as 'total' effects.[12]

Table 4.2 *Results of bilateral IO-simulations of employment effects of competitiveness differences, 1980s, in percentages of 1980 total employment by country*

Country Patents R&D Wages Investment Total* Total**	Germany	Trading partner United Kingdom	Italy	Total
Germany		0.03	0.13	0.16
		0.00	0.10	0.11
		−0.04	−0.05	−0.08
		0.00	−0.09	−0.09
		−0.00	−0.01	−0.01
		−0.03	−0.03	−0.06
United Kingdom	−0.06		0.05	−0.01
	−0.00		0.06	0.05
	0.07		0.01	0.09
	−0.01		−0.06	−0.07
	0.00		0.01	0.01
	0.06		0.01	0.07
Italy	−0.27	−0.06		−0.33
	−0.19	−0.06		−0.25
	0.09	−0.02		0.07
	0.17	0.07		0.24
	−0.01	−0.01		−0.02
	0.07	−0.01		0.05

Notes
* Summed effects of patents, wages and investment.
** Summed effects of R&D, wages and patents.

A number of interesting features emerge from Table 4.2. First, it is interesting to see that the largest employment effects exist in the combinations where Italy is present. The combination between Germany and the UK yields much smaller changes. This results from the fact that the differences in competitiveness between the UK and Germany are much smaller than those between Italy and each of the two other countries. This holds, however, only for the partial effects, and much less so for the overall effects (that is, the sum of the partial effects). The overall effects are documented in the last two lines of each cell in the table. There are two summed effects: one in which R&D is the technology indicator, and one in which patents take this role. It is clear that Italy lags behind in technology, which implies a tendency to lose market share on its local markets, but this tendency is (slightly) more than made up for by the lead Italy has in the two other indicators (that is, it has relatively low wages and high investment). Overall, it is clear that although there are significant differences in employment effects between these countries inside the EU, the net effect of these differences is often small.

Another interesting finding is that the employment effects of technology variables are mostly larger than those associated with wages and investment. It appears that in this sample of countries, differences in wage levels have the smallest impact on employment. This result seems to refute the relatively large attention the 'wage factor' is usually assigned in public discussions, contrary to technology factors, for example.

4   CONCLUSIONS: PERSPECTIVES ON EUROPEAN COHESION

What do these results imply for cohesion in the European Union? For the three countries and the time period analysed here, the outcomes in Table 4.2 indicate that only rather small (aggregate) employment effects result from the differences in competitiveness between the three countries. Thus, these countries have evolved in such a way that the differences in 'scores' for the individual competitiveness indicators more or less cancel each other out.

We want to put forward the interpretation that this result is an illustration of the working of (general equilibrium) mechanisms (which have remained outside our analysis), such as differential rates of growth of wages or capital accumulation, 'reacting' to performance in international and domestic markets, although we do not have empirical evidence to support this. Thus, for example, an initial Italian lag in technology might have led to downward pressure on employment levels, which, in turn, put downward pressure on wages, thereby leaving 'net' Italian competitiveness largely unaffected.

The results, however, clearly show that although such mechanisms seem to exist, it is not necessarily true that their working also ensures 'cohesion', or 'even development' in a broader sense. For example, a country may have a clear lag with regard to innovation performance, relying to a large extent upon traditional, low-tech (and low-wage) industries, without major employment effects resulting. It is only through relatively low wages and high investment that such a country can keep up in international competition *vis-à-vis* the more advanced countries in the European Union. Thus, below the surface of 'converging aggregate competitiveness', there might be a tendency for different countries to achieve differential rates of productivity growth, incomes or real wage growth, or growth of innovation potential. Such convergence in 'aggregate' competitiveness is thus likely to go together with divergence in the long-term growth of real income between different parts of the Union (for example, Tylecote, 1992), for example, with one part of the Union on a track of fast productivity growth, technological development and wage growth, and another part on a track of slow technological change and slow wage growth. Fagerberg and Verspagen (1995), in an analysis of regional growth and technology gaps in Europe, have indeed found a pattern which is broadly compatible with such an interpretation.

In such a situation, the mainstream recipe for curing unemployment (increased flexibility of labour markets), is likely to reinforce such 'real' long-term divergence (by allowing markets to adjust faster to the new circumstances). In short, a vicious circle is likely to develop in some countries, adjusting 'downwards' their specialization pattern, leading to a short-term burst of investment-led growth, but a decline in those countries' long-term technology-based growth. We thus call for prudence in the application of these policies, which, in the longer term, may well be harmful for an even and balanced development inside the European Union.

NOTES

*   We thank participants at the Royal Economic Society Conference, Canterbury, UK, March 1995, as well as Reinoud Joosten, Luc Soete, Adriaan van Zon and the editors of this volume for helpful comments and discussions. Bart Verspagen's research has been made possible by a fellowship from the Royal Dutch Academy of Arts and Sciences.
1. The OECD Jobs Study put it as follows: 'The theoretical mechanisms of international trade … imply that an increasing intensity of trade will lead to higher incomes and will displace labour and capital resources from one activity to another, with little or no impact on labour utilisation as long as markets function well and wages are flexible' (OECD, 1994, p. 98).
2. Dosi et al. (1990), Chapter 6, develop this argument in more detail, without, however, referring to the formal framework of the replicator equation.
3. Estimating an exact replicator equation puts heavy demands on data availability, because the population weighted average competitiveness cannot be computed in the presence of missing values for some data points. The present functional form can be seen as maintaining the idea of absolute advantages having an impact on changes of market shares, while using the

competitiveness of the domestic producers as a proxy for average competitiveness (this requires a bilateral specification, however).

4. The countries are: Canada, Denmark, Germany, France, Italy, Japan, Norway, Sweden, the United Kingdom and the United States.

5. R&D expenditures are essentially an input–indicator of technological change, while patents measure technological output. Neither of the two indicators is perfect for measuring technology, but given the available data, they are the only measures that are feasible. See Soete and Verspagen (1991) for a more detailed discussion of the pros and cons of the indicators. US patents are used because they are available on a sectoral (ISIC) basis, and because they provide a common patent market for all countries in the sample (national patents are subject to different national patenting laws).

6. Amable and Verspagen (1995) estimate a similar model, and provide a more detailed discussion.

7. That is, exogenous to the input–output part of the model. The analysis below will use the estimation results for equation (4.1) to endogenize changes in market shares.

8. See, for example, Chenery et al. (1962, 1986), Martin and Evans (1981), and Sakurai (1993).

9. z and z' were calculated by multiplying the value for $(z + z')$ in the input–output table by s and $(1 - s)$, respectively, where s is the share of the partner country in total imports of the domestic country (taken from OECD databases). This way, differences between the trade data in the input–output data and the OECD database are neutralized (these differences are in some cases considerable). Note that because of the lack of bilateral trade data outside manufacturing, it had to be assumed that all trade in these sectors is with the 'rest of the world' (in other words, z' is set to zero in these sectors).

10. Two coefficients were set to zero because their (significant) signs do not have a useful theoretical interpretation. Setting these coefficients to their actual (negative) value does not, however, change the results presented in this section in any significant way.

11. The effects documented in Table 4.2 appear to be rather small, for example, the largest effect is –0.33 per cent of the 1980 labour input in Italy. One has to keep in mind, however, that these percentages measure the impact of trade with only *one* partner on *total* initial employment.

12. For example, for the combination Germany–United Kingdom, the effect of differences in technological competitiveness as measured by patents is 0.03 per cent employment change in Germany, and –0.06 per cent change in the United Kingdom. Implicitly, we see that Germany has a technological lead over the United Kingdom. Overall, that is, including wages and investment, however, Germany is less competitive than the United Kingdom, as indicated by the negative signs for the total effects in Germany, and the positive signs in the United Kingdom. The United Kingdom, apparently, has a large lead over Germany for wage competitiveness, as indicated by the 0.07 per cent increase in employment in the United Kingdom, and the 0.04 per cent decrease in Germany. Looking at the last column of the table, we see that Germany has indeed a larger technology lead, as indicated by the 0.16 and 0.115 per cent increases in employment because of its 'total' (that is, over trading partners) effects related to patents and R&D, respectively.

REFERENCES

Amable, B. and B. Verspagen (1995), 'The role of technology in market share dynamic', *Applied Economics*, **27**, 197–204.

Amendola, G., G. Dosi and E. Papagni (1993), 'The dynamics of international competitiveness', *Weltwirtschaftliches Archiv*, **129**, 451–71.

Arthur, W.B. (1989), 'Competing Technologies, Increasing Returns and Lock-in by Historical Events', *Economic Journal*, **99**, 116–31.

Boggio, L. (1996), 'Growth and International Competitiveness in a Kaldorian Perspective', *Structural Change and Economic Dynamics*, **7**, forthcoming.

Chenery, H.B., S. Robinson and M. Syrquin (1986), *Industrialization and Growth: A Comparative Study*, London: Oxford University Press.

Chenery, H.B., S. Shishido and T. Watanabe (1962), 'The Pattern of Japanese Growth', *Econometrica*, **30**.

Cornwall, J. (1977), *Modern Capitalism. Its Growth and Transformation*, London: Martin Robertson.

David, P.A. (1990), 'The Dynamo and the Computer: An Historical Perspective on the Modern Productivity Paradox', *American Economic Review. Papers and Proceedings*, **80**, 355–61.

Dosi G., S. Fabiani, R. Aversi and M. Meacci (1994), 'The Dynamics of International Differentiation: A Multi-Country Evolutionary Model', *Industrial and Corporate Change*, **3**, 225–41.

Dosi, G., K. Pavitt and L. Soete (1990), *Economics of Technical Change and International Trade*, London: Harvester Wheatsheaf.

Fagerberg, J. (1988), 'International Competitiveness', *Economic Journal*, **98**, 355–74.

Fagerberg, J. (1994), 'Technology and International Differences in Growth Rates', *Journal of Economic Literature*, **XXXII**, 1147–75.

Fagerberg, J. and B. Verspagen (1995), 'Heading for Divergence? Regional Growth in Europe Reconsidered', MERIT Research Memorandum 95–014, Maastricht.

Greenhalgh, C. (1990) 'Innovation and Trade Performance in the United Kingdom', *Economic Journal*, **100**, 105–18.

Grossman, G. and E. Helpman (1991), *Innovation and Growth in the Global Economy*, Cambridge, MA: MIT Press.

Hofbauer, J. and K. Sigmund (1988), *The Theory of Evolution and Dynamical Systems*, Cambridge: Cambridge University Press.

Kaldor, N. (1966), 'The Case for Regional Policies', *Scottish Journal of Political Economy*, **XVII**.

Levine R. and D. Renelt (1992), 'A Sensitivity Analysis of Cross-Country Growth Regressions', *American Economic Review*, **82**, 942–63.

Lundvall, B.A. (ed.) (1993) *National Systems of Innovation: Towards a Theory of Innovation and Interactive Learning*, London: Pinter.

Magnier, A. and J. Toujas-Bernate (1994), 'Technology and Trade: Empirical Evidence from Five Industrialized Countries', *Weltwirtschaftliches Archiv*, **130** (3), 494–520.

Martin, J.P. and J.M. Evans (1981), 'Note on Measuring the Employment Displacement Effects of Trade by the Accounting Procedure', *Oxford Economic Papers*, **33**, 154–64.

Metcalfe, J.S. (1988), 'Trade, Technology and Evolutionary Change', University of Manchester, mimeo.

Nelson, R.R. (ed.) (1993), *National Innovation Systems: A Comparative Analysis*, New York: Oxford University Press.

OECD (1994), *The OECD Jobs Study: Evidence and Explanations*, Paris: OECD.

Posner, M. (1961), 'International Trade and Technical Change', *Oxford Economic Papers*, **XIII**, 323–41.

Sakurai, N. (1993), 'Structural Change and Employment: Empirical Evidence for Eight OECD Countries', paper presented at the conference on 'Technology, Innovation and Employment', 7–9 October 1993, Helsinki.

Silverberg, G. and B. Verspagen (1995), 'An Evolutionary Model of Long Term Cyclical Variations of Catching Up and Falling Behind', *Journal of Evolutionary Economics*, **5**, 209–27.

Silverberg, G and B. Verspagen (1996) (in press), 'Evolutionary Theorizing on Economic Growth', in K. Dopfer (ed.), *The Evolutionary Principles of Economics*, Norwell, MA: Kluwer Academic Publishers.

Soete, L. and B. Verspagen (1991), 'Recent Comparative Trends in Technology Indicators in the OECD Area', in OECD (ed.), *Technology and Productivity. The Challenge for Economic Policy*, OECD: Paris, pp. 249–74.

Tylecote, A. (1992), 'Core-Periphery Inequalities in European Integration, East and West', in W. Blaas and J. Foster (eds), *Mixed Economies in Europe*, Edward Elgar: Aldershot, pp. 236–71.

Verspagen, B. (1993), *Uneven Growth Between Interdependent Economies. The Evolutionary Dynamics of Growth and Technology*, Aldershot: Avebury.

Wood, A. (1994), *North–South Trade, Employment and Inequality: Challenging Fortunes in a Skill-Driven World*, Oxford: Clarendon Press.

5. New theory and evidence on the standard good hypothesis

Arne Melchior

1 INTRODUCTION*

Product innovation is frequently seen as an essential prerequisite for the competitiveness of firms: they should find 'market niches'; that is, develop differentiated products that give them some market power and sales potential in limited market segments. If prices are above marginal costs, it is trivially true that individual firms may increase their profits by developing products that increase their sales. When all firms make differentiated products, however, the question becomes different: then we may ask how product differentiation as such affects specialization and trade. In this chapter, the role of horizontal differentiation in this context will be examined. We shall assume that all firms and countries have the same capacity for product innovation, derive the aggregate effects, and examine how the degree of product differentiation affects the outcome. While research on technology is normally interested in differences between countries or firms with respect to technology, we assume away these differences and concentrate on the macro implications of technology patterns.

An early approach to these issues was the so-called 'standard good hypothesis' by Dreze (1961). Dreze maintained that if products are nationally differentiated and there are economies of scale in production, small countries should specialize in production of goods for which the international demand is relatively standardized. Because of their limited market size, small countries would be at a disadvantage in the production of more differentiated goods. These questions may be important for explaining the pattern of trade, and also in the context of recent trade policy developments where product standardization has been an important issue. According to Dreze, a process of international product standardization, as in the EU internal market, would clearly be in the interest of the smaller European countries.

During recent years, a whole body of trade theory has been developed where scale economies and product differentiation play an important role. It is now textbook theory that intra-industry trade may be caused by a combination of scale economies and product differentiation. In spite of this, it has not been made clear what the relationship between the degree of product differentiation and the trade pattern actually is. The purpose of this chapter is to shed some light on this issue, and to test empirically some of the theoretical predictions obtained.

Ethier (1982) considered the role of technology in a two-factor model with one differentiated good sector, and concluded that the levels of fixed and marginal costs, or the degree of product differentiation, had no impact on the trade pattern. While the existence of fixed costs and product differentiation was crucial for the results, their levels did not matter. The reason why the degree of product differentiation did not matter in the model of Ethier, is that intermediate levels of trade barriers were not analysed. As in most other Heckscher–Ohlin-based models with one sector with monopolistic competition (see, for example, Dixit and Norman, 1980), autarky and completely free trade are compared, and not intermediate solutions. As will be shown in this chapter, some of the results are fundamentally changed when intermediate levels of trade barriers are considered.

This chapter takes the following format: Section 2 sets out a model of monopolistic competition. Section 3 considers the role of the technology parameters in the model. Section 4 presents some preliminary evidence from Norwegian data, and Section 5 contains some final comments.

2   A BASIC MODEL

The basic point can be shown using a model of monopolistic competition along the lines of Krugman (1980) and Venables (1987), with one factor of production and two sectors. The basic framework is well known; here we shall use it to address an issue that has not been explicitly considered.

Following the two-stage procedure of Dixit and Stiglitz (1977), consumers first choose between 'food' (Y_i) and an aggregate of manufactured (differentiated) goods (X_i). Food is produced under constant returns to scale and may be traded costlessly between all countries, so the price for food is the same in all countries and it is used as the numeraire. The price index for manufactures in country i is denoted P_i. There is one factor of production, labour, and country i has an endowment of L_i, expressed in terms of the numeraire. Since there will be no pure profits in the model (because of monopolistic competition and zero profits), total income will be L_i and we therefore have $L_i = Y_i + X_i P_i$ (thus, there is no transfer of profit between countries). Costless trade in 'food' assures that nominal wages are equalized, although real wages may be different because of different prices for manufactured goods.

We use a Cobb–Douglas utility function of the form $U_i = Y_i^{1-\alpha} X_i^{\alpha}$, where α is the expenditure share of manufactures in all countries. From this we derive the demand function for manufactured goods, $X_i = \alpha L_i P_i^{-1}$, and the demand for food, $Y_i = (1 - \alpha)L_i$. $a_i = \alpha L_i = X_i P_i$ is then the value of manufactured goods consumed. The Cobb–Douglas form implies that the expenditure shares are constant, so a_i is also a measure of relative market size.

In country i, there are n_i identical firms, each producing a distinct variety of the differentiated product, with sales to market j denoted as x_{ij} ($i = 1, \ldots ,N, j = 1, \ldots,N$) with prices p_{ij}. The sub-utility function for manufactures will have a CES (constant elasticity of substitution) form:

$$X_i = \left[\sum {}_j n_j x_{ji}^{\frac{\varepsilon-1}{\varepsilon}} \right]^{\frac{\varepsilon}{\varepsilon-1}} \tag{5.1}$$

ε is the elasticity of substitution between all pairs of products, and we assume that $\varepsilon > 1$. The corresponding price index is:

$$P_i = \left[\sum {}_j n_j p_{ji}^{1-\varepsilon} \right]^{\frac{1}{1-\varepsilon}} \tag{5.2}$$

The demand functions for individual products will then be

$$x_{ij} = a_j p_{ij}^{-\varepsilon} P_j^{\varepsilon-1} \tag{5.3}$$

We assume that all manufacturing firms have the same cost function, which involves a fixed cost f and constant marginal costs c. In addition, there are trading costs, expressed as a mark-up on marginal costs, in the form ct_{ij}, with $t_{ij} \geq 1$. We shall generally assume $t_{ii} = 1$ so that there are no trading costs in the home market. Trading costs are real costs, not taxes. Total costs for a firm in country i are then

$$C_i = f + c \sum {}_j t_{ij} x_{ij} \tag{5.4}$$

We assume that the market structure is one of monopolistic competition. In this case, firms maximize profits while neglecting the influence of their actions on the aggregate price indices P_i. The perceived elasticity of demand is therefore $\in$. Firms in country i maximize total profits

$$\pi_i = f + \sum {}_j x_{ij} (p_{ij} - ct_{ij}) \tag{5.5}$$

We obtain the first-order condition

$$p_{ij} = \frac{ct_{ij}\varepsilon}{\varepsilon - 1} \qquad (5.6)$$

Denoting the sales of an individual firm from country i to country j as v_{ij}, we have, using (5.3) and (5.6):

$$\frac{v_{ij}}{v_{jj}} = \frac{x_{ij}p_{ij}}{x_{jj}p_{jj}} = t_{ij}^{1-\varepsilon} \qquad (5.7)$$

Under monopolistic competition, the number of firms will adjust so that the profits of each firm are zero. Setting (5.4) equal to zero and using the first-order condition (5.5), we obtain

$$\sum_j x_{ij}p_{ij} = \varepsilon f \qquad (5.8)$$

The value of each firm's output is uniquely determined by ε and f, and all manufacturing firms in all countries are of equal size.

For simplicity, we may solve the system for the case of two countries ($i, j = 1,2$). We assume $t_{12} = t_{21} = t$, that is, symmetrical trade barriers. Using (5.8) for firms in countries 1 and 2 we gain two equations which can be solved for the sales of firms in the two markets. Using (5.7) we obtain:

$$v_{11} = v_{22} = \frac{\varepsilon f t^{\varepsilon-1}}{1 + t^{\varepsilon-1}} \qquad (5.9)$$

$$v_{12} = v_{21} = \frac{\varepsilon f}{1 + t^{\varepsilon-1}} \qquad (5.10)$$

Summing the total sales of manufactured goods in the two markets, we obtain:

$$\begin{aligned} n_1 v_{11} + n_2 v_{21} &= a_1 \\ n_1 v_{12} + n_2 v_{22} &= a_2 \end{aligned} \qquad (5.11)$$

The solution for the number of manufacturing firms in the two countries is then:

$$n_1 = \frac{a_1 t^{\varepsilon-1} - a_2}{\varepsilon f\left(t^{\varepsilon-1} - 1\right)}$$
(5.12)

$$n_2 = \frac{a_2 t^{\varepsilon-1} - a_1}{\varepsilon f\left(t^{\varepsilon-1} - 1\right)}$$
(5.13)

A basic result from this type of model is the creation of a home-market effect; large countries will have a disproportionately large share of manufacturing production and be net exporters of manufactured goods. In Melchior (1996, Chapter 7) it is confirmed that for intra-OECD trade this home-market effect is present for the majority of manufacturing sectors. Trade liberalization will increase the home-market advantage of large countries, unless this is offset by cost advantages in smaller countries (Krugman and Venables, 1990).

3 PRODUCT DIFFERENTIATION AND TRADE

We may first observe from (5.8) that the level of fixed costs f will affect firm size; higher fixed costs will make firms larger. From (5.12) and (5.13), we see that the absolute number of firms in each country will be affected by f, but not the relative number of firms in the two countries. By combining (5.9)–(5.10) and (5.12)–(5.13), we also notice that the total volume of trade between the two countries will be unaffected by the size of fixed costs. It is therefore evident that the introduction of trade barriers in the monopolistic competition framework does not change the conclusions reached by Ethier (1982): the presence of fixed costs is vital for the results, but the level of fixed costs does not matter for aggregate trade or the specialization pattern.

The case is different with respect to the degree of product differentiation, since the elasticity of substitution interacts with the trade barriers in determining the trade and production pattern. From (5.8) we may notice that individual firms will become larger when products become more homogeneous. Average costs will thus decline, as well as the number of product varieties. The total number of firms in both countries combined must therefore decrease when products become more standardized. Looking at the impact of a change in ε for the number of firms in country 1, we have:

$$\frac{\partial n_1}{\partial \varepsilon} = \frac{\varepsilon f t^{\varepsilon-1}(\ln t)(a_2 - a_1) - f\left(a_1 t^{\varepsilon-1} - a_2\right)\left(t^{\varepsilon-1} - 1\right)}{\left[\varepsilon f\left(t^{\varepsilon-1} - 1\right)\right]^2}$$
(5.14)

If $a_1 > a_2$, both terms in the numerator will be negative. Therefore *when the products are more homogeneous, the number of firms in the larger country will be lower*. If country 1 is the smallest ($a_1 < a_2$), the sign of this derivative will be ambiguous, that is it is possible that the number of firms in the smaller country may increase when products become more standardized.[1] What is certain, is that the *relative* number of firms in the smaller country will increase when ε gets larger. This is seen by differentiating the ratio n_1/n_2. We obtain:

$$\frac{\partial\left(\dfrac{n_1}{n_2}\right)}{\partial\varepsilon} = \frac{t^{\varepsilon-1}(\ln t)\left[1-\left(\dfrac{a_1}{a_2}\right)^2\right]}{\left(t^{\varepsilon-1}-\dfrac{a_1}{a_2}\right)^2} \qquad (5.15)$$

If $a_1 < a_2$ the expression is positive, and this confirms that *when the products are more homogeneous, the smaller country will have a higher share of manufacturing production*. We have thus obtained an interesting parallel to the 'standard good hypothesis' by Dreze (1961). Although Dreze considered national differentiation, not symmetrical and horizontal differentiation, the theme is the same. The model thus confirms Dreze's assumption that *small countries will be at a disadvantage in the production of differentiated goods under economies of scale, and this disadvantage will be larger when the products are more differentiated.*

In Melchior (1996, Chapter 6), this conclusion is generalized to the case with many sectors with monopolistic competition. In this case, the home-market advantage of the larger country will be more pronounced, the more differentiated the products in a sector are. The level of fixed costs will still not matter for the patterns of trade and production.

The mechanism behind these results is a higher elasticity of substitution between products, implying that trading costs will 'bite harder'; firms will sell a larger share of their production in the home market. In the limit, when ε becomes very large, we will approach autarky. A higher elasticity of substitution will thus reduce the possibility of firms in the larger country exploiting their home-market advantage.

It is thus evident that the degree of product differentiation will have an impact on the trade pattern. Using (5.11), (5.12), (5.14) and (5.15), we have

$$GROSS = n_1 v_{12} + n_2 v_{21} = \frac{a_1 + a_2}{1 + t^{\varepsilon-1}} \qquad (5.16)$$

Similarly, the net exports of manufacturing products from country 1 to country 2 (NET_{12}) will be

$$NET_{12} = n_1 v_{12} - n_2 v_{21} = \frac{a_1 - a_2}{t^{\varepsilon-1} - 1} \qquad (5.17)$$

By differentiating these expressions with respect to ε, it is easily established that *a higher elasticity of substitution will reduce the volume of trade, and the magnitude of the trade deficit of the smaller country.*

The net export ratio (sometimes called the Balassa index of export specialization) for manufactured goods, B_{12}, will then be

$$B_{12} = \frac{NET_{12}}{GROSS} = \left\{\frac{a_1 - a_2}{a_1 + a_2}\right\}\left\{\frac{t^{\varepsilon-1} + 1}{t^{\varepsilon-1} - 1}\right\} \qquad (5.18)$$

We differentiate this with respect to ε:

$$\frac{\partial B_{12}}{\partial \varepsilon} = \frac{-2t^{\varepsilon-1}(a_1 - a_2)\ln t}{(a_1 + a_2)(t^{\varepsilon-1} - 1)^2} \qquad (5.19)$$

For $a_1 > a_2$ the expression is negative, and for $a_1 < a_2$ it is positive. It is thus evident that *the proportion of net trade in total trade in manufactured goods will decrease when products become more homogeneous.* Since the Grubel–Loyd index of intra-industry trade is equal to $1 - |B_{ij}|$, this also implies that *the more differentiated the products are, the lower will be the proportion of intra-industry trade'.*[2] Several empirical studies have taken for granted the view that the relationship between product differentiation and the proportion of intra-industry trade should be a positive one (see, for example, Pagoulatos and Sorensen, 1975; Loertscher and Wolter, 1980; Balassa and Bauwens, 1988). Our result shows that this may be wrong in the context of monopolistic competition and horizontal product differentiation, when trade barriers are present.[3]

If factor-endowment differences are taken into account in a model with trading costs (Markusen and Venables, 1996), the relationship between product differentiation and the pattern of trade becomes more complex, and the full implications have not deen derived. The results regarding net trade and product differentiation would be expected to hold; if products are more differentiated, the advantage of the larger country could be reinforced by a factor-based comparative advantage, or weakened by a factor disadvantage. The two effects will in a sense be additive. Regarding intra-industry trade, however, the sign of the effect could be changed; if the small country has a factor-based trade surplus, more homogeneous products will tend to increase this surplus and reduce the proportion of intra-industry trade. Our results on intra-industry trade thus only apply to the stylized case when the small country has a trade deficit in all sectors. Because of this ambiguity concerning intra-industry trade, the empirical analysis of this chapter will focus on net trade – for which factor-based advantages may not reverse the effect of product differentiation.

A paradoxical implication of the model is that when the products become almost perfect substitutes (when ε becomes very large), the proportion of intra-industry trade will in the limit approach a maximum equal to $[2^*\min(a_1,a_2)]/(a_1 + a_2)$. When the products become fully homogeneous, however, we should expect no intra-industry trade at all, since product differentiation is a precondition for intra-industry trade in the model. This 'discontinuity at the margin' applies to other features of this kind of model: when trade barriers become very low, the small country will become deindustrialized; but when trade barriers disappear, there will be no market-size effect left. In defence of these unrealistic features of the model it may be said that trade is never costless, and fully homogeneous manufactured goods seldom, if ever, exist. Theory of the type presented here is a stylized tool for deriving hypotheses; empirical research has to confirm whether they hold true or not.

4   SOME EMPIRICAL EVIDENCE

In the following, the theoretical predictions above will be tested on Norwegian data. The dependent variable in the analysis will be the net export ratio, that is, net trade divided by gross trade. According to the earlier results, we expect that this measure will be positively related to the elasticity of substitution in all bilateral trade flows where Norway is the smallest country. Since Norway is smaller than all its major trading partners, the relationship will also hold for total trade, and we shall therefore use total exports and imports for individual sectors as data.

The estimates of elasticities of substitution made by Hansson (1989) will be used as measures of horizontal product differentiation, since this is the best source of information available for the purpose. Hansson estimated the elasticities of substitution between imports and domestic Swedish production at a disaggregated level. We will assume that the ranking of sectors according to this measure is also representative for the ranking of inter-product elasticities of substitution. This would be true in a world exhibiting CES technology. In practice, there may be demand asymmetries which imply that the measure of national differentiation measured by Hansson deviates from the measure we should have according to the theoretical model. This ambiguity has to be taken into account when interpreting the results.[4]

The model used above is a stylized case which abstracts from other forces that are important for the determination of the trade pattern. For the analysis of net trade, it is particularly important to take into account factor endowments; if not, a bias due to omitted variables could occur. Since the model developed in Section 3 does not account for factor-endowment differences, we shall in the empirical study have to account for such variables in an *ad hoc* manner, based on the results in, for example, Helpman and Krugman (1985) and Ethier (1982). Basically, the Heckscher–Ohlin theorem on net trade and relative factor abundance holds also in the case with a differentiated good sector. We face, however, the same problem of indeterminacy in the case with more goods than factors (see Ethier, 1984), but we shall assume that there is a chain of comparative advantage linking factor intensities and net trade. This may be supported by a small-country assumption, or non-equalization of factor prices (Jones and Neary, 1984, p. 19). On the empirical problems involved in cross-sector studies of this kind, see Leamer (1984, p. 56).

The following variables reflecting factor-endowment differences will be used (for more details on variables, see Melchior, 1994b):

- *Capital* measures sectoral capital intensity in Norwegian production, proxied by non-wage value added per employee (that is, a flow measure).
- *Skills* measures the use of skilled labour in each sector, proxied by the average wage level in each sector. The correlation between sectoral wages and the proportion of skilled labour is empirically confirmed (see, for example, Hansson, 1989, p. 78).
- *Electricity* measures the importance of hydroelectricity in each sector, measured by the share of electricity consumption in gross value of production. This variable, as well as *Capital* and *Skills*, is based on Norwegian Manufacturing Statistics.

Previous evidence suggests that we should expect Norway to be exporting capital-intensive (see Haaland and Norman, 1989) and electricity-intensive goods. The sign of the skill variable is less easy to predict: Norway is generally a net importer of such goods, but this does not determine the ranking of the sectoral net export ratios according to skills.

Our model also predicts that the net export ratio will be influenced by the level of trade barriers in each sector. We shall therefore include variables reflecting the sectoral level of trade barriers. Since aggregate trade data are used, the possible influence of differences in trade policies across countries or regions will not be taken into account. We use separate variables reflecting (i) Norwegian trade barriers and (ii) trade barriers in Norwegian export markets. Based on Venables (1987) who examined asymmetrical trade barriers in a similar model, we expect net trade to be positively related to Norwegian trade barriers, and negatively related to barriers in export markets. The following variables will be used:

- *Norwegian barriers* is a dummy variable measuring the importance of Norwegian non-tariff barriers, based on EFTA (1992) and Golombek (1991).
- *EU barriers* is a dummy variable that measures the importance of non-tariff barriers facing Norwegian exports (Buiges et al., 1990). Because of data availability and the position of the EU as Norway's largest trading partner, EU data were used.

The empirical test will be made based on cross-section data on Norway's trade in six selected years from 1976 to 1991. Cross-section regressions will be run for each year in turn. Because of missing data and certain data problems (see Melchior, 1994b for details), some sectors were deleted. For such reasons, oil/gas, fish products and some transport equipment subgroups are not covered by the analysis. The analysis thus concerns the remaining manufacturing sectors, that is, 111 to 114 observations for each year.

The model to be tested will have the form

$$B_{ky} = \alpha_{0y} + \sum_i \alpha_{iy} Z_{iky} + \beta_y \varepsilon_k + \sum_j \gamma_{jy} T_{jk} + u_{ky} \qquad (5.20)$$

where

B_{ky} = net export ratio for total Norwegian trade in sector k and year y
α_{0y} = constant term in year y
Z_{iky} = factor intensity variable i for sector k, year y, with the corresponding parameter estimate α_{iy} in year y
ε_k = substitution elasticity for sector k, with parameter estimate β_y in year y
T_{jk} = trade barrier variable j for sector k, with parameter estimate γ_{jy} in year y
u_{ky} = error term for sector k in year y.

As the subscripts indicate, annual data for the six selected years will be used for the net export ratio and the factor intensity variables, while only a single vector of observations is available for the substitution elasticities and the variables reflecting the level of trade barriers. We will obtain different estimates for all the parameters for each year in turn. When interpreting the results, we can in some cases observe patterns over time; it should be remembered that the number of observations over time is too limited to draw 'significant' conclusions about time trends.

4.1 Econometric Considerations

The net export ratio is a censored variable, and for this reason Tobit regressions should be considered. In fact, however, there are virtually no censored observations (except for one observation in 1976), and Tobit regressions did not change the results in any significant manner. For that reason, only ordinary OLS regressions will be reported.

Problems of heteroscedasticity are considerably reduced by using the net export ratio (instead of net export volume) as dependent variable. Heteroscedasticity-corrected standard errors are reported. Although some heteroscedasticity is present, the basic results from the analysis are unaffected by this.

Outliers may also be expected to be a problem in this kind of analysis; therefore regressions were also run with influential observations excluded. The procedure used was to calculate the influence statistics

$$\hat{u}_{ky} h_{ky} / (1 - h_{ky}) \qquad (5.21)$$

where $\hat{u}_{ky}$ is the sector k residual in year y and $h_{ky} = X_{ky} (X_y^T X_y) X_{ky}^T$, where X_y is the matrix of regressors in year y. The influence diagnostic (5.21) measures the impact on the k'th residual brought about by omitting sector k in the regression, and then comparing the predicted and actual values for sector k (see Davidson and MacKinnon, 1993, p. 35). The influence statistics were examined, and observations with relatively high absolute values were deleted. In this way, between three and nine observations were deleted for each year. Deleting influential observations generally increased the explanatory power of the regressions, and in general also the levels of significance. Deleting influential observations thus indicated that the results were not unduly affected by such observations.

Multi-collinearity will generally also increase the influence of extreme observations. If, for example, two variables are identical except for one observation, this observation will have a strong influence on the parameter estimates. Therefore, our handling of influential observations may also be partially relevant for multi-collinearity.

4.2 Results

Tables 5.1 and 5.2 report the results. In each cell, the upper figure is the parameter estimate, with *** indicating a significance level of 1 per cent or less, ** between 1 per cent and 5 per cent, and * between 5 per cent and 10 per cent. The middle figure is the P value under the T distribution, that is, the probability under the null hypothesis that the observed t value or a value greater than it could occur by chance. These values, and the significance levels marked by the asterisks, are based on the ordinary covariance matrix estimates. The lower figure in each cell reports the heteroscedasticity-consistent (White-corrected) standard error estimates.

Table 5.1   OLS regressions, all observations included
Dependent variable: net export ratio.

Variable	1976	1980	1984	1987	1988	1991
Intercept	−1.34***	−1.37***	−0.91***	−1.16***	−1.04***	−1.28***
	0.000	0.000	0.000	0.000	0.000	0.000
	0.251	0.231	0.249	0.263	0.335	0.211
Capital	2.60*	1.82**	1.84***	1.07**	0.57	−0.05
	0.063	0.050	0.002	0.041	0.123	0.903
	1.989	1.110	0.686	0.661	0.446	0.402
Skills	8.54**	6.88**	0.72	1.65	1.95	2.79***
	0.034	0.017	0.656	0.219	0.106	0.003
	3.654	2.220	1.433	1.148	1.163	0.805
Electricity	8.64***	7.83***	6.09***	7.57***	5.89**	11.83***
	0.002	0.004	0.010	0.001	0.016	0.000
	3.485	3.603	2.556	2.874	2.488	3.222
Elasticity	0.10**	0.10**	0.07*	0.10**	0.04	0.03
	0.033	0.033	0.064	0.023	0.378	0.498
	0.050	0.046	0.043	0.056	0.057	0.047
Norwegian	0.19*	0.18*	0.14*	0.16*	0.13	0.16*
barriers	0.059	0.055	0.084	0.067	0.136	0.074
	0.095	0.090	0.076	0.080	0.075	0.079
EU	−0.12	−0.13	−0.12	−0.17**	−0.17*	−0.04
barriers	0.229	0.165	0.149	0.046	0.055	0.680
	0.094	0.089	0.089	0.093	0.110	0.082
R^2	0.34	0.36	0.36	0.36	0.28	0.35
Obs (N)	111	113	113	113	113	114

Note: See text for explanation.

The most important result from the regressions is that the 'standard good hypothesis' is supported. The sign is positive in all cases, but the significance levels and the parameter values suggest that the relationship is becoming weaker over time. While the results for 1976, 1980 and 1987, are significant at the 5 per cent level or better, the result for 1984 is significant at this level only when influential observations are deleted, and the results for 1988–91 are not significantly different from zero. In Melchior (1994a) the expectation of a positive relationship between product homogeneity and the proportion of intra-industry trade is confirmed for Norwegian data.[5]

Table 5.2 OLS regressions, influential observations deleted

Variable	1976	1980	1984	1987	1988	1991
Intercept	-1.29^{***}	-1.60^{***}	-1.26^{***}	-1.23^{***}	-1.31^{***}	-1.37^{***}
	0.000	0.000	0.000	0.000	0.000	0.000
	0.233	0.234	0.166	0.242	0.179	0.218
Capital	4.78^{**}	1.72	2.60^{***}	1.02	0.73^{**}	-0.04
	0.039	0.254	0.000	0.119	0.035	0.918
	2.634	1.533	0.508	0.689	0.343	0.359
Skills	5.83	7.89^{***}	1.61	1.50	2.27^{**}	2.52^{***}
	0.119	0.006	0.274	0.225	0.015	0.005
	3.335	2.275	1.106	0.956	0.778	0.790
Electricity	13.06^{***}	11.79^{***}	7.52^{***}	11.64^{***}	9.50^{***}	16.54^{***}
	0.000	0.001	0.001	0.000	0.000	0.000
	3.603	3.972	2.116	3.149	2.111	2.831
Elasticity	0.10^{**}	0.13^{***}	0.13^{***}	0.09^{**}	0.03	0.06
	0.037	0.009	0.002	0.041	0.363	0.208
	0.046	0.050	0.038	0.055	0.034	0.047
Norwegian barriers	0.21^{**}	0.16^{*}	0.11	0.11	0.04	0.18^{**}
	0.026	0.081	0.124	0.160	0.482	0.031
	0.090	0.087	0.071	0.072	0.059	0.077
EU barriers	-0.11	-0.06	0.00	-0.08	0.03	-0.01
	0.251	0.512	0.951	0.338	0.605	0.920
	0.094	0.090	0.074	0.085	0.065	0.081
R^2	0.39	0.40	0.50	0.38	0.45	0.43
Obs. (N)	102	107	109	106	106	111

Note: See text for explanation.

The signs regarding the impact of trade barriers are also in conformity with the theoretical predictions, with an improved net export ratio for sectors with high Norwegian barriers (a positive sign in all cases), and with a negative sign on EU barriers in 10 out of 12 cases. The significance levels are rather low, however, and the results are significantly different from zero only in a few cases.

The factor-intensity variables confirm the strong and important role for cheap hydroelectricity for Norwegian manufacturing exports, and a positive but declining role for capital abundance as a basis for Norway's manufacturing competitiveness. Skills also play a positive role for the net export position: in an apparent cyclical fashion with increased imports of skill-intensive goods during the consumption boom in the mid-1980s, and returning to a level around 1990 with lower 'skill performance' than 10 years before.

The explanatory power of the regressions, measured by R^2, varies from 0.28 to 0.36 when all observations are included, and from 0.38 to 0.50 with influential observations deleted. We can therefore conclude that the model has a reasonably high – although not impressive – explanatory power.

5 CONCLUDING COMMENTS

This chapter shows that in trade models with monopolistic competition (scale economies and product differentiation) and trading costs, the net export position of smaller countries will improve when products become more homogeneous. The theoretical results thus provide a parallel to the 'standard good hypothesis' suggested by Dreze (1961), implying that when there are economies of scale in production, small countries will be specialized in goods for which international demand is relatively standardized. While Dreze focused on national differentiation, it has been shown that a similar logic is relevant in the context of horizontal product differentiation. The focus is therefore different from Dreze's, although the theme is the same.

The chapter also presents empirical evidence from Norway's foreign trade for the years 1976–91, which gives some support to this suggested relationship between horizontal product differentiation and trade pattern.

The results imply that to the extent that international product standardization, for example in the EU internal market, reduces horizontal product differentiation across countries, this will improve the manufacturing competitiveness of small countries. They also suggest that if technologies develop according to the 'product cycle', with maturing technologies and product homogeneity over time, the manufacturing competitiveness of smaller countries should increase over the product cycle. In order to improve their international competitiveness, small countries should 'look abroad' in order to develop products for which there is an international demand. If they try to develop highly differentiated goods, this will be like swimming against the tide. The analysis suggests that this is the general rule. As always, there is no rule without exceptions. The analysis here abstracts from nationally biased preferences; development of national varieties may always be important for the position in the domestic market.

This chapter also illustrates the need to take market structure into account when drawing conclusions about technology and specialization. This interplay between technology and the market should be focused on in future research, since technology is always embedded in and shaped by the market.

NOTES

* I thank Pär Hansson, Lars Lundberg, Jan Fagerberg and in particular Karolina Ekholm for useful comments to the first draft. The responsibility for remaining errors is mine.

1. The first term in the numerator will be positive, and the second term will be negative within the range when there is a weakly positive number of firms in both countries. This range is here defined by setting the number of firms in country 1 equal to zero, which implies that $a_1 \geq a_2 t^{1-\varepsilon}$ is a precondition for having a positive number of firms in country 1. This implies that the expression $a_1 t^{\varepsilon-1} - a_2$ in the numerator is also positive when $a_1 < a_2$.

2. In empirical research, economies of scale are sometimes measured by firm size. In this model, this will be εf. Because of the influence of ε it may be related to the trade pattern although f is not. If economies of scale are measured by the ratio of average to marginal costs, which will here be equal to $\varepsilon/(\varepsilon - 1)$, there will be a negative relationship between this measure and the proportion of intra-industry trade.

3. The theoretical results above relate to horizontal differentiation, not vertical differentiation (see, for example, Falvey, 1981; Flam and Helpman, 1987). Vertical product differentiation is an important aspect of the international trade pattern (see, for example, Greenaway, Hine and Milner, 1994).

4. Based on an 'Armington' approach, Hansson himself expected and found a negative relationship between this measure and the sectoral proportion of intra-industry trade in Swedish trade. This result is contrary to our hypothesis. A possible interpretation is the following: intra-industry trade is positively linked to skills (Melchior, 1994a), and Sweden is a relatively skill-abundant country (Hansson and Lundberg, 1995, p. 62). To the extent that Sweden had a trade surplus for such goods with larger countries during the period studied by Hansson (until 1983), the degree of product differentiation might be positively related to the proportion of intra-industry trade, that is, negatively related to the substitution elasticity.

5. Since intra-industry trade is linked to skills and Norway has a large trade deficit for skill-intensive goods (Melchior, 1994b), this may explain why factor-endowment differences do not reverse the relationship suggested by our model.

REFERENCES

Balassa, B. and B. Bauwens (1988), 'The determinants of intra-European trade in manufactured goods', *European Economic Review*, **32**, 1421–37.

Buiges, P., F. Ilzkovitz and J.-F. Lebrun (1990), 'The impact of the internal market by sector: the challenge for the member states', *European Economy*, Special Edition 1990.

Davidson, R. and J.G. MacKinnon (1993), *Estimation and Inference in Econometrics*, New York/Oxford: Oxford University Press.

Dixit, A.K. and V. Norman (1980), *Theory of International Trade*, Cambridge: Cambridge University Press.

Dixit, A.K. and J. Stiglitz (1977), 'Monopolistic competition and optimum product diversity', *American Economic Review*, **67**, 297–308.

Dreze, J. (1961), 'The standard goods hypothesis', in A. Jaquemin and J. Sapir (eds) (1989), *The European Internal Market: Trade and Competition. Selected Readings*, Oxford: Oxford University Press, pp. 13–32.

EFTA (1992), 'Effects of "1992" on the manufacturing industries of the EFTA countries', *EFTA Occasional Paper*, No. 38.

Ethier, W. (1982), 'National and international returns to scale in the modern theory of international trade', *American Economic Review*, **72** (3), 389–405.

Ethier, W. (1984), 'Higher dimensional issues in trade theory', in R.W. Jones and P.B. Kenen (eds), *Handbook of International Economics*, Amsterdam: North-Holland, pp. 131–84.

Falvey, R.E. (1981), 'Commercial policy and intra-industry trade', *Journal of International Economics*, **11**, 495–511.

Flam, H. and E. Helpman (1987), 'Vertical product differentiation and North–South trade', *American Economic Review*, **77** (5), 810–22.

Golombek, R. (1991), 'The impact of 1992 on Norwegian manufacturing industries', *SNF–rapport*, 1/91.

Greenaway, D., R. Hine and C. Milner (1994), 'Country-specific factors and the pattern of horizontal and vertical intra-industry trade in the UK', *Weltwirtschatftliches Archiv*, **130** (1), 77–100.

Haaland, J.I. and V.D. Norman (1989), 'EFTA and the world economy. Comparative advantage and trade policy', Bergen: Senter for Anvendt Forskning, Rapport No. 10/89.

Hansson, P. (1989), 'Intra-industry trade: Measurement, determinants and growth. A study of Swedish trade', Umeå: *Umeå Economic Studies*, No. 205.

Hansson, P. (1993), 'The effects of trade barriers on domestic market performance – evidence from Swedish and Norwegian manufacturing industries', in J. Fagerberg and L. Lundberg (eds), *European Economic Integration: A Nordic Perspective*, Aldershot, Avebury, pp. 107–28.

Hansson, P. and L. Lundberg (1995), *Från basteknologi till högteknologi. Svensk näringsstruktur och strukturpolitik*, Stockholm: SNS Förlag.

Helpman, E. and P. Krugman (1985), *Market Structure and Foreign Trade*, Cambridge, MA/London: MIT Press.

Jones, R.W. and P. Neary (1984), 'The positive theory of international trade', in R.W. Jones and P.B. Kenen (eds), *Handbook of International Economics*, Vol. I, Amsterdam: North-Holland, pp. 1–62.

Krugman, P. (1980), 'Scale economies, product differentiation, and the pattern of trade', *American Economic Review*, **70**, 950–59.

Krugman, P. and A. Venables (1990), 'Integration and the competitiveness of the peripheral industry', in C. Bliss and J. Braga de Macedo (eds), *Unity with Diversity in the European Economy*, London: Centre for Economic Policy Research, pp. 56–75.

Leamer, E. (1984), *Sources of International Comparative Advantage. Theory and Evidence*, Cambridge, MA: MIT Press.

Loertscher, R. and F. Wolter (1980), 'Determinants of intra-industry trade: Among countries and across industries', *Weltwirtschaftliches Archiv*, **116**, 280–93.

Markusen, J. and A.J. Venables (1996), 'The theory of endowment, intra-industry and multinational trade', *Centre for Economic Policy Research Discussion Paper Series*, No. 1341.

Melchior, A. (1994a), 'Intra-industry trade: A matter of scale or skills?', Norwegian Institute of International Affairs, Oslo: *NUPI Report*, No. 183/94.

Melchior, A. (1994b), 'Export specialization in small countries: A case for the standard goods hypothesis? Determinants of Norwegian trade specialization 1976–1991', Norwegian Institute of International Affairs, Oslo: *NUPI Report*, No. 184/94.

Melchior, A. (1996), 'On the economics of market access and international economic integration', Ph.D. dissertation at the University of Oslo.

Pagoulatos, E. and R. Sorensen (1975), 'Two-way trade in international trade: An econometric analysis', *Weltwirtschaftliches Archiv*, **111**, 454–65.

Statistics Norway, Manufacturing Statistics, various issues.

Venables, A. (1987), 'Trade and trade policy with differentiated products: A Chamberlinian–Ricardian model', *Economic Journal*, **97** (387), 700–717.

6. Dynamic comparative advantages in a Ricardian model

Jørgen Drud Hansen

1   INTRODUCTION

This chapter examines the specialization of international trade in a Ricardian model with an extremely large number of goods. The basic model is developed by Dornbusch, Fisher and Samuelson (1977). For given labour productivities, their model allows for a determination of sector menus of exportables and importables for a country. Krugman (1987) extends the model by taking *learning by doing* into account in the individual production activities. The productivity in the individual sector is determined by experience which depends on the cumulated production of the sector, that is, productivity is determined by history. As temporary manipulations of production may lead to long-run changes in trade patterns and terms of trade in an open economy, *hysteresis in specialization* may arise, that is, permanent effects on trade of temporary shocks in production. In policy analysis, the model thus elucidates formally the *infant industry argument*.

The purpose of this chapter is to generalize Krugman's analysis in two respects. First, contrary to Krugman, it is assumed in this chapter that fundamental sector-specific differences in productivity exist between countries, that is, productivity differences for an identical level of experience. The reason for such fundamental productivity differences could, among others, be differences in factor endowments or possible technical know-how from other sources than learning, for example, R&D. In the model presented in this chapter, labour productivity in the individual sector is a combined result of both the fundamental labour productivity and the accumulated experience through learning by doing. Because of learning by doing, history still matters to some degree in explaining the patterns of specialization under free trade. However, because of the *fundamental productivity structure*, there is a risk that free trade may lead to global non-efficient long-run specialization. Such cases are illustrated in this chapter. However, the room for inefficient long-run specialization is constrained by the diffusion of knowledge between countries. The policy conclusion is to improve international mobility of knowledge in order to diminish possible inefficiencies

Second, in another version of the model, it is assumed that the potential for productivity growth varies between sectors. Krugman applies identical parameters for all sectors in relation to learning by doing. By dropping this simplifying assumption, the way is paved for introducing a classification of sectors in accordance with the *degree of dynamism*. If a country in the initial situation is well represented by experience in dynamic sectors, this superiority will be enhanced if the country opens up to trade. Because of a high relative wage in the country, less-dynamic sectors will be expunged, leaving only dynamic sectors, that is, as regards the degree of dynamism, the industrial structure will be homogeneous. This is in stark contrast to a country which initially is less represented by experience in dynamic sectors. The comparatively few dynamic sectors in this country will survive and represent the spearhead of the industries of the country. The outcome will be a mixed industrial structure with both dynamic as well as non-dynamic sectors.

The chapter is organized as follows. Section 2 presents the basic model, that is, Krugman's dynamic version of Dornbusch, Fisher and Samuelson's model. In Section 3, we introduce fundamental differences in relative productivities between countries. Relative productivities in the current period are determined partly by fundamentals and partly by experience from past periods. It is shown that history may lead to a specialization pattern which is not in harmony with the fundamental productivity structure. In Section 4, a version of the model is presented where the potential for efficiency growth through learning differs between sectors. The consequences of differences in the degree of sector-specific experiences on the terms of trade and the industrial structure are analysed in this section. Section 5 summarizes the main conclusions and points to some generalizations.

2   THE BASIC MODEL

The following model is based on *Ricardian assumptions* about production and trade. The world is assumed to consist only of two countries: a home country (H) and a foreign country (F). Each country produces an extremely large number of goods by linear production activities where homogeneous labour is the only input. The production in sector i in the two countries is given by:

$$X_i = a_i L_i, \quad X_i^* = a_i^* L_i^*, \quad i = 1,2,3,...,n \tag{6.1}$$

where X_i is the output in sector i, L_i the input of labour devoted to production in sector i in the home country (without asterix) and in the foreign country (with asterix). The sectors are aligned in order of decreasing relative labour productivity for the home country, $A_i = a_i/a_i^*$. As the number of sectors are extremely large A_i is perceived to be a continuous function of i, $A(i)$ (see Figure 6.1).

To keep the model simple, all goods are assumed to be tradables. Perfect competition prevails, and relative wage rates, that is, w/w^*, determine the *specialization pattern*. For any value of relative wage rates (w/w^*), a marginal industry $\bar{i}$ could be determined by the equation:

$$(w/w^*) = A(\bar{i}) \tag{6.2}$$

that is, all industries in the interval $0 < i < \bar{i}$ are exportables for H whereas all industries for $i > \bar{i}$ are exportables for F.

The relative wage rate is determined by the menu of relative productivities $A(i)$ and the *balance-of-payments equilibrium*. The *budget share of each sector* is assumed to be constant and identical for both countries. The *cumulated budget share* for goods produced in H, λ, is an increasing function of $\bar{i}$, or stated alternatively a decreasing function of (w/w^*). The reason is that a decrease in the relative wage enhances the number of sectors belonging to country H's exportables, compare the A-curve, and the cumulated budget share of goods produced in country H thus increases. The balance-of-payments equilibrium is given by the condition:

$$w/w^* = \frac{\lambda}{1-\lambda}\left(L^*/L\right) \tag{6.3}$$

where L and L^* is the total labour force in H and F, respectively. Dornbusch, Fisher and Samuelson (1977) present this condition by the positively sloped curve B in Figure 6.1. By combining the two curves A and B in Figure 6.1, the relative wage rate and the specialization pattern is determined by the intersection point E.

The model so far is based on Dornbusch, Fisher and Samuelson's presentation. Krugman (1987) adds to this a *dynamic specification* of labour productivities. The labour productivity at time t is determined solely by cumulated experience K_i for the sector. Krugman uses the following specification:

$$a_i(t) = K_i^\varepsilon(t), \quad a_i^*(t) = K_i^{*\varepsilon}(t), \quad 0 < \varepsilon < 1 \tag{6.4}$$

Experience is endogenously given in a dynamic framework by a sector-specific *learning process* determined by the volume of production in the sector. Krugman includes spillovers of learning across borders in his specifications:

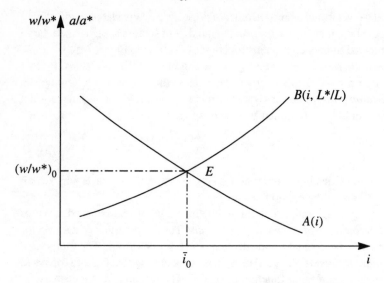

Figure 6.1   Determination of specialization and the terms of trade

$$K_i(t) = \int_{-\infty}^{t} \left(X_i(\tau) + \delta X_i^*(\tau) \right) d\tau$$

and:

$$K_i^*(t) = \int_{-\infty}^{t} \left(X_i^*(\tau) + \delta X_i(\tau) \right) d\tau; \quad 0 < \delta < 1 \qquad (6.5)$$

The parameter δ represents the cross-border *diffusion of knowledge* or the degree of internationalization of learning.

The relative change in experience is given by:

$$\frac{dK_i}{K_i} - \frac{dK_i^*}{K_i^*} = \frac{\left(X_i + \delta X_i^* \right)}{K_i} - \frac{\left(X_i^* + \delta X_i \right)}{K_i^*} \qquad (6.6)$$

As all sectors are totally specialized, except the marginal sector $\bar{i}$, $X_i > 0$ implies $X_i^* = 0$ and vice versa. Utilizing this in (6.6) and solving for:

$$\frac{dK_i}{K_i} = \frac{dK_i^*}{K_i^*}$$

the *steady-state values* of relative experience, K_i/K_i^* are determined. The solutions turn out to be:

$$K_i/K_i^* = 1/\delta \tag{6.7}$$

for exportables for H and:

$$K_i/K_i^* = \delta \tag{6.8}$$

for exportables for F.

Figure 6.1 illustrates a free trade equilibrium in the *short run* where productivities are given. However, if the dynamic effects are taken into account, relative productivities a_i/a_i^* will gradually change to their *long-run* steady-state values $(1/\delta)^\varepsilon$ for exportables for H and δ^ε for exportables for F.[1] Accordingly, the shape of the long-run relative productivity curve thus consists of two horizontal segments connected to the marginal industry by a vertical line (see Figure 6.2). During the adjustment to the long-run steady-state, both the specialization pattern and the relative wage will remain unaffected. The productivity gains will lower prices relative to the wage rate. As the budget shares are assumed to be constant, price elasticity is -1, and the expenditure on the individual good measured in wage units is therefore unchanged. The relative wage rate will only be affected by a *cross-over* of sectors in the trade pattern from one country to the others. However, this will never occur since the short-run specialization pattern will be consolidated by the subsequent changes in productivities.[2]

In the long run, relative wage rates and specialization patterns are constrained to the intervals $\delta^\varepsilon \le w/w^* \le (1/\delta)^\varepsilon$ and $\bar{i}_{min} \le \bar{i} \le \bar{i}_{max}$ respectively (see Figure 6.2). Relative wage rates reflect *terms of trade*, and a trade-off in welfare therefore exists between the two countries when alternative long-run equilibria are compared.

As productivities are endogenously determined in the long run a rationale for *strategic trade policy* exists. If, for example, the home country wants to enhance its menu of exportables, it needs to obtain sufficient superiority in experience in more sectors. This could be done by temporary protection, or by subsidizing production in sectors which the home country wants to capture as exportables. A successful outcome of such a strategy is illustrated in Figure 6.3. Initially, the marginal sector is $\bar{i}_0$. By activating the production in the sector segment $\bar{i}_1 - \bar{i}_0$

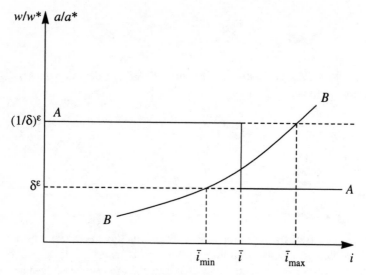

Figure 6.2   Long-run equilibrium

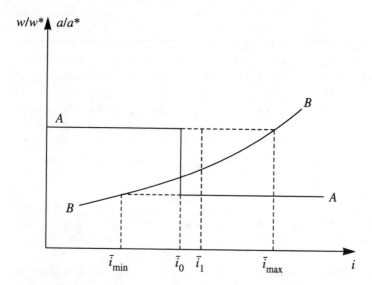

Figure 6.3   Strategic trade policy

the home country succeeds in raising relative productivity above the existing relative wage. Having done this, the home country gains competitiveness in these sectors, and resuming free trade, this segment is added to the country's list of exportables. More generally, short-run exogenous disturbances of production and trade may have a long-run impact on specialization, and in this sense hysteresis exists in international trade.

The main purpose of Krugman's article is to give a formalized presentation of the point that *history matters* in explaining the pattern of trade and specialization. In order to focus on this point, extreme assumptions are chosen. All countries are potentially identical, and each individual sector has the same chance to take the role as exporter. Furthermore, a distinction between high- and low-technology sectors is disregarded. In the following two sections, the model will be generalized in these directions.

3 FUNDAMENTAL PRODUCTIVITY DIFFERENCES: CLEAN VERSUS DIRTY SPECIALIZATIONS

In this section, we take into account the existence of fundamental productivity differences between countries. As such differences could be caused by differences in *relative factor endowments*, the version could be seen as an attempt to capture core elements from the traditional neoclassical trade theory.

Productivity is a combined result of a country-specific term and experience. This leads to the following specifications:

$$a_i(t) = K_i(t)^\varepsilon \tag{6.9}$$

$$a_i^*(t) = i^\psi K_i^*(t)^\varepsilon \quad 0 < \varepsilon < 1; \psi > 0$$

The quantity of output in country H produced by an input of one unit of labour and one unit of 'the stock of experience' is chosen as *numeraire* for output of the specific sector. The productivity of the individual sectors in country H thus only depends on experience. In country F, productivity depends both on a sector-specific term and experience.[3] The sectors are ranked according to increasing productivity in F for given experience in each sector.

Relative productivity is given by:

$$a_i(t) / a_i^*(t) = i^{-\psi}(K_i(t) / K_i^*(t))^\varepsilon \tag{6.10}$$

which is a decreasing function of i for constant experiences in all sectors in each country. The formation of experience is given by (6.5). The solutions (6.7) and (6.8) for steady-state values for relative experience thus still hold true. The relative productivity of the home country in the steady state thus takes the value $i^{-\psi}(1/\delta)^\varepsilon$ for exportables for H and $i^{-\psi}\delta^\varepsilon$ for exportables for F. The interval for relative productivity in the steady state is illustrated in Figure 6.4.

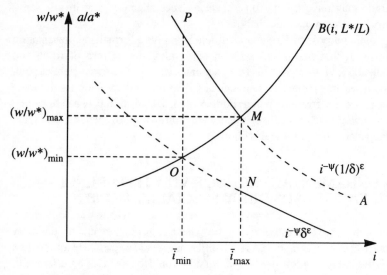

Figure 6.4   Clean specializations

The free-trade equilibrium with *long-run efficiency* prevails when there exists a marginal sector $\bar{i}$ which unambiguously specifies the specialization, that is, all sectors $i < \bar{i}$ are exportables for H and all sectors $i > \bar{i}$ are exportables for F. Such specializations are, in what follows, denoted *clean specializations* as they rest on a clean cut in the sector menu based on fundamental relative productivities. However, the long-run outcome of free trade does not always need to be a clean specialization. Because of learning by doing, cases may arise where the menu of country H's exportables overlaps with the menu of exportables for country F. In other words, no marginal sector exists. Such cases are denoted *dirty specializations*.

Let us first describe the possible clean specializations. Because of the existence of a marginal sector $\bar{i}$, the budget share for exportables from country H, λ, is an increasing function of $\bar{i}$. Relative wage rates for equilibrium on the balance of payments thus depend on $\bar{i}$ (for given values of L and L^*) (see 6.3)). This functional relationship is illustrated in Figure 6.4 by the curve B. The intersection points of the B-curve and the two limiting bands of relative productivity in the steady state indicate an interval for possible steady-state specializations, that is, the relevant interval of industries is $\bar{i}_{\min} \leq \bar{i} \leq \bar{i}_{\max}$, which correspond to the relative wage rates in the interval $(w/w^*)_{\min} \leq w/w^* \leq (w/w^*)_{\max}$.

Figure 6.4 illustrates the case where $\bar{i}_{\max}$ is the marginal sector. The relative productivity is indicated by the fully drawn part of the curves $i^{-\psi}(1/\delta)^{\varepsilon}$ and $i^{-\psi}\delta^{\varepsilon}$, that is, in the marginal sector, relative productivity changes discontinuously by the amount MN. In the case where $\bar{i}_{min}$ represents the steady-state equilibrium, PO indicates the spread in the relative productivity in the marginal sector. Between the two extreme cases of steady-state equilibria, the vertical distance between the two curves indicates the spread in relative productivity. As the relative wage rate w/w^* is at a maximum in $\bar{i}_{max}$, this steady-state equilibrium constitutes the best case for country H and the worst case for country F as regards welfare. Conversely, $\bar{i}_{min}$ is the worst case for country H and the best case for country F.

However, history may lead to long-run specialization patterns which are not in accordance with the fundamental productivity conditions. If relative productivities in the initial situation are arbitrarily distributed inside the band of relative productivities in the steady state in Figure 6.4, learning by doing will lead to a *dirty specialization* in the long run. In the short run, that is, for given productivities, the balance-of-payment constraint allows for a determination of an equilibrium-relative wage rate. Given the current positions of relative productivities for all sectors, the relative wage divides unambiguously the sectors in exportables for H and exportables for F. An increase in (w/w^*) removes sectors from the menu of exportables of H to the menu of exportables of F, and the cumulated budget share for exportables for country H is thus a decreasing function of w/w^*. For successive increases in w/w^* from 0 to infinity the right-hand side of the balance-of-payment equilibrium condition (6.3) decreases monotonically from infinity to zero. At the same time, the left-hand side of (6.3) increases along a 45-degree ray from origin. Assuming that the right-hand side is a continuous function, a solution for an equilibrium relative wage rate therefore exists. This equilibrium relative wage rate is indicated in Figure 6.5 by $(w/w^*)_0$. All sectors $i < i_1$ are exportables for H, while all sectors $i > i_2$ are exportables for F. In the intermediate interval $i_1 < i < i_2$, the situation consists of a mixture. Because of experience inherited from the past, the industries a and b are exportables for H, while the industries c and d are exportables for F.

For all sectors $i < i_1$, production only takes place in H, and in the long run, relative productivities increase to $i^{-\psi}(1/\delta)^{\varepsilon}$. For $i > i_2$, only F is producing, which in the long run will push the relative productivities to the values $i^{-\psi}\delta^{\varepsilon}$. In the intermediate interval $i_1 < i < i_2$ where there is a messy specialization determined by history, some industries, for example a and b, will take on a path towards long-run relative productivities of the sizes $i^{-\psi}(1/\delta)^{\varepsilon}$ as they are exportables for H. Conversely other industries, for example, c and d, will follow a path towards long-run relative productivities of sizes $i^{-\psi}\delta^{\varepsilon}$. The dirty specialization pattern will thus be fixed also in the long run, that is, c belongs to the menu of exportables for F, while b are exportables for H. As country F has a stronger comparative advantage in producing in sector b than in sector c

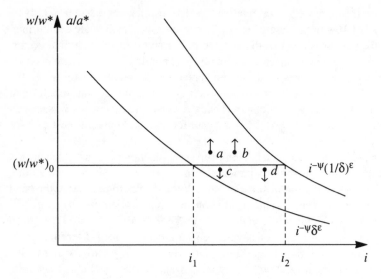

Figure 6.5   Dirty specializations

for given experience, the specialization pattern is inefficient from a long-run point of view.

Turning to the *policy aspects* of the model, manipulations of the specialization pattern may affect both distribution of welfare between countries (the terms of trade) and global efficiency. If, for example, country H captures sector *c* in Figure 6.5, then H improves its terms of trade, and the change in trade pattern represents a move towards a clean specialization. It will be possible to eliminate distributional effects, if both countries could agree to a suitable exchange of sectors, for example, country H takes over the production of sector *c*, and country F takes over the production of sector *b* (see Figure 6.5). However, such arrangements demand full information about fundamental productivities, which is not available.

A more cautious strategy seems to be to impose a temporary moderate tariff on all goods. As protection is moderate, trade still takes place in most sectors where one of the countries has strong cost advantages. For sectors where only weak cost advantages exist for a country, the tariff will be prohibitive, and production will take place in each individual industry in both countries. This roughly corresponds to the segment of sectors where the risk of dirty specialization is largest, that is, the segment of sectors in the interval $i_1 < i < i_2$ (see Figure 6.5).

During the period of protection, production will take place in each individual industry for these sectors in both countries. Assuming that there are identical budget shares for identical goods, the fraction of the labour force devoted to a specific sector among sectors of non-tradables will be identical for the two countries. This will secure a steady-state rank of industries by relative productivities in accordance with the fundamental conditions.[4]

This conclusion seems to support a *gradualist strategy*, when a country should adapt to free trade with new partners. The risk of developing a dirty specialization will be especially large, if the economy has experienced profound changes in the preceding years before opening up its markets for free trade. Most of the Eastern European countries have recently gone through a period of radical changes in their organizational structure, demand and production conditions. Recently some of them have applied for membership of the European Union. This points to a strategy of allowing these countries to maintain temporary protection or subsidies of industrial sectors in their process towards full participation in an internal market.

Another more promising strategy will be to improve the conditions of *transfer of experience* between countries. International spillovers of experience generally constrain the possibilities for dirty specializations. Formally, an increase in the parameter for spillovers, δ, reduces the overlapping interval of possible sectors for exportables for the two countries in Figure 6.5. Efforts should therefore be made to increase international mobility of knowledge so as to create the most favourable environment for securing long-run efficiency in specialization. The specific *assistance programmes* of the European Communities aimed at easing the transformation process towards open-market economies for the Eastern European countries include, among others, educational assistance (for example, the Tempus programme) and technical and economic assistance (for example, the Phare programme). These measures should speed up the transfer of knowledge and thus reduce the risks of long-run inefficiency in specialization. Liberalization of foreign direct investments intensifies imitation of new technology through Western companies' establishment of subsidiaries in the Eastern European countries, and as a side-effect foreign direct investment thus enlarges the channel of spillovers of knowledge.

4 DYNAMIC AND NON-DYNAMIC SECTORS

Until now, we have assumed that the potential for productivity growth through learning was identical for all industries. In other words, all sectors are assumed to have the same degree of dynamism. In the model, the *elasticity of productivity* with regard to experience is therefore assumed to be not only constant but also industry-invariant.

However, much growth literature stresses the importance of differences in growth rates in productivity among industries.[5] Many sectoral empirical studies point to the fact that productivity growth rates vary significantly among industries. In order to include this aspect in the model, the elasticity of productivity with regard to experience is assumed to be sector specific, that is:

$$a_i(t) = K_i^{\varepsilon(i)}(t)$$

$$a_i^*(t) = K_i^{*\varepsilon(i)}(t) \qquad (6.11)$$

where $0 < \varepsilon < 1$, $d\varepsilon/di < 0$ and $\varepsilon \to 0$ for $i \to \infty$.

The industries are now ordered by decreasing potential for learning. To simplify, we disregard fundamental productivity differences between countries, that is, for given experience in an industry in the two countries productivities are equal.

The other assumptions in the basic model for formation of experience and equilibrium on the balance of payments are maintained unchanged. The relative productivity in the steady state in the case of total specialization a_i/a_i^* appears to be $(1/\delta)^{\varepsilon(i)}$ for exportables for H, and $\delta^{\varepsilon(i)}$ for exportables for F. These limits for productivities in the steady state form a *funnel-shaped* figure (see Figure 6.6).

Let us assume that relative productivities are arbitrarily distributed in the initial situation inside the interval given by the funnel in Figure 6.6. The actual relative productivities for selected industries are illustrated by the position a, b, c, d and e. Given the size of relative wage rates w/w^*, all industries where the relative productivity de facto exceeds the relative wage rates are exporters for H. Conversely, all industries where relative productivity falls below the given relative wage rates are exporters for F. Given the distribution in the current period of relative productivities from the past, relative wage rates thus determine the cumulated budget share λ of exportables for H, and, obviously, this share is negatively related to the size of relative wage rates w/w^*. As in the former model version, this makes it possible to determine relative wage rates by using the condition of balance-of-payment equilibrium.

In Figure 6.6, a short-run equilibrium is shown by the relative wage rates $(w/w^*)_0$. The industries a and b belong to the menu of exportables of H, whereas the industries c, d and e belong to the exportables of F. In the subsequent process towards a steady state, neither the relative wage rates nor the specialization pattern change. Only relative productivities change because of the accumulation of experience. All exportables for country H obtain the relative productivities of $(1/\delta)^{\varepsilon(i)}$, and exportables for country F the relative productivities of $\delta^{\varepsilon(i)}$. Graphically in Figure 6.6, the process towards a steady state means that a and b move vertically to the curve $(1/\delta)^{\varepsilon(i)}$ and c, d and e move vertically to the curve $\delta^{\varepsilon(i)}$.

'History matters' also in this version of the model. In the illustrated case, the relative productivities a_i/a_i^* are comparatively high in many dynamic sectors

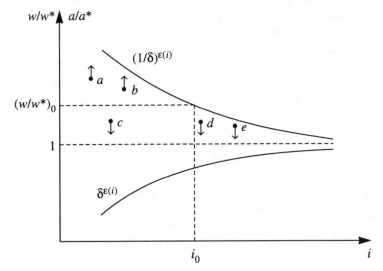

Figure 6.6   Long-run industrial structure in open economies

in the initial period, and this causes a high relative wage rate as w/w^* exceeds 1. At the same time, the high relative wage rate excludes less-dynamic sectors in the menu of exportables in H, that is, only industries of a rank not higher than i_0 are included in the menu of exportables for country H. This advantage in the initial period is consolidated in the subsequent periods as relative productivities move towards a steady state.

While country H is specialized exclusively in dynamic industries, the specialization pattern is mixed for country F. However, dynamic industries which initially belong to the exporters of country F, for example, the industry corresponding to point c in Figure 6.6, maintain their position in the industrial structure of country F.

4.1 Infant Industry Strategies

If country F takes up an aggressive *trade policy*, it may be difficult to snatch dynamic industries from country H. If the population in country F is small compared with that of country H, learning will be limited if the production should serve only the domestic demand. It may appear impossible to obtain a satisfactory change in relative productivities for competitiveness when trade is re-opened. However, it is obvious that country F should target its efforts on the most *vulnerable industries* of country H, that is, exportables for country H where only a modest change in relative productivities in favour of country F makes country

F competitive. In other words, in the illustrated case in Figure 6.6, country F should concentrate on taking exporting industries of country H in the vicinity of i_0.

In a world with several countries it is obvious that *coalitions of countries* could make an infant industry strategy more effective. If, for example, a group of countries creates a *customs union* or an *internal market*, the home market for fostering new industries will be enlarged. Through temporary protection or subsidies, it will be easier to develop competitiveness through learning.

5   CONCLUDING REMARKS

The endogenous character of comparative advantage in trade is accentuated in this chapter. This point is already elucidated in Krugman's basic version of the model, and it holds true in the generalizations presented here. Once a country has obtained competitiveness in a sector, its competitiveness will be strengthened by accumulation of experience in the subsequent periods, and the trade pattern will therefore be preserved.

Fundamental differences in relative productivities among countries constrain potential specialization patterns, and the room for action for changes in the specialization through an active trade policy will be limited. Furthermore, there will be a risk of inefficient long-run specialization patterns. The introduction of a sector-specific parameter in the relation between productivity and experience gives rise to interesting conclusions as regards the industrial structure in an open economy. If the economy in the initial period has the upper hand in high-productivity industries, there will only be room in the economy for dynamic sectors when the economy is opened up to trade. The disadvantaged economy could, in contrast, end up with a mixed structure consisting of both dynamic and non-dynamic sectors.

Although the model focuses on specialization and comparative advantages, it has implications for the overall economic growth in open economies. Free trade and specialization lead not only to the traditional *static efficiency gains* but also to *dynamic gains* in the form of higher growth rates in productivity. However, the elasticity of productivity with regard to experience is assumed to be lower than 1, that is, productivity shows *diminishing returns* as regards experience. In the growth process, the increase in experience thus has a still lower effect on productivity and growth as the stock of experience increases. This *flavour of decreasing growth* in the long run in the model could be overcome if the model was generalized to take into account the main elements from the *'new' growth theory* which establishes a relationship between market size, R&D, *product innovations* and the emergence of new industries and growth (compare Rivera-Batiz and Romer, 1991). Infusion of new industries creates a new potential for learning and *process innovations* which could keep up the overall growth rate in the economy. It may also point to new possibilities for trade policy and industrial policy as new industries in a sense create 'new' initial situations for scenarios of dynamic specializations.

NOTES

1. The *equation of motion* of relative experiences for exportables for H appears to be, compare (6.6):

$$d(K_i/K_i^*)\,/\,(K_i/K_i^*) = X_i\,(1 - \delta\,(K_i/K_i^*))\,/K_i$$

As:

$$d(K_i/K_i^*)\,/\,(K_i/K_i^*) \gtreqless 0 \text{ for } K_i/K_i^* \lesseqgtr 1/\delta$$

the steady-state equilibrium is stable. Similarly, the steady-state equilibrium δ for exportables for F also appears to be stable.

2. In a more general context, this result does not hold true. If, for example, country H is specialized mainly in activities characterized by income elasticities above (below) 1 the relative wage will change in favour (disfavour) of country H on the path towards a long-run equilibrium.

3. For $i > 1$, the absolute productivity in F exceeds that in H in all sectors for a given stock of experience. This property could be avoided without changing the conclusions in the following by introducing a positive constant a in the slightly more general specification $a_i^*\,(t) = \alpha\,i^\psi\,K_i^*(t)^\varepsilon$.

4. Inserting,(6.1) and (6.9) into (6.6), the steady-state solution appears to be:

$$\left(\frac{K_i}{K_i^*}\right)^{\varepsilon-1} = i^\psi\,\frac{L_i^*}{L_i}\left(\frac{1 - \delta/\left(K_i\,/\,K_i^*\right)}{1 - \delta K_i\,/\,K_i^*}\right)$$

This solution is identical to Krugman's (1987), when we disregard the term i^ψ. The ratio of sector-specific employment L_i^*/L_i is identical to the ratio of the total labour force L^*/L because of identical budget shares. Using Krugman's geometrical procedure for solving the steady-state values of K_i/K_i^* it follows that K_i/K_i^* is negatively related to i. Relative productivity $a_i/a_i^* = i^{-\psi}(K_i/K_i^*)^\varepsilon$ therefore decreases monotonically for increasing i, because both terms $i^{-\psi}$ and K_i/K_i^* decrease when i increases.

5. For example, Chadha (1991), who presents a two-sector growth model based on sector-specific parameters for learning by doing. A more general specification of productivity growth with sector-specific parameters has recently been used in a growth model of Verspagen (1992). Buiges et al. (1990) discuss the industrial structure in a growth strategic perspective for the poor member states in the European Community. The point that growth in a region or a nation depends crucially on the industrial structure because of sector-specific learning was earlier stressed by Kaldor (1970) and Thirlwall (1974).

REFERENCES

Buiges, P., F. Ilzkowitz and J.-F. LeBrun (1990), 'The Impact of the Internal Market by Industrial Sector: The Challenge for the Member States', *European Economy*, 'Social Europe' (special edition), Commission of the European Communities.

Chadha, B. (1991) 'Wages, Profitability, and Growth in a Small Open Economy', *IMF Staff Papers*, **38**, 59–82.

Dornbusch, R., S. Fisher and P.A. Samuelson (1977), 'Comparative Advantage, Trade, and Payments in a Ricardian Model with a Continuum of Goods', *American Economic Review*, **67**, 823–39.

Kaldor, N. (1970), 'The Case for Regional Policies', *Scottish Journal of Political Economy*, **17**, 337–48.

Krugman, P. (1987), 'The Narrow Moving Band, the Dutch Disease, and the Competitive Consequences of Mrs. Thatcher: Notes on Trade in the Presence of Dynamic Scale Economies', *Journal of Development Economics*, **27**, 41–55.

Rivera-Batiz, R.A. and P.M. Romer (1991), 'Economic Integration and Endogenous Growth', *Quarterly Journal of Economics*, **106**, 531–55.

Thirlwall, A.P. (1974), 'Regional Economic Disparities and Regional Policy in the Common Market', *Urban Studies*, **11**, 1–12.

Verspagen, B. (1992), *Uneven Growth Between Interdependent Economies – An Evolutionary View on Technology Gaps, Trade and Growth*, Maastricht, Holland: University of Limburg.

7. Trade and growth: a survey

Steve Dowrick

1 INTRODUCTION

It has become an article of faith in many policy circles that opening up the economy to international trade will produce substantial benefits in terms of greater consumer choice and higher living standards. Higher productivity is expected to be realized through competitive pressure and through opportunity to specialize in productive activities where a country has a comparative advantage or where it can gain from economies of scale.

Belief in the beneficial effects of trade liberalization has been fuelled by comparisons of the relatively moribund postwar performance of the protected and inward-looking economies of Latin America with the dynamic growth in trade and living standards in the more open economies of East Asia. Such casual empiricism can, however, be quite misleading as it ignores a host of other explanations for the East Asian economic 'miracles' including the opportunity for less-developed economies to import technology as they industrialize. It is also recognized by the World Bank (1993) that governments of some of these fast-growing economies have in fact intervened heavily in trade and have protected domestic industry, especially in the early stages of industrialization.

There is, nevertheless, a strong consensus among economists that openness to trade, even if combined with elements of direction and protection, tends to promote economic welfare. There are indeed good theoretical reasons to believe that trade liberalization should increase economic welfare under a wide range of plausible circumstances. It has, however, proved rather more difficult to come up with good reasons why such welfare gains should be at all sizeable. Conventional economic modelling typically estimates the benefit of trade liberalization as an increase in the level of national income of about one per cent. While such figures are not negligible, they are hardly the basis on which to justify a radical re-structuring of the economy with all of its inevitable adjustment costs. So trade optimists have a long tradition of appealing to beneficial effects of trade on the growth prospects of the economy.

Concepts of 'dynamic gains from trade' and 'dynamic comparative advantage' have long been banded about as justifications for trade liberalization, just as trade pessimists and protectionists have supplemented their analyses of terms of trade deterioration and strategic advantage with concepts of 'immiserizing growth'. It is only recently, however, that developments in the modelling of long-run growth have enabled a more formal examination of the consequences of trade for growth.

The main purpose of this chapter is to survey some of these recent developments in the economic theory of growth to see if they do provide a sound basis for trade optimism. The chapter then goes on to examine evidence on the link between countries' trade positions and their economic performance, before surveying recent empirical results.

The broad conclusion that emerges from the theoretical survey is that trade liberalization can indeed be expected to stimulate growth in the aggregate world economy by enhancing the international flow of knowledge and innovation and by allowing economies of specialization not only in the production of goods but also in the generation of new knowledge and new inputs into production. This is not to say, however, that each and every country must necessarily benefit. While trade may have substantial positive benefits for some countries, it may conversely lock other countries into a pattern of specialization in low-skill, low-growth activities. In the absence of perfect markets, such low growth can be immiserizing. To avoid the low-growth trap, it is important to link trade liberalization with appropriate policies on education, training and research and development; otherwise failures in the markets for investment in skills and knowledge may be compounded by inappropriate trade-induced specialization.

Empirical estimates of growth returns to trade liberalization emphasize that such returns are not automatic for all countries. Nevertheless, there is confirmation that in aggregate increased trade does stimulate growth.

2   MODELS OF ENDOGENOUS GROWTH AND TRADE

The standard economic textbook treatment of gains from trade deals with comparative advantage and the efficiency loss associated with tariffs or other impediments to mutually advantageous trade, as in Corden (1984). However, the predicted size of static gains from trade is usually quite small. For example, Richard Baldwin (1992, p. 162) refers to the body of empirical research which 'consistently find[s] that trade liberalizations raise aggregate income by an amount that is negligible (0.1 percent ...) or small'.[1]

Given the problems of finding large-scale gains from static models of trade liberalization, there has been a long tradition of appealing to 'dynamic gains' to justify trade optimism. Such gains may be associated with capital accumulation, with external economies of scale, with learning by doing, or with technology transfer. In many formal models, the dynamics are transitional in the sense that the model will eventually approach a steady-state level, as in the Solow–Swan model of growth. Dynamic gains have also been analysed in the sense of changing the long-run growth path of the economy – as in the work of Schumpeter and Kaldor. There has been a recent upsurge of interest in formal economic modelling of long-run growth, typically under the labels of 'new growth models' or 'the theory of endogenous growth'.

The essential feature of supply-side models of economic growth is the accumulation of factors of production – generic capital which might consist of machines and buildings and infrastructure, but can also consist of human skills and knowledge. There are three distinguishing features to these models. First are the technical features which provide sufficient conditions for accumulation to generate long-run growth. Second, there is an emphasis on the accumulation of non-tangible capital such as skills and knowledge. Third is the implication that any policies which affect the rate of accumulation will affect rates of growth, for example taxation which alters the private returns to capital accumulation.

Romer, Lucas, Barro and others have extended the neoclassical growth model, characterized by formal modelling of investment decisions by a forward-looking, rational agent, to clarify the conditions which are required for long-run growth to occur. Hammond and Rodriguez-Clare (1993) have produced a coherent synthesis of the technical features of these models of endogenous growth. The driving force of all these models is capital accumulation. By building up stocks which increase productive capacity, and using that enhanced capacity to further build up stocks, it may be possible that incentives to continue investing are sufficient to generate continuous growth – but it is also possible that decreasing returns to capital may inhibit growth in the long run. Much of the recent theoretical literature is concerned with the technical conditions under which accumulation can drive growth.

It is useful to distinguish between three different sorts of technological interaction – flexibility, feedback and spillovers – which make long-run growth technically feasible without relying on the 'manna from heaven' of exogenous technological progress.

1. Flexibility in the production of final goods is a measure of the extent to which capital can substitute for fixed factors of production such as labour and natural resources. Long-run growth is not feasible if increasing capital intensity drives the marginal product of capital to zero. This occurs if capital is not readily substituted for labour, for example in the case of a Cobb–Douglas production function. Labour is 'essential' in production, in the sense that the marginal product of capital approaches zero as the ratio of capital to labour rises. In the absence of feedback or spillover the long-run growth of output is

constrained by the growth of the labour supply and by the growth of exogenous technology. Agents can accumulate human capital and physical capital as much as they like, but they will always run aground on the rock of diminishing returns in the long run. Hence the 'investment pessimism' traditionally associated with the Solow–Swan model.

If, on the other hand, the elasticity of substitution between fixed and accumulable factors exceeds unity, then the marginal product of capital no longer declines to zero; labour is no longer 'essential'. In effect, robots can replace humans on the production line; they can even replace humans in the production of further robots. Of course, labour is still required to organize and direct the production process; but the essential point is that if there is sufficient substitutability between capital and labour, then investment will always contribute to growth. This case is analysed by Pitchford (1960) and more recently by Jones and Manuelli (1990). As long as the return on investment is above the inter-temporal discount rate, then rational agents should choose to invest and the economy will keep on growing.

2. Feedback in the accumulation of capital occurs if the stock of capital reduces the cost of generating further capital. The supply of capital may then be capable of increasing sufficiently fast as to outweigh diminishing returns in the production of final goods. Feedback models are often used in a neo-Schumpeterian framework where new goods and new ideas produce further goods and further ideas and they typically involve temporary monopoly power. Romer has particularly argued the case that such feedback is a vitally important feature of the generation of new ideas or blueprints which are intermediate inputs into the production of capital goods but are also inputs into the production of the next generation of blueprints. Grossman and Helpman have modelled direct feedback in the generation of new goods. Learning by doing can be interpreted as a feedback mechanism too.

3. Spillovers occur if the output or the stock of capital owned by one producer affects the productivity of other producers. Models based on spillovers use notions related to the Kaldorian concepts of external economies and Verdoorn's Law of dynamic economies of scale. There are several features of investment which may produce such spillovers. The public good qualities of knowledge are a prime example, suggesting positive spillovers from R&D or from learning by doing. Not surprisingly, private investment decisions which ignore positive spillover benefits to other producers generate a suboptimal rate of growth. On the other hand, in some circumstances new ideas may be substitutes rather than complements, as in the case of patent races or quality upgrading, in which case the common pool problem implies that there may be over-investment in research.

In the standard neoclassical tradition, the Heckscher–Ohlin–Samuelson analysis, trade will affect the level and composition of output and welfare, but not long-run growth. The new growth models have something in common with the classical tradition of Ricardo and Marx, as developed by Lewis (1980) in his Nobel lecture, where trade can increase the rate of profit and hence the rate of investment and growth. We can distinguish three sorts of trade growth models by reference to the ideas of three classical economists of the last century: Smith, Ricardo and Mill.

An important class of models follows Adam Smith in emphasizing the role of trade in enabling specialization which yields increases in productivity through learning by doing or through specialization in research. Such models rely on spillover and/or feedback mechanisms to generate cumulative increases in productivity and specialization.

Then there are models where Ricardian comparative advantage leads to specialization in particular activities. If some activities are characterized by higher rates of productivity growth, countries which specialize in these will tend to grow faster. However, productivity growth is not derived from the specialization *per se* – it is an inherent feature of each activity.

Third, there are models which, in the spirit of some of the ideas put forward by John Stuart Mill, emphasize the role of trade as a conduit for the international dissemination of ideas and technology.

2.1 Neo-Smithian Models: Specialization as the Source of Growth

The idea of specialization lies behind the notion of internal economies of scale in production. Access to foreign markets allows the realization of potential economies as each country concentrates on the activities in which it has comparative advantage. In traditional models, realization of scale economies affects the level of output without influencing the long-run growth path. Once the minimum efficient scale of production has been reached in a particular activity, there may be no opportunity for further productivity gains. It is only if there are sufficient feedback or spillover effects that the opportunity to specialize through trade may raise long-run growth. One can imagine this occurring, for example, through the development or acquisition of machine tools which enable production of superior tools, and so on in a continuous feedback loop. Equally, it seems plausible that we might find such positive feedback in the information technology industry where new computers help to design even better and faster computers.

An obvious avenue for positive feedback lies in the acquisition of intangible skills and knowledge. Feedback might occur where training or research activity increases the individual's stock of knowledge or human capital. It may be the case, for instance, that the larger the stock of knowledge, the easier it is to increase it. Better educated and more knowledgeable people learn faster and develop new ideas more easily. The underlying idea is appealing, that existing knowledge and understanding, combined with further education and research, generate further knowledge.

However, even though knowledge acquisition may drive growth, it is not necessarily the case that trade will always be growth enhancing. Rivera-Batiz and Romer (1991) argue that the effects of trade depend on the precise nature of the relationship between physical investments and knowledge flows. To illustrate this point they develop a model of knowledge-driven R&D which concentrates on the non-rival nature of knowledge as the prime determinant of growth. As in Romer (1990), production design knowledge or 'blueprints' can be re-used at practically zero marginal cost. Patent protection can enable inventors to extract payment from manufacturers who use their designs, so there is an economic incentive to produce new designs. But the very act of registering a patent has the effect of offering the ideas behind the blueprint to other designers. They are free to use these ideas in the production of the next generation of designs.

In this framework, Rivera-Batiz and Romer argue that trade in goods enhances the level of output, by giving producers access to a wider range of capital goods, but it does not necessarily increase the long-run rate of growth. For growth to increase, it is necessary that researchers in one country should also have access to the ideas and designs produced in the other. Foreign designs will, however, only raise domestic research productivity if they are distinct from the home designs. In an extreme example, if the two countries' production and research activities are identical, the free flow of knowledge leads to no increase at all in new designs, hence to no change in either the level or growth rate of output. In other words, it is only to the extent that research activities are specialized that international knowledge flows enhance productivity. In their model, the primary growth-enhancing effect of trade in final goods arises because it enables countries to specialize in production and thus to avoid the duplication of R&D efforts which would occur if each had to produce the entire range of both goods and designs for its domestic market.

Rivera-Batiz and Romer do not, however, claim that access to other countries' designs is necessarily facilitated by trade – a hypothesis which is discussed later under the heading of neo-Millian theories. Nor do they insist that international knowledge flows are a necessary condition for trade to enhance growth. For instance, they consider the possibility that production blueprints might be produced purely by the application of skilled labour and physical capital, what they call their lab equipment model. In this model, disembodied ideas play no role but trade is still growth enhancing as the increased demand for patents attracts resources into inventive activity.

2.2 Neo-Ricardian Models: Dynamic Comparative Advantage as a Source of Growth

In the neo-Ricardian class of models, trade again drives growth by allowing specialization. Unlike the neo-Smithian models, where products and technologies are differentiated but essentially identical and the gains from trade are symmetric, the distinguishing feature of the neo-Ricardian models is that activities are not symmetric. Some countries will specialize in activities which have inherently faster or slower productivity growth, according to the technological possibilities and the stage of development of a particular activity. It follows that trade may produce divergence in growth rates of real output. (When changes in terms of trade are taken into account, however, it is not necessarily the case that welfare levels will diverge.)

A key determinant of patterns of growth is the extent to which skills and knowledge spill over national boundaries. In the case where there are no impediments to the transfer of knowledge, that is to say where knowledge is a global public good, the predicted pattern of specialization in production and trade depends on relative supplies of the other factors of production: natural resources, labour and human capital (or skilled labour). Grossman and Helpman find that their analysis of dynamic comparative advantage does not necessarily overturn the traditional Heckscher–Ohlin predictions of static trade theory. Countries with relatively high endowments of skilled labour will specialize in production of innovative or high-technology goods, while others will specialize in production of traditional manufactured (unskilled labour-intensive) goods or resource-based goods.

The rate of growth of output (real GDP) will be higher in the skill-intensive country which specializes in innovative products. Grossman and Helpman cite the experience of the Japanese economy in the 1960s and 1970s as it rapidly built up its skill base and transformed the structure of output towards innovative products. But a crucial point in their welfare analysis of trade and specialization is that this does not necessarily mean that the 'high-tech' country will be better off than the labour- or resource-intensive countries. In a long-run equilibrium with free trade and rational expectations, their model predicts similar rates of growth of real consumption for all countries.

The point here is that with free trade in goods and free transmission of knowledge, it may not matter to consumers whether they are located in the labour-intensive or skill-intensive country; they can enjoy the benefits of innovation through the purchase of traded goods. Faster growth of output in the skill-intensive country is offset by deteriorating terms of trade. High-tech goods become relatively cheaper in direct proportion to their faster rate of innovation. An extreme example of this phenomenon is the case of oil producers like Saudi Arabia in the 1970s where real output growth was often negative but was massively offset by improvements in the terms of trade. Specialization in oil production may have slowed the growth of real output (that is, fewer barrels of oil) but certainly did not harm Saudi consumption.

These conclusions change somewhat if knowledge is not transmitted freely across national boundaries. With knowledge a national public good, but not an international public good, the more technologically advanced country will have a comparative advantage in the production of further knowledge; hence it will tend to extend its technological lead and expand its share of world production of the innovative products. This cumulative causation will, in a simple model where no knowledge spills over to other countries, lead to a situation of complete specialization. The country with a head start in the accumulation of knowledge will tend to widen its lead, unless the laggard country government intervenes to overcome the initial disadvantage.

In Young's (1991) model of learning by doing, where the learning does not spill over national boundaries, a similar prediction emerges: the larger and more advanced countries will grow faster as a result of free trade. They have a comparative advantage in the industries with learning-by-doing economies of scale, so those industries will expand in response to the opening up of trade and the realization of further economies will compound their comparative advantage.

Thus, where knowledge is contained within national boundaries, success can breed success. It also follows that intervention can affect the subsequent growth path. Countries are not necessarily constrained by an exogenous factor endowment. However, once again it does not necessarily follow that gaining a technological lead will make a country better off. International trade in assets and goods still allows the residents of the country which specializes in the production of labour-intensive 'traditional' goods to invest their savings in foreign assets and to import the new and cheaper innovative goods.

If private incentives for accumulation of human and knowledge capital reflect social costs and benefits, then, although it may be possible to increase output growth by intervening to change the pattern of dynamic comparative advantage, doing so can actually reduce welfare.

In practice, however, capital market imperfections typically imply suboptimal investment in human capital; given that human capital is a complement to research, there is then a presumption that incentives to invest in R&D are also suboptimal, compounding failures in the market for knowledge. A 'revealed comparative disadvantage' in knowledge-intensive production may in fact reflect these market failures. In this case, trade liberalization may lower welfare in technologically backward countries if it encourages specialization in low-learning, low-knowledge industries which further decreases incentives for investment in human capital and knowledge.

2.3 Neo-Millian Models: Trade as the Conduit of Technology Transfer

In both the Smithian and Ricardian models, trade affects growth by influencing the degree or pattern of specialization. Of course, trade may have a more direct influence on growth if it acts as a direct transmission mechanism for the international dissemination of knowledge – an idea attributable to John Stuart Mill. There are various ways in which trade in goods and services might be expected to increase the flow of knowledge between countries. The direct exchange of ideas between buying and selling agents is one route. Reverse engineering of products is another. Additionally, reverse engineering of concepts may be important; even if the buyer of an imported good does not directly copy the production technique, he or she may find that the concept underlying a new good stimulates ideas for further varieties adapted to local conditions.

Grossman and Helpman (1991a) discuss the implications of this type of trade-assisted technology transfer. Increases in trade will increase the dissemination of knowledge and will thereby increase the level of output. Ben-David and Loewy (1995) simulate such a model of knowledge-disseminating trade and confirm that there is a positive impact on the level of output of the trade-liberalizing country. Moreover, they find that unilateral trade liberalization also improves the growth potential of the non-liberalizing trading partners. To the extent that the Millian hypothesis is valid, it follows that extra weight should be given to policies that promote trade.

2.4 Summary

The general import of the new growth models is that trade liberalization should increase world growth and welfare in aggregate. In the neo-Smithian analysis, gains are spread evenly – everyone grows faster as a result of economic integration. This is also true under the Millian hypothesis that trade speeds the international diffusion of knowledge. In the neo-Ricardian analysis, however, some countries whose comparative advantage is in low-growth activities may find that their growth is retarded by increased opportunity to trade and specialize. Low growth need not be a welfare problem if markets are complete – the citizens of that country will gain from falling prices of the high-tech goods which are more efficiently produced elsewhere. It is only a problem if there are market failures in the acquisition of skills and knowledge which are compounded by trade specialization. If so, a 'lucky' country with abundant natural resources may find itself regretting that it is locked out of the areas of dynamic learning and growth.

3   EXAMINING THE DATA ON TRADE AND GROWTH

It is useful to examine the data. The source is the Penn World Tables (5.5), an earlier version of which is described by Summers and Heston (1991). Sub-Saharan African countries are excluded along with the major Middle Eastern oil exporters because the growth patterns of these countries are typically very different from those of the rest of the world and are extremely difficult to model. Countries are also excluded if more than three annual data points are missing from any decade. This leaves the sample of 74 countries listed in Table 7.1.

Table 7.1   Trade intensity, openness and growth, 1960–1990

		1960 GDP	Growth	Trade intensity	Openness
Below-average openness					
1	URUGUAY	3,829	0.4%	33.7	**−0.76**
2	PARAGUAY	1,215	2.1%	36.4	**−0.69**
3	ARGENTINA	3,293	0.2%	20.1	**−0.66**
4	MYANMAR	296	2.3%	19.6	**−0.65**
5	ICELAND	5,172	3.1%	77.8	**−0.64**
6	BRAZIL	1,758	2.7%	15.7	**−0.51**
7	HAITI	873	−0.4%	36.9	**−0.51**
8	GUATEMALA	1,641	0.8%	37.2	**−0.45**
9	TURKEY	1,604	2.8%	23.0	**−0.41**
10	USA	9,776	2.1%	14.5	**−0.40**
11	MEXICO	2,809	2.2%	20.7	**−0.40**
12	AUSTRALIA	7,879	2.0%	31.5	**−0.39**
13	COLOMBIA	1,652	2.2%	27.9	**−0.36**
14	BANGLADESH	798	1.4%	21.0	**−0.32**
15	NICARAGUA	1,466	−0.2%	55.7	**−0.30**
16	NEW ZEALAND	7,920	1.3%	53.7	**−0.28**
17	GREECE	2,088	3.9%	39.3	**−0.28**
18	BOLIVIA	1,112	1.2%	46.9	**−0.27**
19	PERU	1,917	0.2%	34.5	**−0.27**
20	INDIA	665	1.6%	12.7	**−0.25**
21	DOMINICAN REP.	1,162	1.9%	48.0	**−0.25**
22	ECUADOR	1,433	2.2%	44.1	**−0.24**
23	CHILE	2,893	1.1%	40.6	**−0.22**
24	COSTA RICA	2,021	1.9%	64.5	**−0.21**
25	SURINAME	2,097	0.2%	103.9	**−0.20**

		1960 GDP	Growth	Trade intensity	Openness
26	FINLAND	5,367	3.2%	51.3	**–0.20**
27	FIJI	2,046	2.0%	92.6	**–0.19**
28	SPAIN	3,196	3.7%	30.2	**–0.17**
29	JAPAN	3,033	5.3%	22.1	**–0.17**
30	CYPRUS	2,043	4.6%	94.0	**–0.15**
31	EL SALVADOR	1,372	0.8%	56.4	**–0.15**
32	HONDURAS	1,007	0.8%	61.0	**–0.13**
33	CHINA	825	4.8%	13.1	**–0.10**
34	TRINIDAD & TOBAGO	5,577	1.4%	88.2	**–0.08**
35	VENEZUELA	6,194	–0.2%	44.7	**–0.06**
36	BOTSWANA	552	6.1%	98.6	**–0.04**
37	PANAMA	1,520	2.3%	79.1	**–0.04**
Averages					
1–37		2,831	2.0%	46	**–0.30**
1–19		3,005	1.6%	34	**–0.45**
20–37		2,389	2.4%	58	**–0.16**
Above-average openness					
38	SWEDEN	7,492	2.2%	54.2	**0.01**
39	PAKISTAN	618	2.6%	29.7	**0.01**
40	DENMARK	6,751	2.4%	62.5	**0.01**
41	CZECHOSLOVAKIA	2,468	3.0%	46.5	**0.02**
42	MOROCCO	790	3.1%	46.0	**0.06**
43	YUGOSLAVIA	1,955	2.8%	43.7	**0.06**
44	PAPUA N. GUINEA	1,128	0.6%	77.0	**0.06**
45	TUNISIA	1,088	3.2%	64.2	**0.08**
46	JAMAICA	1,788	1.0%	86.3	**0.08**
47	FRANCE	6,013	2.8%	36.0	**0.11**
48	CANADA	7,288	2.9%	46.1	**0.13**
49	SWITZERLAND	9,639	1.9%	66.4	**0.14**
50	AUSTRIA	5,176	3.0%	63.2	**0.14**
51	JORDAN	1,141	2.3%	85.4	**0.15**
52	ITALY	4,636	3.3%	37.2	**0.16**
53	ALGERIA	1,717	1.5%	52.3	**0.17**
54	GUYANA	1,524	–0.8%	125.6	**0.17**
55	PORTUGAL	1,869	4.2%	61.2	**0.17**

		1960 GDP	Growth	Trade intensity	Openness
56	PHILIPPINES	1,119	1.5%	42.9	**0.23**
57	NORWAY	5,665	3.2%	84.5	**0.25**
58	THAILAND	929	4.5%	45.3	**0.27**
59	LUXEMBOURG	8,112	2.3%	173.5	**0.30**
60	IRELAND	3,184	3.5%	94.6	**0.30**
61	SOUTH AFRICA	2,109	1.4%	54.0	**0.32**
62	EGYPT	770	2.9%	49.4	**0.33**
63	KOREA, REP.	907	6.7%	52.0	**0.37**
64	SRI LANKA	1,285	1.9%	68.2	**0.38**
65	INDONESIA	625	3.8%	36.7	**0.39**
66	GERMANY, WEST	6,637	2.6%	45.7	**0.39**
67	UK	6,548	2.3%	48.9	**0.44**
68	TAIWAN	1,382	6.1%	74.5	**0.51**
69	PUERTO RICO	3,069	3.7%	122.6	**0.54**
70	MALAYSIA	1,397	4.2%	92.7	**0.66**
71	NETHERLANDS	6,122	2.5%	97.7	**0.74**
72	BELGIUM	5,583	3.0%	112.4	**0.78**
73	HONG KONG	2,210	6.2%	185.9	**1.07**
74	SINGAPORE	1,712	6.2%	307.0	**1.39**
Averages					
38–74		3,193	3.0%	78	**0.32**
38–54		3,601	2.2%	60	**0.09**
55–74		3,062	3.6%	92	**0.49**

Notes

GDP is 1960 real GDP per capita, measured in 1985 international $, from Penn World Tables.
Growth is annual average growth rate of real GDP per capita, 1960–90.
Trade intensity is $100x$ (imports+exports)/GDP. Openness is the residual from regression (1).

For the purposes of preliminary data analysis I use the country averages over the period 1960–90. Figure 7.1 plots economic growth (in real GDP per capita) against trade intensity (exports plus imports / GDP) for the 74 countries. It is immediately obvious that there are three significant outliers in terms of trade intensity – Singapore, Hong Kong and Luxembourg. The first two of these are also outliers in terms of growth, so we may expect them to have considerable influence on subsequent statistical analysis of the relationship between trade and growth. The presence of Hong Kong and Singapore in the sample gives a weak positive correlation between trade intensity and growth ($r = 0.30$). Excluding the three outliers, it is evident that there is no systematic relationship – the correlation coefficient drops to 0.06.

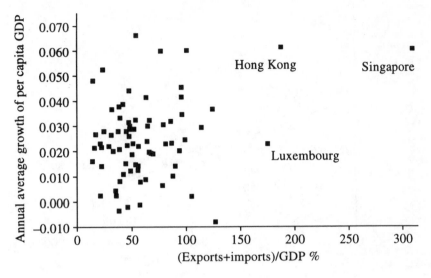

Figure 7.1   Growth and trade intensity, 1960–1990 for 74 countries

A common feature of the three extremely high trading economies is that they are small countries, virtually city states. To ascertain whether their trading intensity is in fact exceptional they should perhaps be compared with other cities rather than with other nations. Here I can approximate that comparison by plotting trade intensity against population size. The scatter plot in Figure 7.2 is drawn to a logarithmic scale which shows that there is a very strong log-linear correlation between trade intensity and population. As we expect, countries like the USA with large populations have ample opportunity for internal trade, so their raw trade intensity is an inadequate measure of their true trade orientation.

The regression line is drawn in Figure 7.2 and some of the principal outliers and countries of interest are labelled. Luxembourg, for instance, is not a significant outlier – its high trade intensity is almost entirely explicable in terms of its tiny population. Singapore and Hong Kong, however, are indeed much stronger traders than other countries of similar size. Japan's relatively low trade intensity is largely explained by its size. The most significant low trade outliers are the Latin American economies.

I take T_i, the deviation from the predicted trade intensity in Figure 7.1, as a measure of underlying openness – the observed trade intensity corrected for the size of the internal market. In Figure 7.2, T_i is the vertical distance between a country's observation and the regression line. This measure is listed in Table 7.1, where countries are arranged in order from the least open economy, Uruguay, to the most open, Singapore. I have also included in the table the trade

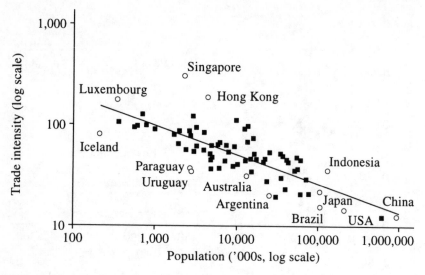

Figure 7.2   Trade intensity and population

intensity (uncorrected for population size), the level of development in 1960, and the rate of economic growth 1960–90. From inspection of the table it is evident that on average the more open economies (numbered 38–74) grew faster than the less open economies (numbered 1–37). But the relationship does not appear to be strongly linear. It is not apparent that there is any strong correlation between openness and growth, other than at the extremes of the distribution. There are some inward-oriented countries which have grown fast and a number of outward-oriented countries which have grown relatively slowly.

To emphasize this point, Table 7.1 also shows the average growth rates for the sample of countries divided into quarters. The least open economies, listed as countries 1–19, grew at only 1.6 per cent, per year which is less than half the rate at which the most open economies grew, 3.6 per cent per year. However, there is no significant difference between the growth rates of the mildly above- and below-average groups. Indeed, the mildly closed economies, countries 20–37, grew slightly faster at 2.4 per cent per year than the mildly open economies, countries 38–54, which averaged growth of 2.2 per cent per year.

These simple bivariate correlations between openness and growth provide some interesting suggestions. They do not take account, however, of differences in technology gaps or rates of growth of population, nor do they allow us to distinguish between the different classes of theories about the mechanism by which trade and growth are related. These issues are addressed in the recent econometric literature which I summarize in the next section.

4 ECONOMETRIC EVIDENCE ON THE IMPACT OF TRADE ON GROWTH

A wide range of studies conducted over the last decade or so have indicated a fairly consistent pattern of positive correlations between trade openness and growth. Some cautionary notes on the empirical literature are important. Lal (1993) is critical of trade and growth studies on the grounds that the indices of trade bias sometimes rely on subjective assessment which is preconditioned on the authors' knowledge of economic success. Such a criticism can be made of the World Bank (1987) study, but is not particularly pertinent to most of those referred to here which are based on objective measures of trade flows or price distortions. Lal also cites Sheehey (1990) as criticizing studies of bivariate correlations between the growth of exports and the growth of GDP for ignoring questions of causation. None of the studies cited here uses this specification of the trade–growth relationship. A different line of criticism comes from Levine and Renelt (1992) who focus on the sensitivity of cross-country partial correlations to the inclusion of other explanatory variables. They find, for instance, that on a single cross-section (averaged over 30 years) the partial correlation between growth and openness is weak when other variables such as investment are included in the regression. While their study sounds a valuable warning about the dangers of inference when important explanatory variables are missing, their approach to 'data under-mining' lacks a theoretical basis for arguing why certain variables should or should not be included in the regression analysis and for distinguishing endogenous from exogenous variables. Despite the limitations of this approach, they report that trade openness is robustly related to levels of investment, hence to growth.

I will briefly summarize some of the main empirical results which have emerged over the last decade. For a summary of earlier work, Edwards (1993) provides a comprehensive overview, particularly of country-specific studies.

The World Bank (1987) divides a sample of 41 developing countries into four categories of more or less inward- or outward-oriented economies. Their classification is based on evidence of rates of protection, direct import controls, export incentives and exchange rate over-valuation plus a considerable element of judgement. GDP growth is strongest in the most outward-oriented countries, and weakest in the most inward oriented. As Evans (1989) points out, however, there is little difference between the weakly outward- and the weakly inward-oriented groups. Moreover, the strong outward-oriented group consists of three very particular outliers – Hong Kong, South Korea and Singapore – where other unmeasured factors may be playing a role in their strong growth performance. This evidence is largely consistent with the data analysed in the previous section.

Other researchers such as Agarwala (1984), Evans (1989) and Dollar (1992) have used measures of price distortion (relative to world prices) for developing countries and find higher growth in those countries with lower price distortions. They find that outward orientation is associated with faster growth, particularly for small countries with a comparative advantage in manufacturing. Lee (1993) estimates trade distortions as a function of tariffs and black market premia for 81 countries, covering developed and developing economies. He finds that, for example, a 20 per cent tariff for a country trading 20 per cent of its output reduces annual growth by 0.6 percentage points, with the effect working mainly through diminished rates of investment.

Further cross-country studies provide econometric support for the growth-enhancing effects of freeing trade, in studies by Helliwell (1992) and Edwards (1992). Van den Berg and Schmidt (1994) find similar results using time-series data from Latin American countries. Dowrick (1994) combined the cross-section and time-series approaches by using a panel of observations. Controlling for unobserved fixed country effects and for reverse causation, this study again found a positive causal relationship from trade openness to growth.

Only a few studies have tried to identify the differential impact of trade on various countries. For instance, Singer and Gray (1988) suggest that the advantages of freer trade are greater for the group of countries whose exports are subject to strong-growing world demand. Kawai (1994) suggests that effective trade policy varies depending on the country's stage of development, with import substitution effective in the early stages of development and a switch to trade liberalization and even export-oriented intervention proving more successful at more advanced stages of development.

A couple of recent studies explore more explicitly some of the ideas thrown up by recent theorizing about growth. Backus et al. (1992) appear to have re-discovered the results if not the work of Kaldor and 'Verdoorn's Law'. They suggest that larger economies and more specialized economies should grow faster than smaller or less specialized economies. They find support for this neo-Smithian hypothesis in cross-country comparisons of rates of growth of productivity in manufacturing, but not for non-manufacturing activities. Coe and Helpman (1995) and Coe, Helpman and Hoffmaister (1995) find support for their neo-Millian hypothesis that trade flows between developed economies interact with the knowledge gap (measured by differences in stocks of R&D) to raise productivity growth. While their evidence does not contradict their contention that trade diffuses knowledge, they do not explicitly confront alternative hypotheses such as that diffusion might be related to foreign direct investment, geographical proximity, language and culture, telecommunication links, and so on.

There is, then, a fairly consistent impression from a wide range of studies of a positive relationship between trade openness and growth. I think this can be interpreted as an average effect: trade stimulates world growth. There is, however, little consistent evidence as yet on the mechanisms by which trade stimulates growth. There is some support for the neo-Smithian hypothesis that growth is increased by the opportunities trade gives for specialization and also for the neo-Millian hypothesis that trade flows facilitate the international dissemination of technological knowledge. But neither of these theories has been subject to rigorous testing against alternative hypotheses. Nor have we yet gained much insight into the differential impacts of trade on different countries, a possibility suggested by the neo-Ricardian models.

5   CONCLUDING COMMENTS

The overall impression from a brief survey of the existing econometric literature is that there are indeed significant gains to rates of economic growth from further opening up of inward-oriented economies. This evidence supports the conclusions of the new models of economic growth which suggest that world growth should be enhanced by the increased specialization which trade makes possible in knowledge-producing and growth-enhancing activities – whether in customized research and development activities or in learning by doing.

These potential gains are not, however, of the order of magnitude suggested by some commentators who point to annual growth rates in the NICs of eight per cent or more and naively suggest that such rapid development should be possible for an already developed economy. The results of a wide range of econometric studies suggest that, at most, gains of the order of one-half of a percentage point per year might be expected.

Moreover, the wide variance in growth rates listed in Table 7.1 should serve as a warning that there is no simple mechanical translation from trade to growth. There are plenty of countries with a measured outward orientation which have nevertheless experienced relatively slow rates of economic growth – notably some of the high trading EC economies such as Switzerland, the UK, Belgium and the Netherlands among the developed economies.

There are also plenty of examples of less-developed countries which have grown quickly despite, or maybe because of, temporary trade restrictions. Many commentators have suggested that the fast-growing East Asian economies have relied on protection, at least in the early stages of industrialization. The econometric evidence does not rule out infant industry arguments, although it does suggest that long-term protection is less likely to be successful. Nor, it should be emphasized, does either the new theory or the econometric analysis contradict the traditional result that optimal tariffs are not necessarily zero when the terms of trade can be altered.

The new growth theories point out that the growth-enhancing effect of trade is an aggregate effect – we expect it to hold on average, as confirmed by the econometric results, but not in every case. In particular, trade can reduce growth for countries which have comparative advantage in industries with low growth potential. Lower growth does not, however, necessarily imply lower economic welfare. Specialization through trade may move the terms of trade in favour of the low-tech country which is enabled to import cheaper high-tech goods. The new theories support the traditional analysis of comparative advantage and the beneficial impact of trade liberalization in a world of complete and competitive markets.

Trade is not, however, necessarily welfare enhancing in the absence of competitive markets. If there are substantial market failures in the accumulation of knowledge and skills and new goods, then trade is a double-edged sword. On the one hand trade acts as a conduit for new ideas, stimulating growth and enhancing welfare. On the other hand, trade liberalization and consequent specialization in 'low-tech' activities may relegate a country which is historically disadvantaged in the accumulation of skills and knowledge to fall further and further behind.

NOTE

1. Somewhat larger estimates of the benefits of trade liberalization come from the analysis of trade in differentiated products with increasing returns to scale, as in Cox and Harris (1986), or taking account of the possibility of new non-rival inputs into production, as in Romer (1994).

REFERENCES

Agarwala, R. (1984), 'Price distortions and growth', *Finance and Development*, **21** (1), March, 33–7.
Agarwala, R. (1993), 'Price distortions and growth in developing countries', *World Bank Staff Working Paper*, No. 575, Washington: IBRD.
Backus, David K., Patrick J. Kehoe and Timothy J. Kehoe (1992), 'In search of scale effects in trade and growth', *Journal of Economic Theory*, **58**, 377–409.
Baldwin, Richard E. (1992), 'Measurable dynamic gains from trade', *Journal of Political Economy*, **100** (1), February, 162–74.
Baldwin, Robert E. (1992), 'Are economists' traditional trade policy views still valid?', *Journal of Economic Literature*, **30**, June, 804–29.
Barro, Robert J. and Xavier Sala-i-Martin (1995), *Economic Growth*, New York: McGraw-Hill.
Ben-David, Dan and Michael B. Loewy (1995), 'Free trade and long-run growth', *Centre for Economic Policy Research Discussion Paper*, No. 1183, London.

Coe, David T. and Elhanan Helpman (1995), 'International R&D spillovers', *European Economic Review*, **39** (5), May, 859–87.

Coe, David T., Elhanan Helpman and Alexander W. Hoffmaister (1995), 'North–South R&D spillovers', *National Bureau of Economic Research Working Paper*, No. 5048, Cambridge, MA.

Corden, W.M. (1984), 'The normative theory of international trade', in Ronald W. Jones and Peter B. Kenen (eds), *Handbook of International Economics*, Vol. 1, Amsterdam: North-Holland, pp. 63–130.

Cox, David and Richard G. Harris (1986), 'A Quantitative Assessment of the Economic Impact on Canada of Sectoral Free Trade with the United States', *Canadian Journal of Economics*, **19** (3), August, 377–94.

Dollar, D. (1992), 'Outward-oriented developing countries really do grow more rapidly: evidence from 95 LDCs 1976–85', *Economic Development and Cultural Change*, **40**, 523–44.

Dowrick, Steve (1994), 'Openness and Growth', in Philip Lowe and Jacqueline Dwyer (eds), *International Integration of the Australian Economy*, Sydney: Reserve Bank of Australia, September, pp. 19–41.

Edwards, Sebastian (1992), 'Trade orientation, distortions and growth in developing countries', *Journal of Development Economics*, **39**, 31–57.

Edwards, Sebastian (1993), 'Openness, Trade Liberalization, and Growth in Developing Countries', *Journal of Economic Literature*, **31** (3), September, 1358–93.

Evans, H.D. (1989), *Comparative Advantage and Growth*, New York: Harvester Wheatsheaf.

Grossman, Gene M. and Elhanan Helpman (1990), 'Trade, innovation and growth', *American Economic Review*, **80** (2), May, 86–91.

Grossman, Gene M. and Elhanan Helpman (1991a), 'Trade, knowledge spillovers and growth', *European Economic Review*, **35**, 517–26.

Grossman, Gene M. and Elhanan Helpman (1992b), *Innovation and Growth in the Global Economy*, Cambridge, MA: MIT Press.

Hammond, Peter J. and Andres Rodriguez-Clare (1993), 'On endogenizing long-run growth', *Scandinavian Journal of Economics*, **95** (4), 391–425.

Helliwell, John F. (1992), 'Trade and technical progress', *National Bureau of Economic Research Working Paper*, No. 4226.

Jones, Larry E. and Rodolfo Manuelli (1990), 'A convex model of equilibrium growth: theory and policy implications', *Journal of Political Economy*, **98** (5), 1008–38.

Kaldor, N. (1981), 'The role of increasing returns, technical progress and cumulative causation in the theory of international trade and economic growth', *Economie Appliquée*, **34**, 593–617.

Kawai, Hiroki (1994), 'International comparative analysis of economic growth: trade liberalization and productivity', *The Developing Economies*, **32** (4), December, 373–97.

Lal, Deepak (1993), 'Does openness matter? How to appraise the evidence?', seminar paper at Australian National University.

Lee, Jong-Wha (1993), 'International trade, distortions, and long-run economic growth', *IMF Staff Papers*, **40** (2), June, 299–328.

Levine, Ross and David Renelt (1992), 'A sensitivity analysis of cross-country growth regressions', *American Economic Review*, **82** (4), September, 942–63.

Lewis, W.A. (1980), 'The slowing down of the engine of growth (the Nobel lecture)', *American Economic Review*, **70** (4), 555–64.

Lucas, Robert E., Jr. (1988), 'On the mechanics of economic development', *Journal of Monetary Economics*, **22**, 3–42.

Martin, Will and Koji Yanagishima (1993), 'Concerted trade liberalization and economic development in the Asia–Pacific region', *Asia–Pacific Economic Modelling Conference – 93*, Australian National University.

Pitchford, J.D. (1960), 'Growth and the elasticity of factor substitution', *Economic Record*, **36** (76), 491–504.

Rivera-Batiz, Luis A. and Paul M. Romer (1991), 'Economic integration and endogenous growth', *Quarterly Journal of Economics*, **106**, 531–55.

Romer, Paul M. (1990), 'Endogenous technological change', *Journal of Political Economy*, **98** (2), S71–S102.

Romer, Paul (1994), 'New goods, old theory, and the welfare costs of trade restrictions', *Journal of Development Economics*, **43**, 5–38.

Sheehey, Edmund J. (1990), 'Exports and Growth: A Flawed Framework', *Journal of Development Studies*, **27** (1), October, 111–16.

Singer, Hans W. and Patricia Gray (1988), 'Trade policy and growth of developing countries: some new data', *World Development*, **16** (3), 395–403.

Summers, Robert and Alan Heston (1991), 'The Penn World Table (Mark 5): an expanded set of international comparisons, 1950–88', *Quarterly Journal of Economics*, **106** (2), 327–68.

Thirlwall, A.P. (1979), 'The balance of payments constraint as an explanation of international growth rate differences', *Banca Nazionale del Lavoro Quarterly Review*, **128** (791), March, 45–53.

van den Berg, Hendrik and James R. Schmidt (1994), 'Foreign Trade and Economic Growth: Time Series Evidence from Latin America', *Journal of International Trade and Economic Development*, **3** (3), November, 249–68.

World Bank (1987), *World Development Report 1987*, New York: Oxford University Press.

World Bank (1993), *The East Asian Miracle: Economic Growth and Public Policy*, New York: Oxford University Press.

Young, Alwyn (1991), 'Learning by doing and the dynamic effects of international trade', *Quarterly Journal of Economics*, **106**, 369–405.

8. Knowledge inflow to Sweden: does geography and international trade matter?*

Fredrik Sjöholm

1 INTRODUCTION

In recent years, growth theorists have emphasized the role of knowledge as one important determinant of economic growth. However, the *character* of knowledge has not been explored to the same extent.[1] One reason for this is the difficulties in measuring knowledge and in tracing knowledge flows. Jaffe et al. (1993) suggest that patents and references in patent documents can be used to trace knowledge flows. Using this method, we examine the determinants of knowledge inflows to Sweden. Our analysis focuses on two issues on transfer of knowledge which have been discussed in growth theory: the roles played by geographic proximity and international trade.

Two different studies have been conducted using patent documents to trace domestic knowledge flows within the United States. Jaffe (1989) studies the relationship between university research and patent applications in 29 US states. The amount of spillover depends on geography: firms are more likely to benefit from R&D conducted in universities in their 'home' states. Jaffe et al. (1993) use data on patent citations, and compare the geographic location of the inventor with the origin of the cited patent. Cited patents in the US are likely to come from the same state as the inventor. Sjöholm (1996) uses Swedish patent data for a number of small-sized firms to examine international knowledge flows. He finds that international trade facilitates the transfer of knowledge. There are also some indications of a geographic component in the flows of knowledge between countries.

This study extends previous work in some important respects. First, we use patents from both large and small Swedish firms. As previously said, the role of international knowledge flows has been examined only for small firms. A large share of R&D and innovations are conducted by large multinational firms; therefore it is desirable to include them in an empirical examination of knowledge flows. Second, we include knowledge flows within Sweden as well as foreign knowledge flows into Sweden. Hopefully, this will give a better estimation of the effect of geographic proximity on knowledge flows. Previous studies concentrate either on domestic or on international flows of knowledge.

We use ordinary least square (OLS) as well as a conditional logit model to estimate the effect from geographic proximity and international trade on knowledge flows. Both geographic proximity and international trade are found to affect the number of references, that is, the amount of knowledge inflow to Sweden.

Section 2 discusses the role of geographic proximity and international trade on knowledge flows. Section 3 discusses the use of patents in tracing knowledge flows, and presents stylized facts on the knowledge inflow to Sweden. Section 4 describes the methodology and variables. Section 5 presents the results from the econometric examination and the conclusions are presented in Section 6.

2　THE ROLE OF GEOGRAPHIC PROXIMITY AND INTERNATIONAL TRADE

The possible geographic component in knowledge flows is of importance in growth theory. Grossman and Helpman (1991) show that the larger the extent that knowledge exhibits the characteristics of a public good for the entire world, the higher is the tendency for different countries' growth rates of real income to converge.

Geographic distance is believed to be an obstacle to knowledge flows through its negative impact on personal contacts.[2] To a certain extent, knowledge spreads through personal contacts. Face-to-face communication facilitates the knowledge recipients' understanding of new ideas, as they can immediately secure clarification or additional information from the source. The more complex the new piece of knowledge, the more important the personal contact, if the recipient is to be able to interpret it successfully.[3]

The channels through which personal contacts and knowledge transfers take place could be research and development projects, educational exchange, foreign direct investment, international trade, and so on. These channels are likely to decrease with geographic distance. We would also expect cultural differences to increase with geographic distance. Sweden has, for instance, strong cultural ties with its neighbouring Nordic countries. Cultural and linguistic similarities are assumed to make transfer of knowledge – via the various channels – more effective.[4]

One channel of knowledge transfer, which will be affected by geographic proximity, might be international trade. In recent growth theory, trade contacts have been argued to deepen knowledge flows between countries.[5] Commercial interactions promote personal contacts and, hence, enhance knowledge transfer.

The impetus for knowledge transfer is increased profits. Both suppliers and recipients of the knowledge are engaged in the transfer as a way of improving their competitive positions and increasing their revenues. A firm which is importing foreign products is dependent on the quality of these products in order to succeed in business. Importers will consequently inform foreign producers about new technology or about possible alterations to the product in order to make it better meet the demand. Accordingly, exporters will inform foreign business partners about better channels of distribution, or how they can use their goods in production more effectively, and so on. The *method* of knowledge transfer includes planning and feasibility studies, product design, seminars and on-the-job training of technical and managerial staff, as well as a host of other similar mechanisms.[6] For instance, Rhee et al. (1984, Chapter 4) find, in a study of 113 Korean firms, foreign importers to be the most important source of new technology. The foreign firms do more than just buy the Korean goods, they 'provide access to information about what product styles are wanted and about how to make products of a desired style. They come in, too, with models and patterns for Korean engineers to follow, and they even go out to the production line to teach workers how to do things.' One well-known example of knowledge transfers in the other direction – from exporters to importers – is IBM, which has transferred computer technology to domestic and foreign buyers by training users, providing software, and servicing computer installations.

3 DATA AND DESCRIPTIVE STATISTICS

A patent is a temporary monopoly awarded for the commercial use of a device. For a patent application to be granted, the invention must be non-trivial and of potential commercial value. When someone applies for a patent in Sweden, the Swedish patent and registration office lets an examiner, who is familiar with the technological area in question, undertake a close investigation of the application. If the patent is granted, the investigation is published. The publication contains detailed information about the inventor, his or her employer, the technical area concerned, and so on. The publication also includes references to existing patents. The references limit the scope of the property rights awarded to the patent holder. The cited patents represent previously existing knowledge on which the new patent builds. Previously existing knowledge, naturally, cannot be included in the new patent. Although the applicant is obliged to include references in his or her application, it is ultimately the examiner who decides which references are to be included. The main aid when selecting references is the examiner's knowledge of the international patent classification system, containing about 60,000 different groups. Each patent application is assigned to one group. It is this classification of the patent documents which makes access to them possible.

When the examiner is searching for references he or she can, using symbols and keywords, let a computer identify possible relevant patent documents. He or she can then study the full text of the documents from paper or microfiche files.

Jaffe et al. (1993) suggest using these references when tracing knowledge flows. They compare the geographic location of the applicant with the cited patent's point of origin. The cited patents represent crucial pieces of knowledge underpinning the new invention. There should thus have been a transfer of knowledge preceding a citation of a patent. As a consequence, citations can be used as a proxy variable for knowledge flows.

The Swedish patent office has supplied investigations of 220 applications for patents. The sample was randomly picked from patent applications in 1986. The sample includes 555 references to domestic and foreign patents. We have excluded references to the applicant's own patents, since self-citations cannot be viewed as traces of knowledge spillovers.

When someone somewhere in the world applies for a patent to protect an invention, he or she can do it in more than one country. For instance, let us assume that there is a German inventor who applies for a patent which he or she wants to be valid throughout Europe. There will now be one patent registered in France, one in Italy, one in Sweden, and so on (all of them to the German inventor). The examiner at the patent office commonly takes the patent from, for instance, Sweden as a reference instead of the identical but original patent from Germany. In our study, it is necessary to have the original patent as a reference because it is from that country that the knowledge originates. Therefore we have, for all references, checked in which country the original application was made. The original patent has then been used as a reference.

A country's stock of patents can be seen as a proxy variable for its stock of commercial knowledge, and the share of references to a certain country – in Swedish patent documents – is a proxy variable for that country's share of the total flow of knowledge into Sweden. Table 8.1 shows individual OECD countries' share of the total OECD patent stock – that is, the countries' share of the total OECD knowledge stock – as well as their share of references in Swedish patent documents – the countries' share of the knowledge flows into Sweden. The figures are from 1986. Japan, followed by the USA, are the two largest countries in terms of shares of the total patent stock. The two countries possess more than 50 per cent of the total patent stock. In terms of references in Swedish patent documents, almost 90 per cent refer to foreign patents. Foreign knowledge is, hence, of significant importance for Swedish inventors. The US has, by far, the largest share of the knowledge inflow to Sweden. More than 30 per cent of the cited patents are from the USA. Germany is the other country with more citations than Sweden. About 23 per cent of the references are to German patents. There are a number of countries with comparably small stocks of patents and which are not cited in our sample of

Swedish patent documents. This group includes Greece, Iceland, Ireland, New Zealand, Portugal, Spain, Turkey and Yugoslavia.

Table 8.1   Countries' share of total OECD patent stock and their share of references in Swedish patent applications

Country	Share of patents (%)	Share of references (%)	Rank of countries' ratio between share of patents and share of references
Australia	1.3	1.3	11
Austria	0.9	1.5	6
Belgium	0.7	0.5	13
Canada	1.0	1.3	8
Denmark	0.6	2.6	2
Finland	0.5	1.8	4
France	5.7	7.7	7
W. Germany	14.6	23.1	5
Greece	0.2	0.0	—
Iceland	0.0	0.0	—
Ireland	0.1	0.0	—
Italy	3.1	1.5	15
Japan	30.6	3.8	16
Netherlands	1.9	1.6	12
New Zealand	0.2	0.0	—
Norway	0.3	1.1	3
Portugal	0.02	0.0	—
Spain	0.5	0.0	—
Sweden	2.2	10.4	1
Switzerland	3.6	2.7	14
Turkey	0.02	0.0	—
UK	7.0	7.3	10
USA	24.8	31.9	9
Yugoslavia	0.2	0.0	—

Note: Figures from 1986. A country's patent stock has been constructed by adding up its patent applications between 1973 and 1986.
Source: References are from Swedish patent documents. The number of patents are from OECD (1991).

Countries' share of the total patent stock and their share of the references differ substantially for some of the countries. In the last column we rank countries in terms of ratios between the share of patents and the share of references.

Countries which are highly ranked, have a large share of the knowledge inflow into Sweden, in comparison to their shares of the total knowledge stock. There seems to be a connection between proximity to Sweden and relative share of references. Sweden has, not surprisingly, the highest ratio. The neighbouring countries, Denmark, Norway and Finland, also have a relatively large share of references. Moreover, other countries such as Germany, France and Austria are relatively close to Sweden and have a large share of references in Swedish patent documents. Finally, a distant country such as Japan has a very low share of references. Looking at Table 8.1, we would assume that there exists a positive connection between knowledge flows and geographic proximity. In the next section, we will conduct a more formal examination where we also examine the effect of international trade.

4   VARIABLES AND METHOD

4.1   Variables

The purpose of this study is to statistically examine the effect of geographic proximity and international trade on knowledge flows. Geographic proximity is measured by the distance between Sweden and other countries in this study.

Geography$_i$ is the distance between Sweden's economic centre and country *i*'s economic centre (in thousands of kilometres). The value of *Geography* for Sweden has been set equal to zero. The data are from the US Naval Oceanographic Office (1975). If geographic distance is an obstacle to knowledge flows, we would expect a negative sign for *Geography*.

International trade is measured by total bilateral trade flows. *Trade*$_i$ is the total trade between Sweden and country *i* (billions of US dollars 1986 prices, average value for 1981–85). Data on Swedish bilateral trade is from *Statistics Sweden* (1992).

We may expect many references to countries which produce and invent within industrial sectors which are important to Sweden. For example, imagine that a relatively large amount of the citations refers to Finnish patents. We could, of course, take it as a proof of a geographic component in knowledge flows. A different interpretation would be that Sweden and Finland both happen to have similar production structures and that they carry out research within the same industrial sectors. Both Sweden and Finland have, for instance, large forests which have led to large pulp and paper sectors in both countries. If the geographic concentration of industries is linked to factors other than knowledge flows, we would observe a geographic pattern in citations although there is no geographic pattern in the knowledge flows.[7] The variable *Production dissimilarities* controls for relative dissimilarities in production structures between Sweden and other countries.

$$Production\ dissimilarities_i = \sum_{j=1}^{n}\left(q_j - q_{ij}\right)^2$$

where

q_j = the share of product group j in total Swedish production
q_{ij} = the share of product group j in total production in country i
j = $(1,2, ...,n)$ the number of product groups.

Data on production are from the OECD database *STAN* (OECD, 1992) and from *Industrial Structure Statistics* (OECD, 1989). q_{ij} and q_j have been measured as the average value for the five years between 1981 and 1985 (billions of US dollars, 1986 prices). Data on International Standard Industrial Classification (ISIC) at a three-digit level have been used. The value on *Production dissimilarities* for Sweden has been set equal to zero.

Countries with production structures similar to Sweden will have low values on *Production dissimilarities*. If a large share of references are to countries similar to Sweden, we would expect a negative sign for *Production dissimilarities*.

The last variable is *Patent stock*. The larger a country's stock of patents or knowledge, the more references to the country we may expect to find. *Patent stock* is included because we seek to examine the effect of geographic distance on the knowledge inflow, for a given foreign knowledge stock.

Patent stock$_i$ is the total number of domestic and external patent applications from domestic applicants in country i between the years 1973 and 1986 (hundred thousands). The data on patent applications is from *Basic Science and Technology Statistics* (OECD, 1991).

4.2 Method

We will use two different estimation methods to examine the effect of geographic distance and international trade on knowledge flows. We start with OLS, which means that we estimate the following expression:

$$R_i = constant + \beta_1\ Patent\ stock_i + \beta_2 Production\ dissimilarities_i + \beta_3 Geography_i + \beta_4 Trade_i + u$$

where R_i is the number of references to country i and u is a residual. One problem with an OLS estimation could be that we do not have a normal distribution since the sample includes a large number of countries which are never cited. There could, therefore, be a risk of a bias in the estimated coefficients. If, instead, one takes every patent application by itself, and controls for whether there has been a knowledge flow or not, then the reference is a qualitative variable. For every patent application, one will observe either a flow of knowledge (a reference) from a specific country, or no flow of knowledge. However, there is no measure of the *amount* of knowledge being transferred. A dummy endogenous model is appropriate for qualitative variables. Our choice is between a logit and a probit model. The two models differ only in their respective assumptions on the distribution of residuals, and they are likely to render similar results. We have decided to use a conditional logit model in the econometric estimation.[8] The dependent variable can take 16 values, the same as our number of countries with citations. One disadvantage with using a logit rather than an OLS estimation is that the estimated coefficients are only dependent on those countries which are cited. We lose some information by excluding countries with no citations. The model is choice specific, that is, the dependent variable is determined by country characteristics such as geographic distance and international trade. We can therefore write our model as:

$$\delta_i = \frac{\exp\left(\beta_1 Patent\ stock_i + \beta_2 Production\ dissimilarities_i + \beta_3 Geography_i + \beta_4 Trade_i\right)}{\sum_{k=1}^{n} \exp\left(\beta_1 Patent\ stock_k + \beta_2 Production\ dissimilarities_k + \beta_3 Geography_k + \beta_4 Trade_k\right)}$$

where δ_i is the odds that country i will be referred to and $k = 1, 2, \ldots, 16$ are the included countries.

5   RESULTS

Table 8.2 presents the empirical results from our OLS estimations. Swedish references are excluded in estimations with international trade. The coefficient for *Patent stock* is significant with positive sign in all estimations, which means that there are many references to countries with large stocks of knowledge. *Production dissimilarities* is not statistically significant in any of our three estimations. There is, hence, no sign of a large number of references to countries with production structures similar to Sweden. Geographic distance was assumed to be an obstacle to knowledge flows; as distances between a given country and Sweden increase, we would expect the number of references to decrease. *Geography* has in regression 1 a negative coefficient and is judged to decrease the number of references. Finally, international trade was hypothesized to be a channel of knowledge transfer. A large amount of trade with a certain country should increase knowledge inflow from this particular country. The coefficient for *Trade* is positive and significant in regression 2. If we compare the effect from *Geography* with the effect from *Trade*, it seems that the latter may be of slightly more importance. First, the $\bar{R}^2$ increases from 0.52 with, the inclusion of *Geography* in regression 1, to 0.63 with the inclusion of *Trade* in regression 2. Moreover, the inclusion of both *Geography* and *Trade* in regression 3 makes the coefficient for *Geography* insignificant while the coefficient for *Trade* is still statistically significant. One explanation could be that the importance of geographic proximity on knowledge flows is through its positive effect on trade flows.[9]

Table 8.2   Results from OLS estimations

Variable	Regression 1	Regression 2	Regression 3
Constant	20.97	–9.99	–5.17
	$(2.15)^{**}$	(0.98)	(0.37)
Patent stock	4.00	2.60	2.86
	$(4.86)^{***}$	$(3.46)^{***}$	$(3.12)^{***}$
Production dissimilarities	–0.11	0.03	0.02
	(0.80)	(0.25)	(0.12)
Geography	–4.1	—	–1.1
	$(2.33)^{**}$		(0.52)
Trade	—	8.8	7.8
		$(3.30)^{***}$	$(2.23)^{**}$
$\bar{R}^2$	0.52	0.63	0.61
Number of observations	24	23	23

Notes
Geography – thousand kilometres. *Trade* – billions of US dollars. *Patent stock* – hundred thousand patents.
** Significant at the 5 per cent level.
*** Significant at the 1 per cent level.

The results from the conditional logit estimations are found in Table 8.3. The results are, with some exceptions, similar to the OLS estimations. One difference is that *Production dissimilarities* is negative and statistically significant in all three estimations. This means that there are many references to countries which are similar to Sweden. Both *Geography* and *Trade* are highly significant. Unlike in the OLS estimation, neither *Geography* nor *Trade* become insignificant when we include both in the same conditional logit estimation.

Table 8.3   Results from logit estimations

Variable	Estimation 1	Estimation 2	Estimation 3
Patent stock	0.13	0.06	0.13
	$(19.69)^{***}$	$(11.7)^{***}$	$(11.01)^{***}$
Production dissimilarities	−0.03	−0.02	−0.02
	$(6.00)^{***}$	$(3.35)^{***}$	$(2.48)^{**}$
Geography	−0.32	—	−0.25
	$(13.47)^{***}$		$(6.44)^{***}$
Trade	—	0.27	0.08
		$(15.2)^{***}$	$(2.63)^{***}$
Number of observations	555	498	498

Notes
Geography – thousand kilometres. *Trade* – billions of US dollars. *Patent stock* – hundred thousand patents.
** Significant at the 5 per cent level.
*** Significant at the 1 per cent level.

5.1 Extensions

The inclusion of references is dependent on the examiner, and they therefore in some sense correspond to the examiner's personal preferences. There is a possibility that personal preferences could bias our results. For instance, the high share of references to the Scandinavian countries could be dependent on language similarities. The case of few references to Japan might, accordingly, be affected by the limited number of examiners speaking Japanese. As the examiners cannot read the Japanese patents, they will instead use a Scandinavian patent or maybe one written in English. There are two arguments against the idea of a bias in favour of patents from countries with a similar language. First, and most important, is the fact that inventors usually patent their innovations in at least some of the other OECD countries.[10] For the Japanese patent, there might be one copy valid in, for example, the United States, written in English. The examiner will probably choose the patent in English as a reference after he or she has consulted the international database. However, we have chosen all the original patents as references, which limits the possibility of a bias in favour of references in the English and Scandinavian languages. Second, an important part of a patent is the blueprint which may be understood despite language differences. However, in order to examine whether our results might be biased because of language similarities, we estimated our OLS and our logit model with inclusion of dummy variables for the Scandinavian and English-speaking countries.[11] Inclusion of dummy variables did decrease the coefficient for *Geography*, but it was still negative and significant.

The trade variable was constructed by computing the value of the total trade flow (imports and exports) between Sweden and the other country. Most of the examined patent applications have been filed by firms in the manufacturing sector. It might, therefore, be more appropriate to examine the relationship between the amount of trade in manufactures and the number of references. Such an examination was carried out, but it did not change previous results. Moreover, we divided international trade into imports and exports, but the results suffered from multi-collinearity since these two variables are highly correlated. Finally, we experimented with several different measures on international trade, such as share of total Swedish exports, imports of machinery, and so on. The results were stable and seemed convincing in showing a positive effect from international trade on knowledge inflow to Sweden.

It has been suggested that Japan has a comparatively high propensity to file domestic patent applications.[12] Japan's share of the total stock of commercial knowledge might therefore be exaggerated. An alternative measure of the stock of knowledge was constructed, where only a country's *external* patent applications were included. There have been no suggestions of country-specific propensities when external patent applications are filed. Re-running the econometric estimations using the new measure of patent stocks, did not alter the previous results.

Finally, we created a subsample of our references. The original sample included a group of references to patents which are up to one hundred years old. It is doubtful whether such old patents contain knowledge of any real benefit for new inventors. The patent examiner might have included old patents as references more for the sake of completeness than for marking out knowledge which is truly of intellectual benefit for the new inventor. A subsample was therefore created, containing references to patents less than 20 years old. It is admittedly quite an arbitrary way of creating a subsample, but our justification for doing so is the fact that patent protection lasts for only 20 years. After this time the knowledge connected with a patent might be considered to be trivial, that is, familiar to a skilled practitioner in the area in question. Changing the sample did not alter the previous results.

6   CONCLUDING REMARKS

In this chapter, we have examined the role of geographic proximity and international trade in the flow of knowledge. Our study of the problem differed from earlier ones in one respect: we study the problem in an *international* context, including both domestic and international knowledge flows. Our results indicate that there exists a geographic component in flows of knowledge into Sweden. The geographic component in flows of knowledge at a domestic level found by Jaffe (1989) and Jaffe et al. (1993), hence, seems to be valid also in an international context. The relationship between international trade and transfer of knowledge seems to be well established. This chapter confirms the picture in Sjöholm (1996), who found international trade to facilitate the exchange of knowledge in small Swedish firms and who also found some indications of a geographic component in the knowledge inflow to these firms.

If we relate our results to endogenous growth models, there is a situation where knowledge does indeed flow across borders but the spillover is not complete. Geographic distance seems to be one determinant to the degree of international spillovers. The results also lend some support for the endogenous growth model by Grossman and Helpman (1991, Chapter 6), which is based on the assumption of a positive connection between international trade and knowledge transfer.

NOTES

*	I thank Bo Södersten and Jan Fagerberg for valuable comments. Jan-Erik Bodin at the Swedish patent and registration office has been most helpful in facilitating the empirical material. Financial support from the Bank of Sweden Tercentenary Foundation, the Swedish Council for Research in the Humanities and Social Sciences, and the Tore Browaldhs Foundation for Scientific Research and Education are gratefully acknowledged.

1. For theoretical work on knowledge and economic growth see, for example, Romer (1986 and 1990), Lucas (1988), Grossman and Helpman (1991).
2. See for example, Jacobs (1984), Porter (1990, p. 157), Glaeser et al. (1992).
3. Rogers and Shoemaker (1971).
4. See, for example, Rogers and Shoemaker (1971, p. 14) and Miyagiwa (1991, p. 745).
5. Grossman and Helpman (1991, Chapter 6).
6. Perlmutter and Sagfi-Nejad (1981, p. 13).
7. For a further discussion of the need to control for production similarities when one is investigating knowledge flows, see Jaffe et al. (1993, pp. 579, 591–2).
8. For a description of a conditional logit model see, for example, Maddala (1983, Chapters 2 and 3) and Green (1993).
9. The correlation between *Geography* and *Trade* is –0.32.
10. See, for example, OECD (1991). All countries, except Japan, have at least three times as many external patent applications as domestic patent applications.
11. We argued in Section 2 that geographic proximity captures cultural and linguistic similarities and that such similarities enhance the transfer of knowledge. It should be noted that with the inclusion of dummy variables for lingual similarities, we therefore control for parts of the effect from geographic proximity on knowledge flows.
12. OECD (1991, p. 370).

REFERENCES

Glaeser, E., H. Kallal, J. Sheinkman and A. Schleifer (1992), 'Growth in Cities', *Journal of Political Economy*, **100**, 1126–52.
Greene, W. (1993) *Econometric Analysis*, New York: Macmillan Publishing.

Grossman, G.M. and E. Helpman (1991), *Innovation and Growth in the Global Economy*, Cambridge, MA: MIT Press.

Jacobs, J. (1984), *Cities and the Wealth of Nations*, New York: Vintage Books.

Jaffe, A. (1989), 'Real Effects of Academic Research', *American Economic Review*, **79**, 957–70.

Jaffe, A., M. Trajtenberg and R. Henderson (1993), 'Geographic Localisation of Knowledge Spillovers As Evidenced By Patent Citations', *Quarterly Journal of Economics*, **108**, 577–98.

Lucas, R.E., Jr. (1988), 'On the Mechanics of Economic Development', *Journal of Monetary Economics*, **22**, 3–42.

Maddala, G.S. (1983), *Limited Dependent Variables and Qualitative Variables in Econometrics*, Cambridge: Cambridge University Press.

Miyagiwa, K. (1991), 'Scale Economies in Education and the Brain Drain Problem', *International Economic Review*, **32**, 743–59.

Perlmutter, H.V. and T. Sagfi-Nejad (1981), *International Technology Transfer: Guidelines. Codes and a Muffled Quadrilogue*, New York: Pergamon.

Porter, M.E. (1990), *The Competitive Advantage of Nations*, London: Macmillan.

Rhee, Y.W., B. Ross-Larson and G. Pursell (1984), *Korea's Competitive Edge: Managing the Entry into World Markets*, Baltimore, MD: Johns Hopkins University Press.

Rogers, E.M., and F.F. Shoemaker (1971), *Communication of Innovations: A Cross-Cultural Approach*, New York: Free Press.

Romer, P. (1986), 'Increasing Returns and Long-Run Growth', *Journal of Political Economy*, **94**, 1002–37.

Romer, P. (1990), 'Endogenous Technological Change', *Journal of Political Economy*, **98**, 71–102.

Sjöholm, F. (1996), 'International Transfer of Knowledge: The Role of International Trade and Geographic Proximity', *Weltwirtschaftliches Archiv*, **132**, 97–115.

STATISTICS

OECD(1989), *Industrial Structure Statistics*, Paris: OECD.

OECD (1991), *Basic Science and Technology Statistics*, Paris: OECD.

OECD (1992), *Structural Analysis (STAN) Industrial Database*, Paris: OECD.

Statistics Sweden (1992), *Statistical Yearbook of Sweden 1992*, Stockholm Official Statistics of Sweden.

US Naval Oceanographic Office (1975), *Distances Between Ports*, H.O. Pub. No. 151, Washington, DC: US Government.

9. Decentralization of research and development by multinational companies: determinants and future prospects

Steven Globerman*

1 INTRODUCTION

Linkages between the activities of multinational companies (MNCs) and technological change have concerned both host- and home-country policy-makers. Much of the concern has focused on the magnitude and nature of the research and development (R&D) carried out by MNCs in different countries. In particular, host-country officials have traditionally been concerned about MNCs centralizing most of their R&D activities in home-country laboratories while assigning local affiliates mandates to 'adapt' home-country innovations to local conditions. Conversely, home-country officials have been worried about a decentralization of R&D activities to overseas affiliates, especially 'early stage' R&D (Dunning, 1993a; Globerman, 1994).

While there has been a modest trend for MNCs to do relatively more R&D in overseas affiliates, there have been recent suggestions in the literature that this trend may be reversed by emerging economic and technological changes (Blank, Krajewski and Yu, 1994; Eaton, Lipsey and Safarian, 1994). The purpose of this chapter is to assess whether recent patterns of international R&D performance of MNCs are likely to change. Several attributes of MNC R&D performance are relevant in this regard. One is the geographical location of the R&D activity. A second is the nature of the R&D activity undertaken in different affiliates. A third is the degree to which R&D decision-making is centralized in the home-country affiliate.

The primary focus of the chapter is on the geographical location of R&D activity, as this is the attribute of MNC R&D performance for which there is the most information and to which most attention has been paid. Decentralization of R&D in this context implies that MNCs are doing relatively more R&D in host-country affiliates compared to home-country affiliates. The increased autonomy of host-country affiliate managers to administer R&D budgets and exploit R&D results is a different manifestation of decentralization. To avoid confusion, we will refer to geographical decentralization to identify increased R&D activity in host-country affiliates and managerial decentralization to identify increased discretion of host-country affiliate managers in allocating MNC R&D resources.

The chapter proceeds as follows. Section 2 presents evidence documenting a trend in recent decades for MNCs to geographically decentralize their R&D activities. Much more speculative evidence is also presented of a tendency towards managerial decentralization over the same time period. Section 3 identifies and discusses alternative possible explanations of the observed trends in MNC R&D behaviour. Section 4 raises and evaluates alternative arguments regarding whether or not past trends will continue, drawing in part upon evidence of recent MNC R&D performance patterns. Section 5 presents several policy implications of the analysis in the preceding sections.

2 MNC R&D PATTERNS IN THE POST-WAR PERIOD

Studies examining the R&D location decisions of MNCs have tended to focus on two measures: R&D expenditures and patents.[1] For either measure, a number of studies document a modest trend through the 1980s on the part of MNCs to carry out relatively more R&D in their overseas affiliates. Dunning (1993b) notes that in the case of US MNCs, for which available data are most comprehensive, 6.5 per cent of global R&D undertaken in 1966 was performed outside the United States. By 1982, this allocation had increased to 7 per cent, and it reached 9 per cent by 1989.[2] R&D employment data for German MNCs tell a similar story. For example, a survey of 11 German MNCs at the end of 1970 revealed that about 15 per cent of their R&D personnel were employed abroad, whereas a survey of 33 major German MNCs in 1989 showed that 18 per cent of their total R&D employees were employed in affiliates outside the home country (United Nations, 1992).

Data for Swedish MNCs also show a propensity towards geographical decentralization, although the trend is not a smooth one. Considering all manufacturing industries, foreign R&D as a share of total R&D increased from approximately 8 to 14 per cent in the first half of the 1970s. Thereafter it remained at that level, or even decreased slightly until 1986. In the second half of the 1980s, the share of R&D undertaken abroad increased from about 13 to 17 per cent of total R&D carried out by Swedish MNCs (Fors and Svensson, 1994).

The trend towards increased geographical decentralization of MNC R&D activities is not characteristic of all countries. Perhaps more importantly, as indicated by the Swedish experience, the trend has not been uniform over the post-war period for major MNCs. Table 9.1 reports the share of patents filed in the United States by MNCs that is credited to research undertaken outside the home country of the parent firm. Over the period 1969–72 to 1983–86, this share increased for seven of the 11 countries cited. Belgium, Sweden and the United States are characterized by relatively large increases, while Canada and Italy are characterized by relatively large decreases. Relatively modest changes are identified for France, Germany and the United Kingdom.

Table 9.1   The share of US patents of the largest firms world-wide attributable to research in foreign locations (outside the home country of the parent company) organized by the nationality of parent firms, 1969–1986 (percentages)

Country	1969–72	1973–77	1978–82	1983–86
Belgium	49.6	54.2	56.1	71.3
Canada	42.0	40.0	39.8	35.5
France	10.2	9.4	8.8	10.9
Germany	13.6	11.5	12.3	14.4
Italy	20.1	18.3	13.7	11.7
Japan	2.9	—	1.9	1.3
Netherlands	63.9	68.8	64.1	70.0
Sweden	20.9	17.8	25.9	31.3
Switzerland	45.0	44.3	44.1	42.6
UK	43.3	40.5	38.7	45.0
USA	4.3	5.5	6.0	7.4

Source: United Nations (1992, Table VI.5, p. 139).

Looking more closely at the patterns from subperiod to subperiod, it is clear that the trend towards decentralization was not monotonic over the full period. Specifically, comparing the first and second subperiods and the second and the third subperiods, there were actually more decreases than increases in the reported percentages. In contrast, comparing 1978–82 to 1983–86, there were seven reported increases in the relevant statistic and only three reported decreases. The pattern observed in Table 9.1 suggests that the geographical decentralization of R&D undertaken by MNCs began in earnest in the late 1970s.

In summary, there was an identifiable trend through the 1980s on the part of most MNCs to geographically decentralize their R&D expenditures. However, certain home countries pose exceptions to this statement. Moreover, the exceptions are not uniformly small home countries, since they include Japan. The fact that some exceptions to this trend can be found suggests that explanations may have to take into account idiosyncratic national characteristics of MNCs. Furthermore, the fact that the trend appears to decelerate and accelerate in different periods suggests that there may be variable lags in the responses of MNCs to underlying determinants of geographical decentralization.

There is much less reliable information available about changes in the nature of R&D undertaken by MNCs in overseas affiliates, as well as the degree of autonomy enjoyed by managers of the R&D process in overseas affiliates. Indeed, it is difficult to suggest unobjectionable measures of the nature of R&D or the degree of autonomy enjoyed by overseas managers. One traditional way of distinguishing the nature of R&D is to categorize R&D activity as being either basic research, applied research or development (Mansfield, 1968). The bulk of the R&D undertaken by MNCs outside the home country has tended to focus on development, rather than on basic or applied research, on product and process improvements rather than on new products and processes, and on relatively short-term, technically safe work (Mansfield, Teece and Romeo, 1979).[3]

What limited information is available suggests that there have been some changes in the nature of R&D carried out in overseas MNC affiliates. Perhaps the most detailed information is available for Swedish MNCs. Fors and Svensson (1994, p. 10) conclude that the R&D undertaken abroad by Swedish MNCs has changed considerably in character over the past 20 years. In the 1970s, the major part of foreign R&D was directed towards adaptation of products and processes developed in Sweden for local use, while in the 1980s there was a shift towards more long-term and generally applicable R&D in the foreign affiliates. By 1990, more than half of foreign R&D by Swedish MNCs was directed towards development of new products and processes. A similar, albeit less dramatic, change in the nature of overseas R&D has been observed for other industrial countries (United Nations, 1992).[4]

The autonomy enjoyed by subsidiary R&D managers is inherently a subjective concept. Hence, it is unsurprising that what limited evidence is available tends to draw upon surveys in which managers are asked to identify changes in the autonomy they enjoy. A related source of evidence is the opinion of consultants and other expert observers of the international R&D management process. These sources tend to suggest that overseas R&D managers have enjoyed increased management autonomy over the post-war period (Blank, Krajewski and Yu, 1994; Howells and Wood, 1993). While it is unclear whether changes in autonomy are directly related to increased geographical decentralization, the two characteristics may well reflect the influence of similar determining factors.

3   DETERMINANTS OF INTERNATIONAL R&D PATTERNS IN MNCS

In order to evaluate whether the post-war patterns identified in the preceding section are likely to continue into the future, it is useful to identify the factors that have influenced MNC R&D strategies over the past few decades and then assess whether the important determining factors are likely to change in the foreseeable future.

In choosing geographical locations for their R&D activities, MNCs will presumably allocate their R&D resources so as to maximize long-run profits. This in turn suggests that R&D resources will be reallocated if such reallocation promises to reduce costs, including the costs of R&D, and/or increase revenues.

3.1   Costs of R&D

The cost savings associated with concentrating R&D activities in one or a few geographical locations have traditionally been associated with exploiting underlying economies of scale and scope in the R&D process. On the other hand, dispersing R&D activities geographically better enables the MNC to take advantage of regional differences in scientific and technological expertise that are 'site specific'. It also better enables the MNC to take advantage of geographical price differentials for scientific and technical personnel. The availability of host-government subsidies or tax incentives for domestically performed R&D can also lower the overall financing costs of the global organization's R&D activities. Finally, locating R&D facilities abroad may accelerate the rate at which the MNC 'learns about' technology being developed elsewhere, particularly if the R&D labs of foreign rivals are at the forefront of technology in specific areas. Faster learning should help the MNC avoid duplicating costly R&D whose benefits might be more cheaply realized through technology licensing or related strategies.

3.2   Revenues Associated with R&D Activities

The revenues derived from R&D activities will, in turn, be related to the scientific and commercial prospects of the R&D undertaken by the MNC. Geographical decentralization of R&D will therefore be encouraged if such decentralization improves the *ex ante* scientific and/or commercial prospects of the MNC's R&D activities.

If specific regions of the world are acknowledged 'centres of excellence' in particular technologies, locating R&D facilities in those regions could enable MNCs to more readily and effectively identify companies and individuals whose services would improve the scientific and/or commercial prospects of the firm's R&D portfolio. It might also improve the 'yield' of the MNC's R&D portfolio by enhancing the ability of the MNC to capture inter-firm technology 'spillovers', although the importance of geographical proximity to the capture of technological spillovers is a matter of some controversy (Hutchinson and Nicholas, 1992; Bernstein, 1994).

Another important potential benefit from locating R&D activities abroad is that it can improve the profitability of new products or production processes introduced into foreign markets by facilitating the adaptation of the new technology to local conditions. This latter consideration is particularly relevant when demand and/or production conditions in the host country differ significantly from conditions in the home country, or when the geographical proximity of research facilities to manufacturing facilities in the host country significantly reduces time lags in adjusting production techniques or product characteristics to changes in host-country conditions. Indeed, in some cases, locating R&D facilities in the host country may be required as a condition for being allowed to establish production facilities, although various international and regional trade agreements have mitigated the use of such investment provisions by host-country governments (Rugman, 1994).

A potentially negative impact of overseas affiliate R&D on MNC revenues is the possibility that geographically decentralizing R&D might accelerate 'leakages' of the MNC's proprietary technology to foreign competitors with a resulting attenuation of the MNC's pricing power and/or market share in international markets (Bradsher, 1995). One possibility in this regard is that foreign-based R&D personnel will defect to foreign competitors or start up their own ventures. A second is that the appropriation of the MNC's technology by foreign firms might be accelerated if the latter can actually observe the interactions between a new technology and existing manufacturing processes in the host country.[5]

3.3 Evaluation of Determinants of Geographical Decentralization

Various factors influencing the geographical decentralization of R&D are summarized in Figure 9.1. The main theoretical factors encouraging the performance of R&D in overseas affiliates are the need to modify process and product technologies to host-country conditions; the existence of technological centres of excellence in overseas locations; lower costs of performing R&D in overseas locations; and host-government requirements or incentives to do R&D locally. The main theoretical factors encouraging the centralization of R&D in the home country are plant-level economies of scale, and scope in the R&D activity (that is, economies related to operations of the local unit), and higher costs of carrying out R&D abroad including reduced productivity and costs associated with monitoring overseas R&D labs.

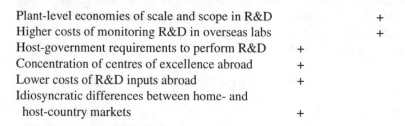

Factor	More Activity	Less Activity
Plant-level economies of scale and scope in R&D		+
Higher costs of monitoring R&D in overseas labs		+
Host-government requirements to perform R&D	+	
Concentration of centres of excellence abroad	+	
Lower costs of R&D inputs abroad	+	
Idiosyncratic differences between home- and host-country markets	+	

Figure 9.1   Summary of factors influencing the location of more MNC R&D activity in overseas affiliates

There tends to be a consensus in the empirical literature that the main factor encouraging the modest trend towards geographical decentralization of R&D identified in the preceding section has been the need to 'adapt' home-country technology to the needs of important foreign markets.[6] Two broad purposes of MNC affiliate R& D have been identified in this context. One is to assist the transfer of technology from the parent company to the affiliate. A second is to adapt products developed for the parent's market to specialized needs of local consumers. The first purpose has been typically associated with a desire to serve host markets from 'within' rather than 'without', perhaps owing to tariff or non-tariff barriers in the host market. The second is typically associated with the need for physical proximity between R&D and manufacturing facilities both for efficiency considerations as well as, sometimes, implicit requirements to perform domestic R&D in order to win orders from public-sector consumers.[7]

A number of case studies and surveys of MNCs conclude that the existence of centres of excellence in foreign markets related to favourable scientific environments and infrastructure is a significant contributing factor to the decentralization of MNC R&D in specific industries. The main industries identified in this regard are pharmaceuticals, consumer chemicals, professional and scientific equipment, office equipment and, to a lesser extent, petroleum products (Pearce, 1992; Casson, Pearce and Singh, 1992). These tend to be industries of above-average R&D intensity and, especially, above-average basic research intensity.

There is no persuasive evidence that lower-cost inputs have encouraged a decentralization of R&D. While this hypothesis is difficult to test formally, since R&D factor input prices are generally not available, the fact that most of the geographical decentralization that has taken place has involved affiliates in developed rather than developing countries suggests that input prices, *per se*, have not been an important determinant of the location of R&D activities.[8] Nevertheless, there have been suggestions in the literature that the growth of high-speed interactive computer communications networks will substantially increase the 'outsourcing' of scientific and technical activities to low-wage countries such as India and Japan (Globerman, forthcoming). These suggestions will be considered in Section 4 of this chapter.

While host-government policies designed to encourage MNC R&D activity undoubtedly have had some influence on the geographical decentralization of R&D, it is unlikely that they have had a major influence. In particular, the relative importance of government funding of R&D decreased over the 1970s and 1980s in developed countries such as Canada. Hence, host-government financial R&D incentives arguably became less important during the period of time that geographical decentralization of R&D was taking place.

There is some evidence that firm-level economies of scale in R&D have been a consideration influencing R&D location decisions. For example, the overall size of the MNC's technological activity appears to be negatively related to the extent to which it decentralizes its R&D, other things constant (Cantwell and Hodson, 1991). Again, however, anecdotal evidence suggests that economies of scale have not been a critical determinant. For example, the concentration of R&D expenditures among the largest corporate R&D performers in Canada was relatively constant over the period of the 1970s and 1980s. If economies of scale were an important influence on the allocation of R&D resources, one would have expected to see the largest R&D performers account for an increasing share of overall R&D over that period.

There is virtually no 'hard' evidence on the linkage between communication costs and the location of R&D activities. The general view on the linkage is expressed by Casson (1991a) who notes that while improved communications mitigates some of the difficulties created by distance, it is an imperfect substitute for physical proximity. In particular, it is not only communications for the R&D activity that is crucial but also communication between R&D and other functional areas, notably marketing and production. The costs of coordinating distant communication across all of these activities has encouraged MNCs in the past to agglomerate the factory, the R&D unit and the local marketing headquarters on the same site.

To be sure, several authors have argued that improved communications technology may have encouraged some geographical decentralization of R&D in recent years. For example, Howells and Wood (1993) argue that improved communication technology, including the spread of shared databases, electronic mail, video-conferencing and workstation technology, has encouraged MNCs to experiment with 'cross-border teamwork' in R&D involving research staff located at two or three different countries working on the same project. The United Nations (1992) has argued similarly that the development of transnational computer-communication networks and on-line systems that permit the smooth flow of data and information among remote sites has facilitated the geographical specialization of R&D and even the on-line conduct of R&D. These authors offer no statistical evidence in support of their arguments.

In summary, the empirical evidence suggests that the main historical factor encouraging the modest geographical decentralization of R&D has been the modest increase in international production by MNCs.[9] Another factor that may have been important in a specific set of industries was the growth of centres of technological excellence which, in turn, encouraged MNCs to engage in more geographical specialization of R&D. The growth of these centres of excellence is, in turn, related to the increasing importance of agglomeration economies, or external economies of scale, in the R&D activity (Zander and Solvell, 1992).

3.4   Managerial Decentralization

Several of the factors theoretically linked to the geographical decentralization of R&D have also been linked to the managerial decentralization of R&D. Idiosyncratic differences between host and home countries are one such factor. Presumably the greater these differences, the greater the imperative to allow affiliates more autonomy, *ceteris paribus*, since the affiliate is likely to enjoy informational advantages relative to the parent. Autonomy in R&D decision-making is often linked to the granting of world product mandates to overseas affiliates. Conversely, the more interdependent are the production and marketing linkages among MNC affiliates, the more important is the need for centralized control of the R&D activities that support production.[10]

The costs of monitoring and evaluating the R&D strategies of overseas affiliate managers are a second potentially significant factor influencing the degree of autonomy granted foreign affiliates. The lower these costs, the lower the risks that managers of foreign affiliates will 'suboptimize' in their allocation of R&D resources. That is, the lower the risks that foreign affiliates will act opportunistically at the expense of global profits by taking advantage of situations in which information between parent and affiliate is asymmetrically distributed. Conversely, the shorter the required response time of foreign affiliates to changes in local competitive conditions, the greater the degree of autonomy the parent is likely to find optimal, since greater autonomy will presumably enable affiliate managers to respond faster to changes in relevant demand and supply conditions in the local market.

As noted earlier, there is relatively little statistical evidence on the extent to which MNCs have been granting more autonomy to managers of R&D activities in foreign affiliates. Several authors argue that increased autonomy has accompanied the modest degree of geographical decentralization identified above (Howells and Wood, 1993; Blank, Krajewski and Yu, 1994). However, these and other experts also argue that the trend towards decentralization of autonomy may be in the process of being reversed.

4 EMERGING FACTORS INFLUENCING MNC R&D STRATEGIES

Several emerging trends in the international business environment have been identified as potentially influencing MNC strategies with respect to international R&D activities. In some cases, these trends reinforce historical influences. In other cases, they oppose such influences.

4.1 Economic Integration

One development that is identified in the recent literature is the 'deepening' of economic integration on both a regional and global basis. The continued economic integration taking place in North America and Europe through formal agreements, in Asia, through both formal agreements and foreign direct investment primarily by Japanese MNCs, as well as further liberalization of trade and investment under the GATT are seen as creating competitive pressures, as well as strategic opportunities, that will encourage MNCs to specialize production more intensively along geographical lines (Eaton, Lipsey and Safarian, 1994; Zander, 1992; Blank, Krajewski and Yu, 1994).

The basic notion that trade and investment liberalization will permit MNCs to locate activities in regions that enjoy location-specific advantages seems unobjectionable. The implications for MNC R&D strategies are less obvious. To the extent that increased specialization of production leads to increased interdependence among MNC affiliates, one implication is that the global R&D process will be more tightly controlled by headquarters. Increased interdependence, in turn, implies that specialization of production will move MNCs away from granting affiliates world product mandates. Rather, specialization will primarily entail 'vertical' specialization in which different affiliates focus on different stages of production. The opportunities to vertically specialize provided by increased trade liberalization are augmented by competitive pressures to specialize which are also a consequence of trade liberalization.

Some evidence linking economic integration to R&D management practices is provided by a survey of 30 large US MNCs undertaken by Blank, Krajewski and Yu (1994). The respondents to their survey indicated overwhelmingly that Canadian affiliates would likely have less rather than more autonomy over R&D decisions in the future. Furthermore, the respondents indicated that this recentralization of managerial authority was part of their firm's intentions to centralize R&D activities across their global operations. The increased opportunities to integrate production in a North American context owing, in part, to the North American Free Trade Agreement (NAFTA), was a major reason cited for reducing the autonomy of affiliate managers.

It is less clear how increased international economic integration will affect incentives to decentralize R&D activities geographically, and the relevant literature is rather confusing on this issue. Presumably, if economic integration accelerates the internationalization of production by MNCs, the share of R&D undertaken by overseas affiliates will increase, all other things constant. This is because relatively more R&D will be required to adapt new process and product technologies to host-country conditions. On the other hand, if economic integration leads to greater production specialization whereby MNCs increasingly supply foreign markets from the home country, the need to customize home-country technology to host-country conditions might actually decrease.

In the past, trade liberalization agreements have generally encouraged increased foreign direct investment (Balasubramanyan and Greenaway, 1992). This may be due, in part, to the partial substitution of non-tariff barriers, such as local purchasing preferences by public-sector customers, for tariff barriers. More recently, economic integration as exemplified by NAFTA and the European Union (EU) is emphasizing the elimination of non-tariff barriers. Recent trade agreements have also focused more on liberalizing rules for foreign direct investment and ensuring that foreign investors are treated the same way as domestic investors. The latter development is likely to be particularly significant for service industries which need to locate in host countries in order to serve host-country consumers. In short, there are potentially countervailing forces associated with recent movements towards economic integration which make it difficult to conclude on purely theoretical grounds whether MNCs will continue to decentralize their R&D activities geographically to the same extent as in the past.[11]

4.2 Growth of Centres of Excellence

Another development indirectly linked to increased economic integration is the emergence and growth of technological centres of excellence. The basic argument here, as developed in Zander (1992), is that the geographical specialization promoted by trade liberalization extends to technological activities. The existence of agglomeration economies implies that specific geographic locations will become increasingly desirable for particular technological activities. MNCs will therefore be increasingly motivated to move skilled personnel to affiliates located in areas where their capabilities are best exploited.[12]

Cantwell (1992) further argues that the growth of centres of excellence is complementary to a life-cycle process whereby, over time, MNCs move technologically sophisticated production activities to centres of excellence in which the research facilities of major international companies agglomerate.[13] This life-cycle process will presumably be further promoted by improvements in communications technology which have the effect of lowering the real costs of coordinating geographically dispersed activities, including technological activities (Eaton, Lipsey and Safarian, 1994).

In summary, the main suggestion in the literature with regard to the geographic decentralization of R&D is that the growing importance of international centres of excellence will encourage MNCs to engage in more geographical specialization of R&D activities. All other things constant, this implies that MNCs will do relatively more R&D in overseas locations, although the number of separate locations in which they perform R&D might actually decline. The R&D stimulated by emerging centres of excellence has been identified by McFetridge (1994) as 'knowledge-seeking' R&D.

4.3 Empirical Evidence

Pearce (1992) offers some evidence based upon surveys of R&D labs in the world's largest enterprises that host-country technological capacities and capabilities are becoming a more distinctive influence on MNC decisions to locate R&D in overseas affiliates. Hakanson (1990) notes a recent trend in Swedish MNCs to establish advanced development and research facilities outside Sweden in order to employ foreign technical expertise and to establish a contact network with foreign research organizations. Hagedoorn and Schakenraad (1993) also remark upon the increasing propensity of European firms to enter into strategic alliances, in part to 'pool' their technological expertise with the expertise of their foreign counterparts. However, they caution that strategic alliancing is not remarkably more prevalent in technology-intensive industries, which calls into question somewhat the strength of the knowledge-seeking motive for geographically decentralizing R&D.

Another reason to question suggestions that knowledge-seeking R&D is becoming relatively more important is provided by data reported in Table 9.2. These data report the geographical distribution of innovating capability over time as measured by two indicators: R&D expenditures in constant (1982) US dollars and patents. Over the period 1970 to 1987, the predominance of the United States as a location for innovation activities decreased (at least in relative terms) by either measure. However, the declining relative importance of the United States is largely mirrored by the increasing importance of Japan. There was also a very modest increase in the relative importance of West Germany which mirrors a modest decline in the relative importance of the United Kingdom. Taken as a whole, the data in Table 9.2 do not suggest a broad geographical dispersion of technological expertise. The major recent development is the growth of the technological capabilities of firms based in Japan. Whether this development by itself will motivate MNCs to decentralize R&D activities to Japan to any significant extent is a matter for conjecture.

Table 9.2   Distribution of innovating capabilities among five leading innovating countries, 1970–1987

	R&D expenditure Constant 1982 $ (billions)		Patents	
	1970 %	1987 %	1970 %	1987 %
USA	61.7	54.0	80.0	58.5
Japan	12.3	20.9	4.5	23.3
West Germany	9.8	10.4	7.5	10.6
France	7.0	7.3	2.9	3.8
UK	9.3	7.4	5.0	3.7
	100.0	100.0	100.0	100.0

Source: Dunning (1992, p. 22).

In evaluating whether knowledge seeking will become a more important influence on MNC R&D strategies in the future, it would be useful to identify whether it has been an increasingly important influence in the recent past. Unfortunately, data bearing upon changes in MNC R&D strategies are not readily available. Hence, one must infer changing motivations from indirect sources of evidence.

Changes in modes of foreign direct investment are one potential source of indirect evidence. For example, if alternatives to 'greenfields' investments, such as mergers and acquisitions or strategic alliances, have become more prominent in recent years, it might suggest a growing importance of knowledge-seeking R&D in MNCs. This inference would be supported by evidence that improved access to foreign R&D skills and technology is an important motive for international mergers, acquisitions and strategic alliances.[14] On the other hand, to the extent that MNCs continue to undertake international R&D primarily to customize technology transferred from the parent, there is no obvious advantage for the MNC to pay a premium associated with acquiring the technology embodied in host-country companies. Rather, it would seem more economical for the MNC to establish a greenfields R&D facility, since the foreign affiliate's R&D activities will be largely derivative of the parent's R&D activities.

There is some evidence that international mergers, acquisitions and strategic alliances have become relatively more important modes of international expansion in recent years (Globerman and Wolf, 1994). In addition, non-US MNCs have emphasized acquisitions and strategic alliances with US companies in technology-intensive industries such as biotechnology and telecommunications. This observation suggests that acquiring or partnering with US firms has been especially motivated in recent years by a desire to acquire US technology. On the other hand, strategic alliances and joint ventures involving European companies have apparently not been disproportionately located in technology-intensive industries (Hagedoorn and Schakenraad, 1993).

To provide additional insight into changing MNC R&D strategies, a simple correlation analysis was carried out using Canadian data. The Canadian experience is arguably informative given the relatively high levels of foreign ownership of domestic industries and the presence of a strong indigenous scientific and engineering capability. The analysis rests upon a simple inference. Namely, if knowledge seeking is becoming a more important motive for overseas R&D on the part of MNCs, we should see evidence of a growing complementarity between the R&D activities of Canadian and foreign-owned firms. This is because R&D undertaken by Canadian-owned firms presumably augments embodied technological expertise in Canada, thereby enhancing the benefits of carrying out knowledge-seeking R&D in Canada.

In the initial correlation test, the ratio of the number of foreign-owned firms carrying out R&D in Canada in 1987 to the number carrying out R&D in 1982 was correlated with a similar ratio defined for domestically owned firms. The correlation was estimated for a sample of 18 industries. It would obviously have been preferable to define the variables in terms of R&D expenditure. Unfortunately, expenditure data did not exist in time series for many of the sample industries. In a second correlation, the numerator of each variable was defined as of 1991, while the denominator was defined as the 1987 value.

Clearly, we could expect the numbers of foreign and Canadian-owned R&D performing firms to increase for a number of reasons, including the growth of the overall Canadian economy. However, it would be suggestive if the correlation coefficient became either more positive or more negative, since this would suggest that factors specific to the R&D process itself may have changed. In fact, there is no significant difference between the two correlation coefficients. The Pearson correlation coefficient for the first period is 0.256. The correlation coefficient for the second period is 0.225.

5 OVERALL POLICY CONCLUSIONS

There have been suggestions in the literature that the underlying determinants of MNC R&D strategies are undergoing profound changes. Two major assertions are that MNCs will increasingly centralize managerial control in the parent affiliate while carrying out more knowledge-seeking R&D in their overseas affiliates. While it is difficult to test these assertions empirically, evidence available, to date, offers no compelling support for these assertions. Adapting parent-company technology to local conditions is still arguably the dominant motive for decentralizing R&D geographically. Nor is there any substantial evidence that changes in communications technology are promoting any significant recentralization of managerial authority in the parent company.

These findings serve as a caution against governments spending large sums of public money to create technological centres of excellence to attract MNC R&D laboratories. Liberalizing restrictions against inward direct investment continues to be a preferred strategy to encourage economic growth by encouraging increased specialization in production. Host countries in particular gain from productivity spillovers associated with MNC activities. Excessive concern about where R&D is performed obscures a more appropriate concern about where R&D results are exploited. Policy-makers should be more concerned about the latter issue than the former.

NOTES

*   The author thanks participants at the Nordic Workshop on Technology and Trade, especially Roger Svensson, for helpful comments on an earlier draft. He also thanks participants at a seminar hosted by the Industrial Institute for Economic and Social Research (IUI) at which an earlier version of this chapter was also presented. The usual caveat applies.

1.   An extensive review of the literature dealing with the geographical location of R&D activities in MNCs is provided by McFetridge (1994).

2.   A survey of 55 US-based MNCs carrying out overseas R&D provides a comparable estimate of the geographical decentralization of R&D by US-based MNCs. The survey reports that the percentage of company-financed R&D expenditures carried out overseas rose from about 2 per cent in 1960 to about 10 per cent in 1980. See Mansfield, Teece and Romeo (1979).

3.   Dunning (1993b, p. 307) characterizes the bulk of innovatory activities of MNCs outside their national boundaries as taking the form of technical and organizational support facilities.

4.   Casson (1991a) argues that there has been some decentralization of basic R&D on the part of MNCs. Amesse, Seguin-Dulude and Stanley (1994) discuss case-study evidence of Canadian telecommunications equipment manufacturers, especially Northern Telecom, which shows that those companies increasingly decentralized applied research activities to overseas affiliates. Pearce (1992) concludes on the basis of a survey of foreign R&D labs in the world's leading MNCs that applied research became more important in those labs relative to development activities designed to support local market commitments.

5.   For a fuller discussion of this concern, as well as references to empirical studies, see McFetridge (1994). The caveat should again be noted that there are a variety of channels through which international technology spillovers can take place. Some studies suggest that reverse engineering is the primary means by which new product technologies are imitated. See, for example, Levin, Klevorick, Nelson and Winter (1987).

6.   A review of many of the relevant studies is provided in McFetridge (1994). In his encyclopaedic review of the literature on MNCs, Dunning (1993b, p. 305) asserts: 'It is perfectly clear from a variety of studies … that the great majority of R&D undertaken by the foreign affiliates of MNCs is directed to the adaptation of particular products, processes or functions and procedures of the firm.'

7.   DeMeyer (1993) among others has argued that technology transfer proceeds faster when manufacturing facilities are combined with R&D facilities in MNC affiliates.

8.   Additional evidence is provided by the observation that the cost of R&D inputs in Europe and Canada increased relative to the cost in the United States from the mid-1960s to the mid-1970s,

notwithstanding that US MNCs increased their share of R&D performed outside the home country. See Mansfield, Teece and Romeo (1979).

9. For empirical evidence on the relatively modest increase in the share of international production undertaken by MNCs, see Lipsey, Blomstrom and Ramstetter (1995).

10. Hakanson (1990) argues in a similar manner that foreign affiliates that are sole manufacturers of a specific product, based on specific technical competence, tend to have relatively great autonomy in setting R&D priorities and in the design of R&D projects. Development and manufacture of products and components that are part of common systems require considerably tighter coordination.

11. Based on survey interviews, Reitsma (1993) suggests that US MNCs may reduce production in Canada as a result of the NAFTA, other things constant. It can be argued that his survey implicitly holds total production constant, whereas production is actually likely to increase.

12. Eaton, Lipsey and Safarian (1994) assert that agglomeration economies are becoming more pronounced with respect to innovation activities, although they offer no evidence to support their assertion.

13. Zander and Solvell (1992) express scepticism about whether the more experienced MNCs are developing into multiple home-based firms as suggested by Cantwell's life-cycle hypothesis.

14. Based upon a very small sample, Hakanson (1993) concludes that the transfer and exchange of technical capabilities and R&D skills constituted a very significant set of benefits motivating acquisitions of foreign firms by Swedish MNCs.

REFERENCES

Amesse, F., L. Seguin-Dulude and G. Stanley (1994), 'Northern Telecom: A Case Study in the Management of Technology', in S. Globerman (ed.), *Canadian-Based Multinationals*, Calgary: University of Calgary Press, pp. 421–56.

Balasubramanyan, N. and D. Greenaway (1992), 'Economic Integration and Foreign Direct Investment', *Journal of Common Market Studies*, **XXX** (2), June, 175–93.

Bernstein, J. (1994), *International R&D Spillovers*, Ottawa: Industry Canada.

Blank, S., S. Krajewski and H. Yu (1994), 'Responding to a New Political and Economic Architecture in North America: Corporate Structure and Strategy', *Northwest Journal of Business and Economics*, Special Edition, 17–30.

Bradsher, K. (1995), 'American Workers Watch as Best Jobs Go Overseas', *International Herald Tribune*, 29 August, 1, 17.

Cantwell, J. (1992), 'Innovation and Technological Competitiveness', in P.J. Buckley and M. Casson (eds), *Multinational Enterprises in the World Economy: Essays in Honour of John Dunning*, Aldershot: Edward Elgar Publishing Ltd., pp. 20–40.

Cantwell J. and C. Hodson (1991), 'Global R&D and UK Competitiveness', in M. Casson (ed.), *Global Research Strategy and International Competitiveness*, Oxford: Basil Blackwell, pp. 133–82.

Casson, M. (1991a), 'Introduction', in M. Casson (ed.), *Global Research Strategy and International Competitiveness*, Oxford: Basil Blackwell, pp. 1–38.

Casson, M. (1991b), 'International Comparative Advantage and the Location of R&D', in M. Casson (ed.), *Global Research Strategy and International Competitiveness*, Oxford: Basil Blackwell, pp. 68–103.

Casson, M., R. Pearce and S. Singh (1992), 'Global Integration Through the Decentralization of R&D', in M. Casson (ed.), *International Business and Global Integration*, London: Macmillan, pp. 163–204.

DeMeyer, A. (1993), 'Internationalizing R&D Improves a Firm's Technical Learning', *Research Technology Management*, **36** (4), 42–9.

Dunning, J. (1992), 'Multinational Enterprises and the Globalization of Innovatory Capacity', in O. Grandstrand, L. Hakanson and S. Sjolander (eds), *Technology Management and International Business: Internationalization of R&D and Technology*, Chichester: John Wiley and Sons, pp. 19–51.

Dunning, J. (1993a), *The Globalization of Business*, London: Routledge.

Dunning, J. (1993b), *Multinational Enterprises and the Global Economy*, Wokingham: Addison-Wesley Publishing Company.

Eaton, B.C., R.G. Lipsey and A.E. Safarian (1994), 'The Theory of Multinational Plant Location: Agglomerations and Disagglomerations', in L. Eden (ed.), *Multinationals in North America*, Calgary: University of Calgary Press, pp. 79–102.

Fors, G. and R. Svensson (1994), *R&D in Swedish Multinational Corporations*, Stockholm: Industrial Institute for Economic and Social Research.

Globerman, S. (1994), 'The Public and Private Interests in Outward Direct Investment', in S. Globerman (ed.), *Canadian-Based Multinationals*, Calgary: University of Calgary Press, pp. 1–52.

Globerman, S. (forthcoming), 'The Information Highway and the Economy', in P. Howitt (ed.), *Knowledge-Based Growth for Micro-Economic Policies*, Calgary: University of Calgary Press.

Globerman, S. and B. Wolf (1994), 'Joint Ventures and Canadian Outward Direct Investment', in S. Globerman (ed.), *Canadian-Based Multinationals*, Calgary: University of Calgary Press, pp. 263–302.

Hagedoorn, J. and J. Schakenraad (1993), 'Strategic Technology Partnering and International Corporate Strategies', in K. Hughes (ed.), *European Competitiveness*, Cambridge: Cambridge University Press, pp. 60–86.

Hakanson, L. (1990), 'Organization and Evolution of Foreign R&D in Swedish Multinationals', in M. Casson (ed.), *Multinational Corporations*, Aldershot: Edward Elgar Publishing Ltd., pp. 273–82.

Hakanson, L. (1993), *Learning Through Acquisition – Management and Integration of Foreign R&D Laboratories*, Stockholm: Institute of International Business.

Howells, J. and M. Wood (1993), *The Globalisation of Production and Technology*, London: Belhaven Press.

Hutchinson, D. and S. Nicholas (1992), 'Technology Transfer and the Strategy of Internationalization by Australian Manufacturing in the 1980s', in P.J. Buckley and M. Casson (eds), *Multinational Enterprises in the World Economy*, Aldershot: Edward Elgar Publishing Ltd., pp. 96–114.

Levin, R.A., R. Klevorick, R. Nelson and S. Winter (1987), 'Appropriating the Returns From Industrial Research and Development', in M. Bailey and C. Winston (eds), *Brookings Papers on Economic Activity*, Vol. 3, pp. 783–820.

Lipsey, R.E., M. Blomstrom and E. Ramstetter (1995), *Multinational Firms in World Production*, New York: National Bureau of Economic Research.

Mansfield, E. (1968), *The Economics of Technological Change*, New York: W.W. Norton and Co.

Mansfield, E., D. Teece and A. Romeo (1979), 'Overseas Research and Development by U.S.-Based Companies', *Economica*, **46** (2) 187–96.

McFetridge, D. (1994), 'Canadian FDI, R&D and Technology Transfer', in S. Globerman (ed.), *Canadian-Based Multinationals*, Calgary: University of Calgary Press, pp. 151–76.

Pearce, R. (1992), 'Factors Influencing the Internationalization of Research and Development', in P. Buckley and M. Casson (eds), *Multinational Enterprises in the World Economy*, Aldershot: Edward Elgar Publishing Ltd., pp. 75–95.

Pearce, R. and S. Singh (1991), 'The Overseas Laboratory', in M. Casson (ed.), *Global Research Strategy and International Competitiveness*, Oxford: Basil Blackwell, pp. 183–212.

Reitsma, S. (1993), *The Canadian Response to Globalisation*, Ottawa: Conference Board.

Rugman, A. (1994), 'NAFTA's Treatment of Foreign Investment', in A. Rugman (ed.), *Foreign Investment and NAFTA*, Columbia: University of South Carolina Press, pp. 47–79.

Statistics Canada (various years), *Industrial Research and Development Expenditures in Canada*, Ottawa: Information Canada.

United Nations (1992), *World Investment Report 1992: Transnational Corporations as Engines of Growth*, New York: United Nations.

Zander, I.(1992), *Patterns of Technological Specialization in an Integrated Europe*, Stockholm: Institute of International Business.

Zander, I. and O. Solvell (1992), *Transfer and Creation of Knowledge in Local Firm and Industry Clusters – Implications for Innovation in the Global Firm*, Stockholm: Institute of International Business.

10. Growth-enhancing policies in a small open economy

Anders Sørensen*

1 INTRODUCTION

The private return to innovating business capital appears to be lower than the social return. In empirical work, the latter return is estimated to be as high as 40 to 100 per cent, see Griliches and Lichtenberg (1984), Griliches (1988) and Coe and Helpman (1995). The existence of this wedge is caused by externalities. Among others are spillovers from R&D, since knowledge is embodied in products and production processes. Therefore, researchers learn from developments created by others through screening of goods and techniques. Moreover, inventors cannot internalize the effect of their own innovations on the overall productivity. Consequently, the private incentive to innovate is too weak to generate the socially desirable level of R&D.

The acknowledgement of a disparity between the private and the social value of innovation has intensified the focus on R&D-promoting policies. Such policies reallocate skilled labour between innovation activity and education if time spent in learning competes with time spent on the job. In this case the accumulation of skills will fall, thereby depressing the effort levels in both activities below what they would have been in the absence of intervention. Hence, the allocation of skilled labour between innovation and education may be important because it affects the stock of human capital embodied in the labour force. This stands in contrast to the literature on endogenous growth driven by R&D where a constant stock of skilled labour is presupposed.

It is often argued that R&D subsidies, as well as tariffs/export subsidies, promote economic growth. This chapter investigates such interventions in a small open economy model where R&D and education compete for skilled labour. Hence, the introduction of an education sector is an extension of the existing literature, implying that the levels of unskilled labour and skilled labour supplied to the production side of the economy are determined endogenously.

A standard result in this model type is that the growth rate depends positively on the quantity of skilled labour devoted to R&D. In this chapter, it is found that

158

the steady-state growth rate is unaffected by an R&D subsidy. Such a subsidy results in a higher incentive to innovate on impact, which reallocates inputs out of education and into innovation. Consequently, the level of skilled labour falls over time. The reallocation effect increases the quantity of the input in R&D, whereas the level effect depresses it. In the long run, the two effects exactly offset each other, such that the steady-state growth rate is unchanged. This knife-edge result follows from the selected functional forms. Presumably, the steady-state growth effect can also be negative or positive in more-general settings.

In contrast to an R&D subsidy, trade policy affects the long-run growth rate. For example, a tariff/export subsidy to skilled-labour-intensive goods reallocates inputs into the protected industry and the education sector. This comes about because the wages are affected according to the Stolper–Samuelson theorem. Hence, it becomes preferable to be employed in the protected sector because the absolute and relative wage of skilled labour increases. On impact, the quantity of inputs in R&D falls, whereas the level of skilled labour increases in the longer run. The positive growth effect dominates in the long run. Conversely, the opposite result applies when protection favours unskilled-labour-intensive goods.

The steady-state growth effects from policy interventions are different from the results in Grossman and Helpman (1991, Chapter 6). An R&D subsidy always increases the steady-state growth rate in their analysis, whereas such a policy leaves the long-run growth rate unaffected in the present model. Furthermore, the introduction of an endogenous stock of skilled labour reverses the long-run growth effect of tariffs/export subsidies compared to the model with a constant stock. Hence, the present analysis suggests that trade policy can be used in promoting long-run growth whereas R&D subsidies cannot.

The chapter is organized as follows: Section 2 describes the model, where the now standard R&D-driven growth model is extended to include an education sector. The steady-state equilibrium and the dynamics of the model are investigated in Section 3. Section 4 analyses the consequences for the economy when an R&D subsidy and trade policies are implemented. Section 5 concludes.

2 THE MODEL

The structure of the production side of the economy follows Grossman and Helpman (1991, Chapter 6). First, skilled-labour-intensive and unskilled-labour-intensive final goods are produced in two separate industries. Second, intermediates are produced by transforming final goods. Third, R&D is undertaken in order to create designs for new intermediate varieties by using skilled labour.

Households have to determine expenditure and saving at all points in time. Agents supply unskilled and skilled labour to the production side and earn labour income, which is used for consumption or is invested in financial capital. Otherwise, they spend time in an education sector in order to accumulate skills.

The analysis is performed within a small open economy (SOE) framework in which some goods are traded internationally, while others are not. First, final goods are traded internationally. Second, patents to specific intermediate varieties are sold to domestic entrepreneurs. Third, there is no international trade in intermediates because this would increase the productivity in the SOE dramatically and thereby violate the theoretical notion of smallness. Consequently, international knowledge flows are absent, which is assumed in order to keep the analysis as simple as possible.[1]

Following Barro, Mankiw and Sala-i-Martin (1995), borrowers have to provide security for foreign loans in the financial capital market by using shares in intermediate firms as collateral. However, agents cannot use their (expected) human capital as collateral, and hence cannot borrow to finance their human capital investment. As a consequence, there is no arbitrage mechanism ensuring that the expected return to education is driven down to the level of the international real interest rate. In the following, it is assumed that the return to education exceeds the return to financial capital, as seems to be the case in the small open economy of Denmark.[2] In this situation foreign creditors finance the flow of new firms into the domestic intermediate sector, whereas domestic households save by accumulating skills. This implies that the restriction on international borrowing is binding.

2.1 Production Side

2.1.1 Final goods sector
Final goods are produced in a skilled-labour-intensive and an unskilled-labour-intensive industry that produces according to

$$y = A_y \left[\int_0^n x_y(j)^\alpha \, dj \right] h_y^{1-\alpha}$$

$$z = A_z \left[\int_0^n x_z(j)^\alpha \, dj \right] l_z^{1-\alpha} \tag{10.1}$$

with $j = [0, n]$. In the following, $i = z, y$. A_i is a productivity parameter, $x_i(j)$ is the quantity of intermediate variety j employed in industry i, h_y is skilled labour used in the y-industry and l_z is unskilled labour in the z-industry. n is the stock of designs available to intermediates. The quantity of physical capital equals $\int_0^n x_i(j)dj$, whereas effective physical capital is given by the square brackets in (10.1). The lower is α, the more complementary are the varieties, and thereby the more productive is a given level of physical capital.

The production functions are homogeneous of degree one in physical capital and labour. Hence, when all rival production factors are changed in the same proportion, output changes by this proportion as well, such that the replication argument for rival production factors is accepted. On the other hand, the change in output is more than proportional if labour, physical capital and the number of designs increase in the same proportion.

For the final goods sector, we assume perfect competition and profit maximizing behaviour, such that the demand for the j'th intermediate variety in industry z and y equals

$$x_z(j) = \left(\alpha p_z A_z / p_x(j)\right)^{\frac{1}{1-\alpha}} l_z$$

$$x_y(j) = \left(\alpha p_y A_y / p_x(j)\right)^{\frac{1}{1-\alpha}} h_y \qquad (10.2)$$

with $j = [0, n]$. It is assumed that a unit of physical capital is fully depreciated over the period in which it is used, such that $p_x(j)$ is the price of one unit of intermediate variety j. p_z and p_y are the prices of final goods, as given from abroad. The demand for labour in the two industries equals

$$l_z = (1-\alpha)p_z z / w_l$$

$$h_y = (1-\alpha)p_y y / w_h. \qquad (10.3)$$

w_l and w_h are the wage rates of unskilled and skilled labour, respectively.

2.1.2 Intermediate goods sector

One unit of intermediate is produced by transforming a_{xy} units of y and a_{xz} units of z, whence the unit costs equal $p_y a_{xy} + p_z a_{xz}$. An intermediate firm possesses the property right to one variety j, which gives it market power. The firm that produces variety j maximizes profit:

$$\pi_{x(j)} = \left(p(j) - \left(p_y a_{xy} + p_z a_{xz}\right)\right) x(j)$$

where $x\,(j) = x_z\,(j) + x_y\,(j)$ is given by (10.2). In the intermediate sector, there is Chamberlinian monopolistic competition implying free entry. Hence, entrepreneurs have coverage of their entry costs, which equals the price of a patent. The profit-maximizing price is independent of j:

$$\bar{p}_x = \frac{\left(p_y a_{xy} + p_z a_{xz}\right)}{\alpha}$$

The wage rates are found by substituting $\bar{p}_x$ into (10.1), (10.2) and (10.3):

$$w_l = (1-\alpha)n\left(p_z A_z\right)^{\frac{1}{1-\alpha}}\left(\alpha/\bar{p}_x\right)^{\frac{\alpha}{1-\alpha}}$$

$$w_h = (1-\alpha)n\left(p_y A_y\right)^{\frac{1}{1-\alpha}}\left(\alpha/\bar{p}_x\right)^{\frac{\alpha}{1-\alpha}} \qquad (10.4)$$

w_l/w_h equals $\omega \equiv (p_z A_z/p_y A_y)^{1/(1-\alpha)}$, which gives a measure of unskilled labour in units of skilled labour, $l' \equiv \omega l$.

Consequently, the market-clearing quantity is also independent of j:

$$\bar{x} = x(j) = \left(\frac{\alpha p_y A_y}{\bar{p}_x}\right)^{\frac{1}{1-\alpha}}\left(l'_z + h_y\right). \qquad (10.5)$$

The intuition for (10.5) follows from (10.1): the larger the quantity of labour devoted to a final good industry, the higher is the marginal product of the single intermediate variety in the specific industry. Hence, there is a positive relation between the quantity of labour devoted to final goods production and the demand for intermediates.

2.1.3 R&D sector

In equilibrium the patent price, p_n, equals the net present value of a patent, because of free entry into the intermediate sector. This condition is used to derive the non-arbitrage condition:

$$\bar{r} = \frac{\dot{p}_n}{p_n} + \frac{\bar{\pi}}{p_n}.$$

A dot above a variable indicates a time derivative. To start activities an intermediate firm issues shares. It is assumed that profit is paid to shareholders as dividends. Hence, the return to shares is given by a dividend plus a capital gain, which is risk free because of arbitrage in the financial capital market. Moreover, this return equals the exogenously given foreign interest rate, $\bar{r}$, since initial capital in intermediate firms is financed from abroad.

Skilled labour and general knowledge are used in the creation of designs. The innovation process generates new general knowledge as a by-product, which is non-rival and non-excludable. Hence, everybody can use it at the same time without paying for it. It is assumed that the creation of a design brings about one unit of general knowledge and that the initial stock equals the initial number of designs. This implies that n is used interchangeably for the number of designs and the stock of knowledge:

$$\dot{n} = Dnh_R \tag{10.6}$$

D is a productivity parameter and h_R is skilled labour employed in the sector. $\dot{n}$ is linear in h_R to satisfy the replication argument in rival goods. The endogenous growth characteristic of the model is generated by the assumption that $\dot{n}$ is homogeneous of degree one in n.

The profit in an R&D firm equals zero due to perfect competition in the sector. Using this fact and (10.6), $p_n = w_h/Dn$. According to (10.4) this results in a constant patent price. Therefore, the non-arbitrage condition for the financial capital market can be expressed as

$$\bar{r} = \frac{\pi}{p_n} = \alpha D\left(l_z + h_y\right). \tag{10.7}$$

(10.7) is derived by substituting for $\bar{p}_x$, $\bar{x}$ and p_n. The quantity of labour in the final goods sector is determined by this relation because of the exogenously given interest rate.

2.2 Consumption and Education

The household sector is characterized by a representative household with an infinite horizon. Preferences are described by the intertemporal utility integral

$$U = \int_0^\infty \frac{\left(c_z^\sigma c_y^{1-\sigma}\right)^{1-\theta} - 1}{1-\theta} e^{-\rho t} dt. \tag{10.8}$$

$\rho > 0$ is the rate of time preferences, $\theta > 0$ is the inverse intertemporal elasticity of substitution and c_i is consumption of final good type i, $i = z, y$. In order to maximize utility, the household allocates endowment of inputs optimally between the education sector and the production side. The endowment consists of skilled labour, h, and unskilled labour, l. Moreover, expenditure is determined for each point in time.

Skilled labour is used in the accumulation of skills. Furthermore, infrastructural services from buildings and equipment are used in the education sector. Hence, the higher is the level of infrastructural service, the higher is the productivity of skilled labour in education. The most satisfying formulation of the learning process would be that final goods and intermediates represent infrastructural services used in education. However, for simplicity I choose to specify infrastructural services as a function of the labour input used to produce infrastructure rather than as a function of the infrastructure itself. Therefore, educational output is a function of labour inputs:

$$\dot{h} = Bh_e^{1-\gamma}l_e^{\gamma} - \delta h. \tag{10.9}$$

h_e and l_e are the levels of skilled and unskilled labour used in education. δ is the depreciation rate of skills and B is a productivity parameter. The functional form of $\dot{h}$ fulfils the replication argument for rival goods.

The budget constraint is given by

$$\dot{f} = w_h \left(l_z' + h_d \right) + \bar{r}f - (p_z c_z + p_y c_y),$$

where h_d is the level of skilled labour on the production side and f is net financial assets. Since the international borrowing constraint binds $(f = \dot{f} = 0)$ labour income equals expenditure:

$$w_h \left(l_z' + h_d \right) = p_z c_z + p_y c_y. \tag{10.10}$$

The dynamic optimization problem is formulated by the present-value Hamiltonian

$$H = \frac{\left(c_z^{\sigma} c_y^{1-\sigma} \right)^{1-\theta} - 1}{1-\theta} e^{-\rho t} + a\left(w_h \left(l_z' + h_d \right) - p_z c_z - p_y c_y \right) + b\left(Bh_e^{1-\gamma}l_e^{\gamma} - \delta h \right).$$

In the following, $(1 - u)$ denotes the share of skilled labour in education, whereas u denotes the remaining share that is devoted to the production side. Hence, $h_d \equiv uh$ and $h_e \equiv (1 - u) h$. Moreover, the stock of unskilled labour is divided between education and goods production, that is, $l = l_e + l_z$. Let a and b represent the shadow prices of income and skilled labour, respectively. The solution is given by the first-order conditions $H_{c_y} = H_{c_z} = H_u = H_{l_z} = H_a = 0$ and $H_h = -\dot{b}$.[3]

As a consequence of the Cobb–Douglas characteristics in (10.8) and (10.9), the optimal expenditure share of z-goods is

$$\sigma = \frac{p_z c_z}{p_y c_y + p_z c_z}. \tag{10.11}$$

and the factor share of unskilled labour in education equals

$$\gamma = \frac{(l - l_z)}{(1 - u)h + (l - l_z)}. \tag{10.12}$$

(10.11) implies that the growth rate of c_z and c_y are of the same size and equal

$$g_c = \frac{1}{\theta}(r_e - \rho), \tag{10.13}$$

where

$$r_e = \tilde{B} - \delta + g_n.$$

$\tilde{B} \equiv B\,(1 - \gamma)^{1-\gamma}\gamma^{\gamma}\omega^{-\gamma}$ and $g_x \equiv \dot{x}/x$ indicates the growth rate of variable x. r_e is the return to education that is composed of the net marginal product of skilled labour in education and the growth rate of the skilled wage rate, see (10.4).

3   REDUCED FORM OF THE MODEL

Of skilled labour supply to the production side, uh, a share v is employed in the y-industry, while a share $(1 - v)$ is used in R&D. Hence, $h_y \equiv uvh$, whereas $h_R \equiv (1 - v)\,uh$. v adjusts such that the market for skilled labour clears. These expressions are substituted into the equations on the production side. The final good markets clear because of perfectly elastic demand in the world economy, whereas the intermediate markets clear since the producers take demand into account when setting prices. Finally, the market for patents clears through Walras's Law.

The solution is given by (10.4), (10.6), (10.7), (10.9), (10.10), (10.12) and (10.13). This system is reduced to two differential equations. To do this, isolate l'_z in (10.12) and substitute in the other six equations. This modifies (10.9) to

$$\dot{h} = \left(\tilde{B} \frac{1-u}{1-\gamma} - \delta \right) h. \tag{10.14}$$

From (10.7) the quantity of skilled labour in final goods production, uvh, is calculated. Subtracting (10.6) from (10.13) and substituting for uvh leads to

$$g_c - g_n = \frac{\left(\tilde{B} - \delta - \rho \right)}{\theta} - \frac{\theta - 1}{\theta} \left(D \left(\frac{u - \gamma}{1 - \gamma} h + l' \right) - \frac{\bar{r}}{\alpha} \right).$$

Next, substitute (10.4) into (10.10), and take logarithms and time derivatives of the resulting equation. Finally, substitute for $\dot{h}$ in (10.14), which gives

$$\dot{u} = \left[(g_c - g_n) \left(\frac{u - \gamma}{1 - \gamma} h + l' \right) - \frac{u - \gamma}{1 - \gamma} \left(\tilde{B} \frac{1 - u}{1 - \gamma} - \delta \right) h \right] \frac{(1 - \gamma)}{h}. \tag{10.15}$$

Accordingly, the solution is given by (10.14) and (10.15).

3.1 Steady-state Equilibrium

The steady-state values of u and h are constant. This is seen from (10.7)

$$\bar{r} = \alpha D \left(uv^* h^* + l' - \frac{\gamma}{1 - \gamma} (1 - u^*) h^* \right).$$

A star denotes a steady-state value. uv^* and u^* are constant, that is, $g^*_{uv} = g^*_u = 0$. If g^*_{uv} was different from 0, uv^* would equal either zero or one, because it is constrained between these values. This implies that g^*_{uv} equals zero, which is a contradiction. A similar argument holds for g^*_u. Since uv^*, u^* and $\bar{r}$ are constants, h^* is constant. u^* and h^* are derived by setting $\dot{h} = 0$ and $\dot{u} = 0$ in (10.14) and (10.15):

$$u^* = 1 - \frac{(1-\gamma)\delta}{\tilde{B}} \qquad (10.16)$$

$$h^* = \frac{1-\gamma}{D(u^* - \gamma)} \left[g^* - Dl^* + \frac{\bar{r}}{\alpha} \right]. \qquad (10.17)$$

$g^* = (\tilde{B} - \delta - \rho) / (\theta - 1)$ is the steady-state growth rate. According to empirical evidence the inverse intertemporal elasticity of substitution is above one, see Mulligan and Sala-i-Martin (1993). Hence, in the following $\theta > 1$ is assumed, which implies that the steady-state equilibrium has saddle-path properties, see Sørensen (1996).

3.2 Dynamics of the Model

In Figure 10.1, the adjustment of the economy is illustrated. The $\dot{h} = 0$ curve is horizontal and intercepts the vertical axis at u^*. Above the curve $\dot{h} < 0$, whereas $\dot{h} > 0$ below. The form of the $\dot{u} = 0$ curve is illustrated in the figure. For a formal proof see Sørensen (1996). If h falls from an initial position of $\dot{u} = 0$, the first element in (10.15) increases leading to $\dot{u} > 0$. In the opposite case $\dot{u} < 0$. This follows from, $dg_c/dh = (dg_n/dh)/\theta$, such that $(g_c - g_n)$ falls in h, see (10.13).

The adjustment process for u can be seen as the net result of an income effect, a relative profitability effect, and an intertemporal substitution effect. First of all, as h rises over time, the wealth of the representative household increases. Because households prefer to smooth consumption, they feel able to forgo larger amounts of consumption by investing more heavily in education as their level of wealth and consumption increases. *Ceteris paribus*, this income effect tends to raise the share of skilled labour employed in the education sector at the expense of skilled labour allocated to the production side, u. Second, an increase in h causes an increase in the demand for intermediates which in turn raises the demand for new designs, thereby drawing skilled labour away from the education sector and into R&D. This effect, stemming from an increased profitability of R&D, clearly increases u. Third, since the growth rate of the wage rate for skilled labour varies positively with the growth rate of the number of designs, the increase in the latter also increases the return to education. Consequently, households are induced to forgo more current consumption by spending more time on education to take advantage of the improved future consumption possibilities of skilled labour. This is the intertemporal substitution effect that works negatively on u. Hence, the total effect on u from a rising h seems theoretically ambiguous. However, it is evident from Figure 10.1 that the dynamic forces imply a stable upward-sloping saddle-point path, such that u rises with h over the transition.

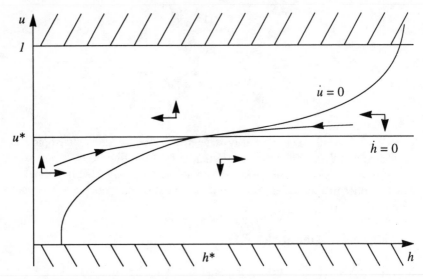

Figure 10.1   The dynamics of the fraction of human capital used in production and human capital

4   POLICIES IN THE MARKET SOLUTION

In this section, growth effects from different policies are investigated. Since one distortion originates from the R&D sector (spillover of knowledge), intervention here corrects the suboptimal allocation of inputs directly. Therefore, an R&D subsidy is introduced. Furthermore, trade policy in the form of tariffs/export subsidies that affect the allocation of inputs indirectly is analysed. Interventions that correct for monopoly pricing in the intermediate sector or the distortion in the financial capital market are not analysed. Hence, the economy can at best end up in a second-best equilibrium. The propositions in the present section are derived in the Appendix.

4.1   R&D Subsidy

The government pays the share S of production costs in R&D, which leads to an aggregate expenditure of $Sw_h h_R$. The non-arbitrage condition in (10.7) is modified to

$$\bar{r} = \frac{\alpha D}{1 - S}\left(l_z + h_y\right).$$

The subsidy increases the incentive to perform R&D and therefore the share of resources devoted to the activity. The policy is financed by lump-sum income taxation, implying a fall in the income of the representative household to $w_h\,(l_z' + h_d - Sh_R)$.

The effect on the growth rate of designs from a marginal change in S is derived by linearization of the dynamic system around the steady-state equilibrium.

Proposition 1   *The change in the growth rate of designs equals*

$$\frac{dg_n(t)}{dS} = \left(1 + \frac{\lambda_S}{\tilde{B} - \delta}\right)\frac{\bar{r}}{\alpha}\exp(-\lambda_S t),$$

when the R&D subsidy is changed marginally from an initial situation characterized by steady-state equilibrium. $-\lambda_S$ is the negative eigenvalue of the linearized dynamic system.

According to Proposition 1, the growth rate increases on impact and adjusts downwards over time to an unchanged steady-state value. The reason is that two opposite effects are working on the growth rate. First, the incentive to innovate increases with S, which reallocates skilled labour into R&D and thereby enhances the growth rate. Second, the stock of skilled labour falls over time because the quantity of inputs in education has fallen. This depresses the incentive to undertake R&D and results in a falling growth rate of designs. In the long run, the level effect exactly cancels out the reallocation effect, such that the steady-state growth rate is unchanged.

Proposition 1 highlights an important issue: education and innovation may compete for skilled labour, implying that promotion of R&D can result in lower learning activity and thereby in a reduction of the skilled labour stock over time. This mechanism is not analysed in the existing literature on endogenous growth. Hence, the present set-up is more general in nature, since it addresses the relation between allocation and accumulation of inputs. This turns out to be a crucial modification for the long-run growth effect from R&D subsidies. In models without the factor accumulation aspect, the stock of skilled labour is assumed to be exogenous and constant (compare Grossman and Helpman (1991, Chapter 6)), such that only reallocation effects influence the economy. Consequently, the long-run growth effect increases when skilled labour is reallocated into R&D.

In order to make the analysis tractable, specific functional forms for technologies and preferences are chosen. As a consequence, the steady-state growth rate is invariant to R&D subsidies. This knife-edge result follows from the Cobb–Douglas production function. Presumably, the reallocation effect and the level effect do not exactly offset each other in a more-general setting. Whether the former or latter effect dominates is hard to tell.

The effect on utility from a marginal R&D subsidy can be studied by rewriting the utility integral in (10.8) to depend on u and h. It can be shown that the utility of the representative household increases, when a marginal R&D subsidy is implemented from an initial situation with steady-state equilibrium and $S = 0$, if

$$\left(g^* + \frac{\bar{r}}{\alpha} \right) \frac{\bar{r}}{\alpha} > g^*.$$

In the market solution, the economy fails to allocate the optimal share of skilled labour to R&D. There are two reasons for this. First, innovators capture a private return different from the social return when a design is developed, since they do not take general knowledge spillovers and effects from designs on the overall productivity into account. This results in a level of R&D below the utility-maximizing level. Second, the outcome is affected by the financial capital market. The lower the foreign interest rate, $\bar{r}$, the lower is the financing cost of patents, and thereby the required return that makes investment in patents profitable. As discussed above, resources are reallocated into R&D until $\bar{r} = \bar{\pi}/p_n$. When $\bar{r}$ is low the extent of R&D may be too large, meaning that utility will increase when the activity is taxed. Hence, a subsidy is optimal when the externality in R&D dominates, whereas a tax is optimal when the distortion in the financial capital market dominates.

4.2   Trade Policy

In this subsection *ad valorem* tariffs/export subsidies are implemented on good i, $\tau_i > 0$, $i = z,y$. When good i is imported τ_i is a tariff, whereas τ_i is an export subsidy when it is exported. Hence, the domestic consumer prices for final goods change to $T_i p_i$, $T_i \equiv 1 + \tau_i$. Two main effects work on the income of the representative household when τ_i is changed. First, wages are affected according to the Stolper–Samuelson theorem when trade policy is implemented. Hence, the wage rate of the labour type that is used intensively in the protected industry increases, whereas the wage rate of the other labour type falls. Second, households pay taxes or receive transfers since the government has net revenues or net costs, and is assumed to run a balanced budget at all points in time.[4] The budget constraint is given by

$$w_h \left(l_z^r + h_d \right) + \tau_y p_y m_y + \tau_z p_z m_z = T_y p_y c_y + T_z p_z c_z. \qquad (10.18)$$

m_i is import of good i, such that taxes/transfers equal $\tau_y p_y m_y + \tau_z p_z m_z$.

The relative and absolute return to skilled labour increases with T_y. Hence, it becomes more preferable to be skilled. This increases the level of unskilled labour in education, and therefore the marginal product of skilled labour in the activity. Hence, two opposite effects work on u: the higher wage tends to increase u, whereas the higher marginal product in education tends to depress it. Therefore, the share of skilled labour devoted to the production side can increase or decrease. In the longer run, the wage effect dominates such that u increases. In the case skilled labour is reallocated out of education on impact (u increases), the higher level of unskilled labour always leads to an increasing stock of skilled labour. Conversely, the opposite scenario applies if T_z is introduced.

Proposition 2   *The growth rate of designs falls on impact and increases over time to a new higher steady-state level when a marginal tariff/export subsidy is introduced in the* y-*industry from an initial situation of steady-state equilibrium. The opposite is the case when a marginal tariff/export subsidy is introduced on good* z.

The growth rate of designs always falls on impact when T_y increases, even in the situation where more skilled labour is devoted to the production side. The reason is that the demand for intermediates falls, which depresses the incentive to perform R&D. This is because the negative demand effect on intermediates from a fall in unskilled labour in the z-industry always dominates a possible positive effect from an increased level of skilled labour in the y-industry. Over time, h increases, which increases the demand for intermediates and thereby the return to shares. The reallocation effect is dominated by the level effect in the longer run, leading to higher steady-state growth.

In Grossman and Helpman (1991, Chapter 6), only the reallocation effect influences the growth rate. Hence, an increase in T_y leads to lower steady-state growth in the set-up without education. Again the results illustrate the point that reallocation may cause level effects. The important result of Proposition 2 is that the level effect turns out to dominate the reallocation effect.

It is hard to determine whether it is desirable to perform trade policy or not. The utility of the representative household is affected through four channels when T_i is implemented. These work through changes in wages, supply of labour to the production side, government revenue and growth. The desirability of a given policy depends on the values of different exogenous parameters.

5   CONCLUSION

This chapter analyses effects of growth-enhancing policies in a small open economy. Two complementary reasons for economic growth are combined: R&D

increases productivity by product innovation, whereas the quality of the labour force is improved through learning. This is an extension of the existing literature. Both growth-generating activities employ skilled labour, implying that innovation and education compete for this input.

Two results are found in the chapter: first, steady-state growth is unaffected by R&D subsidies. On impact such a subsidy results in a higher incentive to innovate. Therefore, resources are reallocated out of education and into innovation. Over time, the level of skilled labour falls as a consequence. The former effect increases growth, whereas the latter depresses it. The two effects neutralize each other in the long run. Even though steady-state growth is unchanged, the policy intervention may be optimal.

Second, trade policy affects long-run growth. For example, wage of skilled labour increases, while wage of unskilled labour falls when skilled-labour-intensive final goods are protected by a tariff/export subsidy. As a consequence, skilled labour is reallocated out of R&D into the protected industry. Inputs are also reallocated into education because it has become more preferable to be skilled. Therefore, the level of skilled labour increases in the longer run. The reallocation effect tends to depress growth, whereas the level effect works positively on it. Steady-state growth increases because the level effect dominates. Conversely, steady-state growth falls when unskilled-labour-intensive final goods are protected. Hence, the analysis suggests that trade policy can be used in promoting long-run growth whereas R&D subsidies cannot.

NOTES

* I thank Peter Birch Sørensen, Johan Torstensson, two anonymous referees and an editor for comments and suggestions. The activities of EPRU are financed by a grant from the Danish National Research Foundation.
1. The knowledge stock can be argued to depend on international contacts, see Grossman and Helpman (1991).
2. In Economic Council (1995) the social return on different types of education is calculated for the Danish economy. It is found that the return to 14 types of training and the average return to the 19 types under investigation exceed the real interest rate.
3. Furthermore, the transversality condition, $\lim_{t \to \infty} [h(t) b(t)] = 0$, must be fulfilled. This implies that the steady-state value of u is larger than γ.
4. This assumption has no impact on the results because of Barro–Ricardo equivalence.

REFERENCES

Barro, R.J., N.G. Mankiw and X. Sala-i-Martin (1995), 'Capital Mobility in Neoclassical Models of Growth', *American Economic Review*, **85** (1), 103–15.
Coe, D.T. and E. Helpman (1995), 'International R&D Spillovers', *European Economic Review*, **39** (5), 859–87.

Economic Council (Det økonomiske råd) (1995), *Danish Economy, Spring 1995*, Copenhagen: Det økonomiske råd.

Griliches, Z. (1988), 'Productivity Puzzles and R&D: Another Explanation', *Journal of Economic Perspectives*, **2** (4), 9–21.

Griliches, Z. and F. Lichtenberg (1984), 'R&D and Productivity Growth at the Industry Level: Is there Still a Relation', in Z. Griliches (ed.), *R&D, Patents, and Productivity*, Chicago: University of Chicago Press, 465–96.

Grossman, G.M. and E. Helpman (1991), *Innovation and Growth in the Global Economy*, Cambridge, MA: MIT Press.

Mulligan, C.B. and X. Sala-i-Martin (1993), 'Transitional Dynamics in Two-Sector Models of Endogenous Growth', *Quarterly Journal of Economics*, **108** (3), 737–73.

Romer, P.M. (1990), 'Endogenous Technological Change', *Journal of Political Economy*, **98** (5), S71–S102.

Sørensen, A. (1996), 'Growth-Enhancing Policies in a Small Open Economy', Working Paper Series 04–1996, Economic Policy Research Unit.

APPENDIX

A.1   Policy Instruments

When the R&D subsidy, S, and *ad valorem* tariffs/export subsidies, τ_i, on good i, $i = z, y$, are implemented in the model, the dynamic system is

$$\dot{h} = h\left(\tilde{B}\frac{1-u}{1-\gamma}\left(\frac{T_y}{T_z}\right)^{\frac{\gamma}{1-\alpha}} - \delta \right) \qquad (10A.1)$$

$$\dot{u} = \frac{\left[(g_c - g_n)K_1 - g_h K_2\right](1-\gamma)}{\left(1 + \gamma\left(T_z^{-1} - T_y^{-1}\right)/(1-\alpha)\right)h}$$

$$g_c - g_n = \frac{\theta - 1}{\theta}\left(g^* - \left(D\frac{u-\gamma}{1-\gamma}h + Dl'\left(\frac{T_y}{T_z}\right)^{\frac{1}{1-\alpha}} - \frac{(1-S)\bar{r}}{\alpha} \right) \right) \qquad (10A.2)$$

Furthermore

$$K_1 = \left(\frac{1}{1-\alpha}\left(\frac{\tau_y}{T_y} + \alpha^2\xi\right) + S \right)\frac{\bar{r}}{\alpha D} + \left(\frac{T_z^{-1} - T_y^{-1}}{1-\alpha} + 1 \right)l'\left(\frac{T_z}{T_y}\right)^{\frac{1}{1-\alpha}} + K_2$$

$$K_2 = \frac{u-\gamma}{1-\gamma}h - \frac{T_z^{-1} - T_y^{-1}}{1-\alpha}\gamma\frac{1-u}{1-\gamma}h.$$

$\xi = (\tau_z a_{xz} p_z + \tau_y a_{xy} p_y)/(T_z a_{xz} p_z + T_y a_{xy} p_y)$ and $T_i \equiv 1 + \tau_i$. The steady-state growth rate is derived by employing the condition of balanced growth, $g_c^* = g_n^* = g^*$:

$$g^* = \frac{\tilde{B}(T_y/T_z)^{\frac{\gamma}{1-\alpha}} - \delta - \rho}{\theta - 1}. \qquad (10A.3)$$

$g_S^* \equiv g|_{T_y = T_z = 1}^*$ and $g_T^* \equiv g|_{S=0}^*$.

A.1.1   Proposition 1

$h*$ is

$$h_S^* = \frac{1-\gamma}{D\left(u_S^* - \gamma\right)}\left(g_S^* - Dl' + \frac{\bar{r}(1-S)}{\alpha}\right)$$

when S is implemented. u^*_S equals the value in (10.16). By linearizing the dynamic system, the eigenvalues are calculated to be

$$\lambda_1 = \tilde{B} - \delta \quad \text{and} \quad \lambda_2 = -\left(g_S^* + \frac{\bar{r}}{\alpha}\right)\frac{\theta-1}{\theta}.$$

The values for $u\,(t)$ and $h\,(t)$ where t is time are given by

$$u(t) = u_S^* + c_{11}\exp(\lambda_1 t) + c_{12}\exp(\lambda_2 t)$$

$$h(t) = h_S^* + c_{21}\exp(\lambda_1 t) + c_{22}\exp(\lambda_2 t).$$

$[c_{11}\;c_{21}]$ and $[c_{12}\;c_{22}]$ are eigenvectors associated with each of the two roots. $c_{11} = c_{21} = 0$ for convergence. In the following, $\lambda_S \equiv -\lambda_2$. Using $t = 0$, $c_{22} = h(0) - h^*_S$. Furthermore, $c_{12} = (\theta-1)(g_S^* + \bar{r}/\alpha)(1-\gamma)c_{22}/(\theta h_S^*\tilde{B}) = \Lambda_S > 0$.

Assuming that the initial situation is characterized by steady-state equilibrium

$$\frac{dh(t)}{dS} = \frac{dh_S^*}{dS}\left(1 - \exp(-\lambda_S t)\right) = -\frac{1-\gamma}{D\left(u_S^* - \gamma\right)}\frac{\bar{r}}{\alpha}\left(1 - \exp(-\lambda_S t)\right)$$

$$\frac{du(t)}{dS} = \frac{du_S^*}{dS} - \Lambda_S\frac{dh_S^*}{dS}\exp(-\lambda_S t) = \lambda_S\frac{1-\gamma}{Dh_S^*}\frac{1}{\tilde{B}-\delta}\frac{\bar{r}}{\alpha}\exp(-\lambda_S t).$$

Proposition 1 is derived by using $g_n = D(u-\gamma)h/(1-\gamma) + Dl' - (1-S)\bar{r}/\alpha$.

A.1.2   Proposition 2

The steady-state values equal

$$u_T^* = 1 - \frac{(1-\gamma)\delta}{\tilde{B}(T_y/T_z)^{\gamma/(1-\alpha)}}$$

$$h_T^* = \frac{1-\gamma}{D(u^*-\gamma)}\left(g_T^* - Dl'(T_z/T_y)^{\frac{1}{1-\alpha}} + \frac{\bar{r}}{\alpha}\right)$$

when T_i is introduced in the i-sector, $i = z, y$. By linearizing the dynamic system, the negative eigenvalue, $-\lambda_T$, is derived. It can be shown that Λ_T is positive. The changes in u and h are calculated as above and derived by substitution of

$$\frac{du_T^*}{dT_y} = \left(1 - u_T^*\right)\frac{\gamma}{(1-\alpha)T_y}$$

$$\frac{dh_T^*}{dT_y} = \frac{1-\gamma}{D(u_T^*-\gamma)}\left(\frac{dg_T^*}{dT_y} + Dl'(T_y)^{-\frac{1}{1-\alpha}}\frac{l_{zT_y}^*}{(1-\alpha)T_y}\right)$$

for $T_z = 1$ and $T_y \neq 1$. $l_{zT_y}^*$ is the steady-state value of unskilled labour in z-industry under trade policy. Using the expression for g_n, we gain

$$\frac{dg_n(t)}{dT_y} = \frac{Dh^*}{1-\gamma}\frac{du(t)}{dT_y} + D\frac{u^*-\gamma}{1-\gamma}\frac{dh(t)}{dT_y} - \frac{1}{1-\alpha}Dl'\left(\frac{T_z}{T_y}\right)^{\frac{1}{1-\alpha}}\frac{1}{T_y}.$$

It can be shown that

$$\frac{dg_n(0)}{dT_y} < -\frac{1}{(1-\alpha)T_y}Dl'\left(\frac{T_z}{T_y}\right)^{\frac{1}{1-\alpha}}l_{zT_y}^* < 0$$

$$\lim_{t\to\infty}\frac{dg_n(t)}{dT_y} = \frac{dg_T^*}{dT_y} > 0.$$

Conversely, g_n increases on impact and falls to a new lower steady-state level, when the z-industry is protected. This gives Proposition 2.

11. A monetary, open economy, R&D-growth model

Juha Honkatukia*

1 INTRODUCTION

In most neoclassical, monetary growth models, there is a negative correlation between monetary growth and capital accumulation. This effect is most apparent in models, where cash has to be used for transactions – the so-called cash-in-advance models (Orphanides and Solow, 1990). In models in this vein, the rent on capital is paid out at the end of each period but can only be used for consumption in the next period. If there is inflation, the purchasing power of rents is reduced; inflation acts as a tax on nominal earnings. Consequently, inflation has the effect of inducing consumers to increase current consumption and to invest less (Abel, 1985). Unless there is productivity growth, this results in a lower, steady-state, capital stock. This result is known as the negative Tobin effect.

In the neoclassical model, growth is due to capital formation. It is well known, however, that capital formation alone explains only a fraction of the growth of production during the current century. In recent years, there has emerged a literature that has improved the neoclassical model. In the simplest models of the literature, long-run growth is made possible by increasing returns to scale to capital. However, the increasing returns explanation to long-run growth does not appear to have empirical support. In particular, Mankiw, Romer and Weil (1992) argue that there are no increasing returns to scale to capital. Instead, growth appears more likely to be driven by productivity growth. Accordingly, more sophisticated models allow for endogenous productivity growth due to R&D innovation (Romer, 1990; Grossman and Helpman, 1991).

Thus far, the endogenous growth literature has only studied monetary growth in the context of constant or increasing returns to scale to capital (Jones and Manuelli, 1993; De Gregorio, 1993). In contrast, the current study examines this relationship in the context of endogenous growth due to innovation. In effect, we impose the cash-in-advance structure of the neoclassical growth model of Abel (1985) on a discrete-time version of the endogenous growth model of

177

Grossman and Helpman (1991). Thus, our results concerning the relationship between money and growth stem from the inflation tax. We accordingly find the conventional negative Tobin effect in capital formation as a special case of the model. But in contrast to the neoclassical model, it is not the effect of monetary growth on capital formation that is essential here, but rather its effect on investment in R&D. This is because growth is driven by externalities in innovation, which sustain productivity growth. The central finding of the current study is that inflation reduces R&D investment. This has the effect of reducing productivity growth, and thereby output growth, capital formation, as well as the marginal productivity of capital, independently of the Tobin effect. As further consequences of endogenous growth, we also find lower rates of steady-state inflation and higher marginal productivity of capital than in the neoclassical model.

Helpman and Razin (1984) study a neoclassical, two-country, growth model and show that optimal growth is possible in open economies under relatively mild conditions. Under the condition that nominal interest rates are constant, real interest rates are equated under flexible exchange rates, which guarantees that there are steady states, where investment takes place in both countries. The exchange rate need not be fixed in the long run.

We consider the two-country, Grossman–Helpman model, where both countries are producing final goods for consumption and investment, using capital, labour and differentiated intermediate goods as inputs. The countries trade final goods and intermediate goods with each other. In contrast to the neoclassical model, growth stems from productivity-enhancing R&D. We concentrate on steady states, where investment takes place in both countries. We allow for heterogeneity of final goods and assume country-specific capital but do not impose restrictions on asset markets. Consumers may also own capital in both countries. Under these assumptions, a flexible exchange rate still guarantees that consumers in both countries will want to invest in new capital in steady states. This does not necessitate equality of marginal productivities of capital, contrary to the homogeneous-good model of Helpman and Razin. Inflation, nominal interest rate and growth differentials may also persist, but the rates of return on investment as well as real interest rates are equated in any of these steady states. The rate of monetary growth affects investment in R&D negatively, thereby slowing down productivity growth. However, if innovation is to take place in both countries, the monetary growth rates must remain in a certain relationship to each other. This relationship depends on the distribution of assets across domestic and foreign investors, the endowments of labour in the two countries, as well as technology parameters. The implications for exchange rates depend entirely on the assumptions about these underlying parameters. The general result is that a flexible exchange rate does not guarantee that innovation takes place in both countries. But this does not imply that a fixed exchange rate generally will. Only if perfect symmetry of the countries is assumed, for example, if final goods are perfect substitutes and the production technologies are identical, and if, furthermore, the countries are symmetric with respect to endowments and asset ownership, does it follow that the exchange rate must be fixed for innovation to take place in both countries.

The chapter is organized as follows. Section 2 presents the model. In Section 2.1 we consider the consumers' problems and in Section 2.2 we consider the firms' problems. As a result, we obtain Euler equations that imply steady-state interest rates, consumption demands, derived demands for factors, and technically feasible growth rates. However, because some of the firms are monopolistic price-setters (choosing profit-maximizing prices subject to given marginal cost and given nominal demand), these exercises do not solve the instantaneous real equilibrium of the economy, contrary to the standard Grossman–Helpman model, where fixed labour supply also gives real prices. In a monetary model, in contrast, nominal prices and nominal wages have to be solved first. Consequently, using the nominal demands for goods and factors implied by the consumers' and the firms' problems, Section 2.3 aggregates nominal demands for final goods; Section 2.4 uses aggregate demands to solve for the nominal exchange rate; and, given nominal demands and the exchange rate, Section 2.5 solves for equilibrium wages and prices and their rates of change. This fixes the equilibrium for the economy and allows us to proceed to the analysis of the steady state. Section 3 then solves for the steady-state interest rates, marginal productivities of capital, and the rate of innovation. Section 4 concludes.

2   THE MODEL

The two countries in the model both consist of an industrial sector, representative consumers and a government. There is also an investment fund in each of the countries, operating in perfect capital markets, and owning the respective domestic firms. Consumers consume the final goods and invest in shares of each of the funds. They work for the domestic industries, and are endowed with fixed amounts of labour. The industrial sector comprises three types of firms, namely, producers of country-specific final goods, producers of intermediate goods, and innovators specializing in R&D. Governments buy final goods from both countries for public consumption. Public consumption is financed by the revenue from lump-sum taxes collected from that country's consumers, and the creation of money. Thus, there is inflation in the steady state. As incomes are received in cash, and since all transactions have to be carried out in cash, money creation imposes an inflation tax on all nominal earnings, increasing current consumption at the cost of saving and investment. This effect leads to reduced productivity growth by reducing R&D; consequently, output growth slows down, as does induced capital formation.

2.1 Consumers' problem

The utility function of the domestic consumer is

$$U_t = \sum_{t=1}^{\infty} \delta^t \log C_t, \quad where \quad C_t = C_{Ht}^{\zeta} C_{Ft}^{1-\zeta}, \tag{11.1}$$

where δ is a subjective discount factor ($\delta < 1$). C_{Ht} is the consumption of the domestic final good by the domestic consumer, and C_{Ft} her consumption of the foreign final good. As the consumer chooses the consumption of domestic and foreign final goods to maximize equation (11.1), she spends a fraction $0 < \zeta < 1$ of her consumption expenditure on the domestic good and $1 - \zeta$ on the foreign good. The foreign consumer is characterized by an identical utility function. As her problem is symmetric to that of the domestic consumer's, it is not stated here.

In each period, the consumer is endowed with L_t units of labour that she supplies to domestic firms. She thus earns a wage income $W_t L_t$. Wages are paid out at the end of the period and thus cannot be used for consumption or saving during the current period. The consumer thus enters period t with holdings of cash M_t^P, which consist of wages earned in the previous period. The consumer owns a portion d of shares of the domestic and foreign funds. We are interested in steady states, where the initial holdings of the shares of investment funds are evenly distributed among consumers and remain so. We assume that they are distributed in proportion to the share of world consumption of each of the countries. If the consumption share of the domestic country is d, the domestic consumer then owns a fraction d of both funds, and the foreign consumer a fraction $(1 - d) \equiv f$. At the beginning of the period, asset and currency markets open and she receives payments $d(1 + r_{t-1})S_{t-1}$ from the domestic fund and $de_t(1 + r_{t-1}^F)S_{t-1}^F$ from the foreign fund, which can be used to acquire consumption goods, to pay taxes τ_t, and to invest in shares of the funds, S_t and $e_t S_t^F$. The consumer might in principle also wish to invest in holdings of money. However, in equilibrium she will have no incentive to do so, as currencies earn no interest, whereas the shares of funds do. Hence, the desired cash balances to be carried over to the next period, denoted by M_{t+1}^P, will equal the nominal compensation for work at the end of the current period, that is, $W_t L_t$.

There are two constraints to the consumer's problem. First, all transactions have to be carried out in cash, which, at the opening of period-t markets consists of M_t^P and the cash paid out by the funds. This cash-in-advance constraint is given by

$$M_t^P - \tau_t - P_t C_t - dS_t - e_t dS_t^F + (1 + r_{t-1})dS_{t-1} + (1 + r_{t-1}^F)e_t dS_{t-1}^F = 0 \quad (11.2)$$

where P_t is an exact price index for final goods – the dual of the utility function – in the domestic country, and is given by

$$P_t = \zeta^{-\zeta}(1 - \zeta)^{-(1-\zeta)}(P_{Yt})^\zeta(e_t P_{Yt}^F)^{1-\zeta}. \quad (11.3)$$

A similar index can be derived for the prices of final goods abroad. Purchasing power parity – PPP henceforth – has to hold for the prices of both goods, as the markets are competitive (and as firms have continuous access to the currency markets); consequently, PPP also holds for the price levels.

Second, the income in each period must be allocated between saving and consumption. This conventional budget constraint is given by

$$M_t^P - \tau_t - P_t C_t - dS_t - e_t dS_t^F + (1 + r_{t-1})dS_{t-1} + (1 + r_{t-1}^F)e_t dS_{t-1}^F$$
$$+ W_t L_t - M_{t+1}^P = 0. \quad (11.4)$$

Then, the following programme implies the solution to the consumer's problem:

$$V_t = \max_{C_t} \left\{ \begin{array}{l} U_t + \dfrac{\lambda_t}{P_t}\left(M_t^P - \tau_t - P_t C_t - dS_t - e_t dS_t^F \right. \\[2mm] \left. +\left(1+r_{t-1}\right)dS_{t-1}+\left(1+r_{t-1}^F\right)e_t dS_{t-1}^F + W_t L_t - M_{t+1}^P\right) \\[2mm] +\dfrac{\mu_t}{P_t}\left(M_t^P - \tau_t - P_t C_t - dS_t - e_t dS_t^F +\left(1+r_{t-1}\right)dS_{t-1}+\left(1+r_{t-1}^F\right)e_t dS_{t-1}^F\right) \\[2mm] +\delta V_{t+1} \end{array} \right\}$$

$$\text{(11.5)}$$
$$\text{(11.6)}$$

where V_t is the value-function for the problem. The first-order conditions for the programme imply Euler-equations

$$\frac{1}{P_t C_t} = \delta(1 + r_t)\frac{1}{P_{t+1}C_{t+1}} \quad (11.7)$$

$$e_t \frac{1}{P_t C_t} = \delta\left(1 + r_t^F\right) e_{t+1} \frac{1}{P_{t+1} C_{t+1}}, \qquad (11.8)$$

which characterize the return requirements on shares of domestic and foreign funds: the interest rates state the price of deferring current consumption to later dates in terms of utility. However, contrary to the neoclassical growth model, under endogenous growth, consumption grows over time. Thus, it is necessary to determine the technologically feasible rate of growth of production in order to evaluate the above expressions.

2.2 Firms, Governments and Funds

2.2.1 Final-good producers

In each country, perfectly competitive final-good producers use labour, capital, and differentiated intermediate goods to produce a homogeneous final good, which they sell to consumers in both countries and to the domestic funds to be used as capital. In particular, domestic final goods are made by competitive firms with technology

$$Y_t = \left(L_{Yt}\right)^\alpha \left(K_t\right)^\gamma \left(\left(\sum_{j=1}^{N_t} X_{jt}^{\frac{\varepsilon-1}{\varepsilon}}\right)^{\frac{\varepsilon}{\varepsilon-1}}\right)^{(1-\alpha-\gamma)}, \qquad (11.9)$$

and foreign final goods with technology

$$Y_t^F = \left(L_{Yt}^F\right)^\beta \left(K_t^F\right)^\kappa \left(\left(\sum_{j=1}^{N_t} X_{jt}^{F\frac{\varepsilon-1}{\varepsilon}}\right)^{\frac{\varepsilon}{\varepsilon-1}}\right)^{(1-\beta-\kappa)} \qquad (11.10)$$

where $0 < \alpha < 1$ and $0 < \beta < 1$ are the respective domestic and foreign input shares of labour (L_{Yt} and L_{Yt}^F) $0 < \gamma < 1$ and $0 < \kappa < 1$ the shares of capital, denoted by K_t and K_t^F respectively, and $1 - \alpha - \gamma$ and $1 - \beta - \kappa$ the shares of the intermediate goods, the domestic use of which we denote by X_{jt} and the foreign use by X_{jt}^F. Of the product varieties indexed by j, we assume that $j = 1, \ldots, n_t$ are produced by domestic firms and $j = n_t + 1, \ldots, N_t$ by foreign firms, the total number of intermediate-good producers (and intermediate goods) equalling $n_t + m_t = N_t$. The elasticity of substitution between the differentiated varieties of the intermediate good are given by $-\varepsilon;\ \varepsilon > 1$.

Final-good producers compete perfectly and thus the prices of final goods equal marginal cost. Setting up a cost-minimization problem, equations (11.9) and (11.10) imply cost functions for final-good producers in a standard manner. In particular, the representative domestic firm takes the demand for its product as well as the prices of inputs as given and chooses inputs to solve the problem

$$\min_{L_{Yt}, K_t, X_{jt}} \left(W_t L_{Yt} + r_{Kt} K_t + \sum_{j=1}^{N_t} P_{jt} X_{jt} \right) \qquad (11.11)$$

subject to the production function in equation (11.9). A similar set-up can be used to derive the cost function for foreign firms. The competitive prices of the final goods are then given by the marginal cost functions

$$P_{Yt} = \alpha^{-\alpha} \gamma^{-\gamma} (1 - \alpha - \gamma)^{-(1-\alpha-\gamma)} (W_t)^{\alpha} (r_{Kt})^{\gamma} (P_{Xt})^{1-\alpha-\gamma}, \qquad (11.12)$$

and $P_{Yt}^{F} = \beta^{-\beta} \kappa^{-\kappa} (1 - \beta - \kappa)^{-(1-\beta-\kappa)} (W_t^{F})^{\beta} (r_{Kt}^{F})^{\kappa} (P_{Xt}^{F})^{1-\beta-\kappa}, \qquad (11.13)$

where W_t and W_t^{F} are the domestic and foreign wage levels, respectively, and $r_{Kt} = F_{Kt} P_{Yt}$ is the value of the marginal product (F_{Kt}) of domestic capital and $r_{Kt}^{F} = F_{Kt}^{F} P_{Yt}^{F}$ is the value of the marginal product (F_{Kt}^{F}) of foreign capital. P_{Xt}, in turn, is a domestic price index for the intermediate goods, and P_{Xt}^{F} is a foreign price index for the intermediate goods, to be defined below.

Equations (11.9) and (11.10) imply, via the cost function and Shephard's lemma, derived demands for labour, capital and intermediate goods. The derived demands for labour are given by

$$L_{Yt} = \frac{\alpha P_{Yt} Y_t}{W_t} \quad \text{and} \quad L_{Yt}^{F} = \frac{\beta P_{Yt}^{F} Y_t^{F}}{W_t^{F}} \qquad (11.14)$$

The derived demands for capital, in turn, are given by

$$K_t = \gamma \frac{P_{Yt} Y_t}{r_{Kt}} \quad \text{and} \quad K_t^{F} = \kappa \frac{P_{Yt}^{F} Y_t^{F}}{r_{Kt}^{F}} \qquad (11.15)$$

The demands for intermediate goods can also be derived using Shephard's lemma, but as intermediate goods are used for final-good production in both countries, the derived demands for, say, the domestic varieties are given by $X^D_{jt} = X_{jt} + X^F_{jt}$. Under the assumptions that intermediate-good producers do not price-discriminate and that they have access to current currency markets, the domestic price of variety j is P_j and the foreign price of the same variety is P_j/e_t. The demand for domestic varieties is then, in domestic terms,

$$X^D_{jt} = (1 - \alpha - \gamma) \frac{P_{Yt} Y_t}{P_{Xt}} \left(\frac{P_{jt}}{P_{Xt}} \right)^{-\varepsilon} + (1 - \beta - \kappa) \frac{e_t P^F_{Yt} Y^F_t}{e_t P^F_{Xt}} \left(\frac{P_{jt}}{e_t P^F_{Xt}} \right)^{-\varepsilon} , \quad j = 1,...,n_t,$$

(11.16)

where the price indices for intermediate goods are given by

$$P_{Xt} = \left(\sum_{j=1}^{n_t} P_{jt}^{1-\varepsilon} + \sum_{j=n_t+1}^{N_t} (e_t P_{jt})^{1-\varepsilon} \right)^{\frac{1}{1-\varepsilon}} \quad \text{and} \quad P^F_{Xt} = \left(\sum_{j=1}^{n_t} \left(\frac{P_{jt}}{e_t} \right)^{1-\varepsilon} + \sum_{j=n_t+1}^{N_t} P_{jt}^{1-\varepsilon} \right)^{\frac{1}{1-\varepsilon}}$$

(11.17)

On steady-state paths with innovation, final-good production may grow at rates which we henceforth will denote by $\sigma_Y = Y_t/Y_{t-1}$ and $\sigma_{YF} = Y^F_t/Y^F_{t-1}$. This growth is made possible by the introduction of new intermediate goods. It is easy to see that the production functions exhibit increasing returns in the number of intermediate goods. Thus, as innovation leads to the introduction of new intermediate goods, productivity rises and makes it possible to increase steady-state production. Under such growth, labour is used in the same amounts by the final-good producers in each period, but as the marginal productivity of capital has to remain fixed in a steady state, the stock of capital must increase at the same rate as output grows (Romer, 1990). Thus $K_{t+1}/K_t = \sigma_Y$. The rate of growth of production is then, by the results of Feenstra and Markusen (1993), given by

$$\frac{Y_{t+1}}{Y_t} = \left(\frac{K_{t+1}}{K_t} \right)^{\gamma} \left(\frac{N_{t+1}}{N_t} \right)^{\frac{1-\alpha-\gamma}{(\varepsilon-1)(1-\gamma)}}$$

(11.18)

The growth rate of foreign final-good production can be obtained in a similar way. Simplifying the expressions, we have

$$\sigma_Y = \sigma_N^{\dfrac{(1-\alpha-\gamma)}{(\varepsilon-1)(1-\gamma)}}, \tag{11.19}$$

$$\text{and } \sigma_{YF} = \sigma_N^{\dfrac{(1-\beta-\kappa)}{(\varepsilon-1)(1-\kappa)}}, \tag{11.20}$$

where $\sigma_N = N_t/N_{t-1}$ is the rate of growth of the number of intermediate goods. Thus, production grows faster in the country that employs more intermediate-good intensive final-good production technology and thus is more affected by technological change.

The fact that the derived demands for capital in equation (11.15) are growing at the rates of growth of output, can be used to express the value of investments as

$$P_{Yt}I_t = (\sigma_Y - 1 + \rho)\gamma \frac{P_{Yt}Y_t}{F_{Kt}} \text{ and } P_{Yt}I_t^F = (\sigma_{YF} - 1 + \rho^F)\kappa \frac{P_{Yt}^F Y_t^F}{F_{Kt}^F}, \tag{11.21}$$

where $I_t \equiv K_{t+1} - (1-\rho)K_t$ and $I_t^F \equiv K_{t+1}^F - (1-\rho^F)K_t^F$ are domestic and foreign net investment, respectively; ρ and ρ^F are the depreciation rates of domestic and foreign capital stock, respectively; and where we have substituted $F_{Kt}P_{Yt}$ for r_{Kt} and $F_{Kt}^F P_{Yt}^F$ for r_{Kt}^F.

2.2.2 Intermediate-good producers

Intermediate goods are produced by monopolistically competitive firms in each country. We assume that the firms are completely symmetric. Their production functions are

$$X_{jt} = \psi L_{jt}, j = 1, \ldots, n_t, \tag{11.22}$$

$$\text{and } X_{jt} = \psi L_{jt}^F, j = n_t + 1, \ldots, N_t. \tag{11.23}$$

Thus, it takes as much labour to manufacture a unit of intermediate goods in each of the countries. This symmetry, combined with the absence of reasons for price discrimination, guarantees that the prices of intermediate goods will be equal to each other in both countries. The simple production functions, together with (11.16) imply the demands for labour by each intermediate good producer, which are simply $L_{jt}^D = X_{jt}^D/\psi$ for domestic firms and $L_{jt}^{DF} = X_{jt}^{DF}/\psi$ for foreign firms.

Producers of the intermediate goods set their prices to maximize monopolistic profits subject to the given wages, and the demands given by equation (11.16), taking the prices of their rivals as given; in other words, price competition is Chamberlinian. The foreign firms are faced with a symmetric problem. The domestic firms set a price to solve

$$\max_{P_{jt}} \left(P_{jt} X_{jt}^D - \frac{W_t X_{jt}^D}{\psi} \right), \quad j = 1, ..., n_t.$$ (11.24)

Optimal prices are easily found to be

$$P_{jt} = \frac{\varepsilon}{\varepsilon - 1} \frac{W_t}{\psi}, \quad j = 1, ..., n_t,$$ (11.25)

$$\text{and } P_{jt} = \frac{\varepsilon}{\varepsilon - 1} \frac{W_t^F}{\psi}, \quad j = n_t + 1, ..., N_t.$$ (11.26)

Thus, the firms set prices according to a simple mark-up rule, the mark-up depending on the elasticity of substitution between the product varieties. The lower is the substitutability – the smaller the ε – the greater is the mark-up. Thus, when products are highly differentiated, firms have substantial market power.

Mark-up pricing implies that intermediate-good producers earn profits. In a symmetric equilibrium, the prices and the price levels of intermediate goods are equal in the two countries, that is $PX_t = e_t P_{Xt}^F$. Thus, these profits can be written as

$$\Pi_{jt} = \frac{(1 - \alpha - \gamma) P_{Yt} Y_t + e_t (1 - \beta - \kappa) P_{Yt}^F Y_t^F}{\varepsilon N_t}, \quad j = 1, ..., n_t.$$ (11.27)

It can be seen that, by symmetry, the profits of the foreign firms are the same in domestic terms.

2.2.3 Research and development
Patents for new products are produced by competitive R&D sectors. Both produce new designs using labour. The domestic R&D technology is

$$N_t = \eta N_{t-1} L_{At} + N_{t-1},$$ (11.28)

and the foreign R&D technology is analogous. The technologies imply that the prices of new designs are

$$P_{At} = \frac{W_t}{\eta N_{t-1}} \quad \text{and} \quad P_{At}^F = \frac{W_t^F}{\eta N_{t-1}}, \tag{11.29}$$

where ηN_{t-1} is a productivity parameter, and $\eta > 0$. Under these technologies, there is an externality in innovation, as each new design raises the productivity of labour in the R&D sector. Thus, productivity is growing at the same rate as the number of designs, $\sigma_N = N_t/N_{t-1}$. This is a crucial assumption in Grossman–Helpman-type models, and it is easy to see that without this externality, exponential growth cannot be sustained, as discussed in Grossman and Helpman (1991).

We assume that fraction d of new patents is produced and applied to production of intermediates in the home country. If innovation takes place in both countries, then the share of domestic innovation of world innovation remains constant in a steady state. The derived demands for labour in the R&D sectors are then

$$L_{At} = d\frac{(N_t - N_{t-1})}{\eta N_{t-1}} = d\frac{(\sigma_N - 1)}{\eta}, \tag{11.30}$$

$$\text{and} \quad L_{At}^F = f\frac{(N_t - N_{t-1})}{\eta N_{t-1}} = f\frac{(\sigma_N - 1)}{\eta}. \tag{11.31}$$

2.2.4 Governments

The governments buy both final goods. We assume government consumptions to be composite indices, G_t and G_t^F, with weights identical to those of the private consumption indices. The domestic government faces the budget constraint

$$P_t G_t = \tau_t + M_t - M_{t-1} \tag{11.32}$$

where τ_t is a lump-sum tax collected from the domestic consumer, and $M_t - M_{t-1}$ is the creation of money. The foreign government's constraint is analogous:

$$P_t^F G_t^F = \tau_t^F + M_t^F - M_{t-1}^F \tag{11.33}$$

Nominal government expenditure P_tG_t has to be met with cash, whence equations (11.32) and (11.33) are the cash-in-advance constraints of the governments. We take it that the domestic money supply is growing at rate $M_t / M_{t-1} \equiv \pi_H$ and the foreign money supply at rate $M_t^F / M_{t-1}^F \equiv \pi_F$. We assume that the shares of government consumption financed by money creation remain constant, which implies that the nominal lump-sum tax grows at the same rate as nominal government expenditure, that is, at the rate of growth of the money supply. We also assume that the share of government consumption to final-good consumption remains constant in steady states.

2.2.5   Funds

The domestic fund holds all domestic capital, K_t, and owns domestic producers. The foreign fund holds all foreign capital, K_t^F, and owns foreign producers. The funds receive the value marginal products of capital of final-good producers and the profits Π_{jt} of the intermediate-good producers at the end of each period in the respective domestic currencies. They then use these earnings and the cash they collect by issue of new shares to pay the interest and principal on shares held by the consumers, and to invest in capital and new designs.

The value of investment in capital by the domestic fund is $P_{Yt}(K_{t+1} - (1-\rho)K_t)$, and that by the foreign fund, $P_{Yt}^F(K_{t+1}^F - (1-\rho^F)K_t^F)$. The cost of the investment in new patents by the domestic fund is $(n_t - n_{t-1})P_{At}$, where P_{At} is the price of domestic patents. The foreign fund invests $(m_t - m_{t-1})P_{At}^F$, where P_{At}^F is the price of foreign patents. Thus the domestic fund's budget constraint in each period is

$$S_t - (1 + r_{t-1})S_{t-1} + \sum_{j=1}^{n_{t-1}} \Pi_{jt-1} - (n_t - n_{t-1})P_{At}$$
$$+ P_{Yt-1}F_{Kt-1}K_{t-1} - P_{Yt}K_{t+1} - (1-\rho)P_{Yt}K_t = 0, \qquad (11.34)$$

and the foreign fund's budget constraint is

$$S_t^F - (1 + r_{t-1}^F)S_{t-1}^F + \sum_{j=n_{t-1}+1}^{N_{t-1}} \Pi_{jt-1} - (m_t - m_{t-1})P_{At}^F$$
$$+ P_{Yt-1}^F F_{Kt-1}^F K_{t-1}^F - P_{Yt}^F K_{t+1}^F - (1-\rho_F)P_{Yt}^F K_t^F = 0. \qquad (11.35)$$

2.3   Aggregate Demand

Having derived the nominal demands for goods and factors, and having stated the nominal investment and public consumptions, it is possible to obtain simple expressions for nominal demands. In particular, aggregating the cash-in-advance constraints of the consumers and the governments, and using equations (11.34) and (11.35), the demand for the domestic final good can be written in domestic terms as

$$
\begin{aligned}
P_{Yt}Y_t &= \zeta(P_tC_t + P_tG_t) + e_t\zeta(P^F_tC^F_t + P^F_t G^F_t) + P_{Yt}I_t \\
&= \zeta(M_t + e_tM^F_t - (n_t - n_{t-1})P^H_{At} - (m_t - m_{t-1})e_tP^F_{At}) \\
&\quad + (1-\zeta)P_{Yt}I_t - \zeta e_t P^F_{Yt}I^F_t.
\end{aligned}
\tag{11.36}
$$

To obtain the second equality, we use the identities that wages, rental earnings on capital, and profits of the intermediate-good producers from the previous period make up the entire nominal compensation of factors of production. By the cash-in-advance constraints they are equal to the money stocks at the end of the previous period. The demand for foreign goods can be stated similarly and is, in domestic terms,

$$
\begin{aligned}
e_t P^F_{Yt} Y^F_t &= (1-\zeta)\left(M_t + e_tM^F_t - (n_t - n_{t-1})P^H_{At} - (m_t - m_{t-1})e_t P^F_{At}\right) \\
&\quad + \zeta e_t P^F_{Yt} I^F_t - (1-\zeta)P_{Yt}I_t.
\end{aligned}
\tag{11.37}
$$

Substituting for investment from equation (11.21), aggregate demands can, after some manipulation, be written as

$$
P_{Yt}Y_t = \zeta\left(M_t + e_tM^F_t - \frac{d(\sigma_N-1)}{\eta}W_t - \frac{f(\sigma_N-1)}{\eta}e_tW^F_t\right),
\tag{11.38}
$$

and $e_t P^F_{Yt} Y^F_t = (1-\zeta)\left(M_t + e_tM^F_t - \frac{d(\sigma_N-1)}{\eta}W_t - \frac{f(\sigma_N-1)}{\eta}e_tW^F_t\right).$ (11.39)

Equations (11.38) and (11.39) can be further simplified by using the fact that in steady states with innovation in both countries, the prices of patents are equalized; thus $W_t = e_t W^F_t$.

2.4   The Exchange Rate

Both country-specific final goods are homogeneous and are on sale in both countries. Thus, PPP holds for both goods. Using this fact, we can solve for the exchange rate. In particular, the nominal value of domestic consumption by consumers and the domestic government, given by the cash-in-advance constraints, is

$$P_t(C_t + G_t) = M_t - dP_{Yt}I_t - de_t P_{Yt}^F I_t^F - d(n_t - n_{t-1})P_{At} - d(m_t - m_{t-1})e_t P_{At}^F,$$

(11.40)

and the value of foreign consumption is

$$P_t^F(C_t^F + G_t^F) = M_t^F - f P_{Yt}^F I_t^F - f\frac{P_{Yt}I_t}{e_t} - f(n_t - n_{t-1})\frac{P_{At}}{e_t} - f(m_t - m_{t-1})P_{At}^F.$$

(11.41)

By PPP, $P_t = e_t P_t^F$. Dividing equation (11.40) by equation (11.41) gives us

$$e_t\frac{d}{f} = \left(M_t^P - dP_{Yt}I_t - de_t P_{Yt}^F I_t^F - d(n_t - n_{t-1})P_{At} - d(m_t - m_{t-1})e_t P_{At}^F\right)$$

$$/ \left(M_t^{PF} - f P_{Yt}^F I_t^F - f\frac{P_{Yt}I_t}{e_t} - f(n_t - n_{t-1})\frac{P_{At}}{e_t} - f(m_t - m_{t-1})P_{At}^F\right),$$

(11.42)

where d/f is the ratio of consumptions by the assumption of symmetry. While in general the net financial flows affect the exchange rate, our assumption of symmetry of holdings of assets implies that the terms consisting of expenditure on patents as well as investment cancel out when rearranging the above equation. We thus have

$$e_t = \Phi\frac{M_t}{M_t^F},$$

(11.43)

where $\Phi = f/d$ remains constant in the steady states we study. This is a fairly standard form of the monetary theory of exchange rates.

It is easy to see that perfect capital markets imply uncovered interest parity for the model. In steady states, the rates of interest in each country must be constant; we denote these equilibrium interest rates by r and r^F, respectively. The Euler equations (11.7) and (11.8) then imply that

$$\frac{e_{t+1}}{e_t} = \frac{(1+r)}{\left(1+r^F\right)}.$$ (11.44)

Thus the rate of change of the exchange rate depends on the difference of the interest rates.

2.5   Wages and Prices

Having solved for the exchange rate and for aggregate demand, the wages that equilibrate the demand for and the supply of labour can now be solved. The demand for labour is given by equations (11.14), (11.16), (11.22), (11.30) and (11.38). The sum of the sectoral demands must be equal to the fixed supply of labour; hence

$$L_t = \left\{\left(\alpha + \frac{(1-\alpha-\gamma)(\varepsilon-1)}{\varepsilon}\right)\zeta + \left(\frac{(1-\beta-\kappa)(\varepsilon-1)}{\varepsilon}\right)(1-\zeta)\right\}$$

$$\times \left(\frac{M_t + e_t M_t^F}{W_t} - \frac{(\sigma_N-1)}{\eta}\right) + d\frac{(\sigma_N-1)}{\eta}.$$ (11.45)

The domestic equilibrium wage is then given by

$$W_t = Y^H(1+\Phi)M_t, \text{ where}$$ (11.46)

$$Y^H \equiv \frac{\alpha\zeta + \left((1-\alpha-\gamma)\zeta + (1-\beta-\kappa)(1-\zeta)\right)^{\frac{(\varepsilon-1)}{\varepsilon}}}{L_t + \left(\alpha\zeta + \left((1-\alpha-\gamma)\zeta + (1-\beta-\kappa)(1-\zeta)\right)^{\frac{(\varepsilon-1)}{\varepsilon}} - d\right)^{\frac{(\sigma_N-1)}{\eta}}}.$$

For the foreign wages, we have by similar reasoning

$$W_t^F = Y^F \frac{(1+\Phi)}{\Phi} M_t^F, \text{ where}$$ (11.47)

$$Y^F = \frac{\beta(1-\zeta) + \left((1-\alpha-\gamma)\zeta + (1-\beta-\kappa)(1-\zeta)\right)^{\frac{(\varepsilon-1)}{\varepsilon}}}{L_t^F + \left(\beta(1-\zeta) + \left((1-\alpha-\gamma)\zeta + (1-\beta-\kappa)(1-\zeta)\right)^{\frac{(\varepsilon-1)}{\varepsilon}} - f\right)^{\frac{(\sigma_N-1)}{\eta}}}.$$

Thus, wages respond fully to monetary growth.

Given equilibrium wages, we obtain equilibrium prices by the pricing rules of the intermediate-good producers and final-good producers. Substituting for the equilibrium wages, the domestic final-good price level is then, for a fixed number of intermediate goods, given by

$$P_t = \Gamma_t M_t F_{Kt}^{\frac{\gamma\zeta}{1-\gamma}} F_{Kt}^{F\frac{\kappa(1-\zeta)}{1-\kappa}} , \qquad (11.48)$$

where Γ_t depends on the technology parameters and is constant for a fixed number of intermediate goods. This implies neutrality of money for a fixed number of intermediate goods. However, if there is innovation, the rate of change of final-good prices does not equal the growth rate of money supply. This is due to the change in the number of intermediate goods. Using the results of Feenstra (1994), the prices of final goods change, by equations (11.12) and (11.13), according to

$$\pi_Y = \sigma_N^{\frac{(1-\alpha-\gamma)}{(1-\varepsilon)(1-\gamma)}} \pi_H = \frac{\pi_H}{\sigma_Y} \quad \text{and} \qquad (11.49)$$

$$\pi_Y^F = \sigma_N^{\frac{(1-\beta-\kappa)}{(1-\varepsilon)(1-\kappa)}} \pi_F = \frac{\pi_F}{\sigma_{YF}}. \qquad (11.50)$$

The rates of change of final-good prices will thus not be equal in general, nor will the change in the consumer-price indices: the rate of change of the domestic final-good price index is

$$\pi_P = \sigma_N^{\frac{\zeta(1-\kappa)(1-\alpha-\gamma)+(1-\zeta)(1-\gamma)(1-\beta-\kappa)}{(1-\varepsilon)(1-\gamma)(1-\kappa)}} \pi_H = \frac{\pi_H}{\sigma_Y^\zeta \sigma_{YF}^{(1-\zeta)}}, \qquad (11.51)$$

and the rate of change of the foreign price index is

$$\pi_P^F = \sigma_N^{\frac{\zeta(1-\kappa)(1-\alpha-\gamma)+(1-\zeta)(1-\gamma)(1-\beta-\kappa)}{(1-\varepsilon)(1-\gamma)(1-\kappa)}} \pi_F = \frac{\pi_F}{\sigma_Y^\zeta \sigma_{YF}^{(1-\zeta)}}. \qquad (11.52)$$

In other words, the rates of change of the price indices are only equated if the rates of monetary growth are. The significance of innovation here is that it reduces the rates of inflation below the rates of growth of the money supplies. It is easy to see that in the absence of innovation, the rates of inflation would be equal to the rates of monetary growth, as they are in the neoclassical growth model.

3 STEADY-STATE GROWTH

3.1 The Rates of Interest

Having solved for the technically feasible rate of growth of production and consumption, we can now turn back to the Euler equations to solve the steady-state rates of interest. In a steady state, consumption is growing at rate σ_c. From the consumption index in equation (11.1), the growth consists of the growth of domestic and foreign production. From equations (11.19) and (11.20), the growth rate of consumption is then

$$\sigma_C = \sigma_{YH}^{\zeta}\sigma_{YF}^{(1-\zeta)} \qquad (11.53)$$

This growth rate applies to both countries, irrespective of the actual shares of innovation taking place in each of the countries.

Substituting the steady-state rates of growth of production and the rates of inflation from equations (11.51) and (11.52) into the Euler equations, we have the constant, steady-state interest rates in both countries:

$$1+r = \frac{\pi_H}{\delta}, \qquad (11.54)$$

$$\text{and } 1+r^F = \frac{\pi_F}{\delta}. \qquad (11.55)$$

Thus nominal interest rates in both countries depend on the growth rates of the money supplies in the standard, neoclassical manner (Abel, 1985). In steady states, nominal interest rates generally differ from each other. However, real interest rates are equated, as is easily seen by dividing the expressions for nominal interest rates by the appropriate rates of change of final-good price indices.

3.2   The Marginal Productivity of Capital

The funds in each country own the final-good producers and thus face an investment decision, since capital is depreciating and the demand for final goods is growing. We assume that the funds maximize firms' intertemporal profits and thus choose K_{t+1+i} in each period to maximize

$$\sum_{i=1}^{\infty}(1+r)^{-i}\left(P_{Yt+i}Y_{t+i} - W_{t+i}L_{t+i} - (1+r)P_{Yt+i}\left(K_{t+1+i} - (1-\rho)K_{t+i}\right)\right), \quad (11.56)$$

where $(1 + r)$ is the interest cost of investment. A first-order condition for this problem is

$$\frac{P_{Yt+1}F_{Kt+1}}{1+r} - (1+r)P_{Yt} + (1-\rho)P_{Yt+1} = 0. \qquad (11.57)$$

Re-arranging, and noting that equation (11.49) gives the relevant rate of change of the domestic final-good price under endogenous growth and that interest rates as well as marginal productivities of capital are constant in steady states, the first-order condition yields a solution for the steady-state marginal productivity of capital:

$$F_K = \frac{\pi_H}{\delta^2}\left(\sigma_Y - \delta(1-\rho)\right). \qquad (11.58)$$

It is easy to set up a similar problem for the foreign fund. As a solution, we have

$$F_K^F = \frac{\pi_F}{\delta^2}\left(\sigma_{YF} - \delta(1-\rho^F)\right). \qquad (11.59)$$

It is noteworthy that, in steady states, the marginal productivities of capital need not be equal (the rates of growth are not); however, their ratio will be constant. But because the consumers can own shares in both funds, the returns on investment in foreign and domestic capital, given that investment in capital is chosen optimally to satisfy (11.58) and (11.59), are equated.

There are two effects of monetary growth on the marginal productivity of capital. Differentiating equation (11.58) with respect to the rate of monetary growth gives us

$$F_{K\pi} = \frac{1}{\delta^2}\left(\sigma_Y - \delta(1-\rho)\right) + \frac{\pi_H}{\delta^2}\frac{\partial \sigma_Y}{\partial \sigma_N}\frac{\partial \sigma_N}{\partial \pi_H}. \tag{11.60}$$

The first term results in the Tobin effect: increases in the rates of monetary growth raise the steady-state marginal productivity of capital. In the stagnant neoclassical model, this effect leads to a decrease in the steady-state capital stock. But there is another effect as well, which stems from the effect of monetary growth to the rates of growth of production. This effect, it will be seen, is negative; thus, increased monetary growth reduces steady-state marginal productivity of capital, and by equation (11.21), the rate of investment. As can be seen from equations (11.58) and (11.59), the effects will not be equal in the two countries.

This result is of some importance, because the latter effect is absent from the increasing-returns growth model. In qualitative terms at least, the current framework may then be more general than the neoclassical model. For example, De Gregorio (1993), in his study of Latin America, argues that the reduction of the marginal productivity of capital caused by inflation is empirically more relevant than the Tobin effect. Yet it cannot be explained by the increasing returns-to-scale model: if, in that model, one allows for endogenous labour supply, monetary growth – or rather, inflation – will reduce the marginal productivity of capital by lowering the steady-state supply of labour. This effect can easily be included in the current framework as well, as in Honkatukia (1994). However, the labour-supply effect does not explain De Gregorio's findings, because he finds no evidence of a correlation between inflation and labour supply. The current framework suggests an alternative explanation: the effect stems from endogenous productivity growth, not labour supply.

The current model reduces to the stagnant neoclassical model, if one abstracts away from endogenous growth. In this case, there is no innovation, and accordingly, no technological change or output growth, so that $\sigma_Y = \sigma_{YF} = 1$. Equations (11.58) and (11.59) then reduce to the basic neoclassical case of Abel (1985).

3.3 The Rate of Innovation

The domestic firms pay their profits to the domestic fund at the end of each period; foreign firms pay them to the foreign fund. Because the funds have to buy a patent for a new design in order to enable a new firm to start production, profits are used entirely for covering the interest on the cost of the patent. For the initial investment to be feasible, profit per firm must thus equal the interest payment on the price of the design. Using this, we have an arbitrage condition for domestic investment in R&D, namely, $\Pi_{jt} = r_t P_{At}$, where P_{At} is the price of a domestic design. Having solved for the interest rates and wages, we can determine the rate of innovation. Using the price of designs implied by the R&D technology, the arbitrage condition becomes

$$\Pi_{jt} - r\frac{W_t}{\eta N_{t-1}} = 0. \tag{11.61}$$

Substituting for the equilibrium wage and profits, we can solve for the rate of innovation. This is given by

$$\sigma_N = (L_t + d/\eta)\Big(\eta\big((1-\alpha-\gamma)\zeta + (1-\beta-\kappa)(1-\zeta)\big)\Big)$$
$$\times \left\{\alpha\zeta er + \big((1-\alpha-\gamma)\zeta + (1-\beta-\kappa)(1-\zeta)\big)\left(d + \left(\frac{\varepsilon-1}{\varepsilon}\right)er\right)\right\}^{-1}. \tag{11.62}$$

Thus, the rate of innovation ultimately depends on technology parameters, the size of the countries, and the nominal interest rate. Substituting for the latter, given by $r = (\pi_H - \delta)/\delta$, it is easy to see that

$$\frac{\partial \sigma_N}{\partial \pi_H} < 0. \tag{11.63}$$

Thus, steady states with increased money creation by the government(s) have lower steady-state rates of innovation. Lower rates of innovation directly imply lower rates of growth of the economy, and, by equation (11.60), lower marginal productivity of capital. This effect can be quite large; in fact, for plausible parameter values, the effect on productivity growth may imply $F_{K\pi} < 0$ in equation (11.60). This may happen, if the cost share of intermediate goods is large and if the goods are highly differentiated (if $\in$ is not very large).

Grossman and Helpman (1991) give an extensive discussion on the conditions under which innovation takes place in different countries. Rather than venture into seeing whether exchange-rate policies could be used to affect innovation, here, we merely point out that the monetary system may play a role in this context as well. For innovation to take place in both countries it is necessary that both domestic and foreign investors' arbitrage conditions are met. As foreign R&D investment is determined from the conditions $\Pi_{jt}^F = r_t^F P_{At}^F$, the foreign rate of innovation is given by

$$\sigma_N^F = \left(L_t^F + f / \eta \right) \left(\eta \left((1 - \alpha - \gamma) \zeta + (1 - \beta - \kappa)(1 - \zeta) \right) \right)$$

$$\times \left\{ \beta(1 - \zeta) \varepsilon r^F + \left((1 - \alpha - \gamma) \zeta + (1 - \beta - \kappa)(1 - \zeta) \right) \left(f + \left(\frac{\varepsilon - 1}{\varepsilon} \right) \varepsilon r^F \right) \right\}^{-1}.$$

$$(11.64)$$

As the technologies and labour endowments need not be equal, it is clear that (11.62) and (11.64) will equal each other only if monetary policies are coordinated so that interest rates equate the two equations. Generally, this implies that one of the currencies is devaluing at a constant rate against the other, which is perfectly consistent with a steady state (Helpman and Razin, 1984), as all return requirements continue to be satisfied. In such steady states, rates of inflation and growth will not be equated, nor will nominal interest rates; however, the real interest rates will be. However, under perfect symmetry the growth rates in equations (11.62) and (11.64) will be equated under a fixed exchange rate. This is easy to see in a special case of such symmetry. If the endowments and technologies of the countries are the same, that is, if $L_t = L_t^F$, $d = f$, $\alpha = \beta$, and $\gamma = \kappa$, then it is easy to see that the equality of the two rates of innovation requires $r = r^F$ – which, by uncovered interest parity, implies a fixed exchange rate.

4 CONCLUSION

The current chapter has presented an open economy, monetary, R&D growth model. The model accounts for growth in open economies much in the spirit of Grossman and Helpman (1991). Contrary to Grossman and Helpman, we consider the determination of nominal prices and exchange rates, physical capital accumulation and government spending.

In the model, the cash-in-advance constraints apply to all transactions. The assumption that all transactions are subject to the cash-in-advance constraints exaggerates the effects of money, but can be generalized, as discussed in Orphanides and Solow (1990). Government expenditure financed by money creation then imposes an inflation tax on nominal earnings. This causes a negative Tobin effect and reduces investment in R&D. Reduction in the latter causes a productivity growth slow-down, thereby reducing output growth as well as capital formation and the marginal productivity of capital. The channels, through which inflation affects growth, are thus quite different from neoclassical models. Furthermore, in Section 2.5, we showed that the rates of price inflation are lower in the presence of endogenous growth due to innovation than they are in monetary, neoclassical growth models. In sections 3.1 and 3.2, we showed that while the nominal rates of interest are equal, the marginal productivities of capital are higher in our model than in the neoclassical model.

We have restricted our attention to steady states, where innovation and capital formation take place in both countries. In such steady states, a floating exchange-rate regime may not guarantee room for independent monetary policies. Generally, the rates of monetary growth have to maintain a certain relationship to each other. In this case, while real interest rates are equated in the steady state, differentials may persist in inflation, nominal interest rates and output growth. However, under the assumption of symmetry, the exchange rate has to be fixed to guarantee that innovation takes place in both of the countries. But while we are arguing that a floating exchange rate does not necessarily guarantee a steady state, where both countries innovate, we do not to seek to advocate a fixed exchange rate either: it is not at all clear that this would guarantee innovation in both countries under asymmetry. Nor do we wish to imply that it would be desirable to innovate in all countries; after all, it is not of importance where innovation takes place, as long as resources are allocated optimally. Rather, we should like to submit that nominal exchange rates appear likely to affect the allocation of these activities. Finally, it should be added that the inflation tax is the only distortionary tax in our model. It is conceivable that other distortionary taxes can be used to counteract the effects of inflation. But because the economies are imperfectly competitive and thus inefficient, the determination of welfare-improving combinations of such taxes can be a formidable task.

NOTES

*   I wish to thank Drud Hansen, Pertti Haaparanta, Seppo Honkapohja, Tapio Palokangas, Margareta Soismaa, and the editors for helpful comments. Financial support from the Helsinki School of Economics, NorFa, and the Yrjö Jahnsson Foundation is gratefully acknowledged. The usual disclaimer applies.

REFERENCES

Abel, A. (1985), 'Dynamic Behaviour of Capital in a Cash-in-Advance Model', *Journal of Monetary Economics*, **16**, 55–71.

De Gregorio, J. (1993), 'Inflation, Taxation and Long-Run Growth', *Journal of Monetary Economics*, **31**, 271–98.

Feenstra, R.C. (1994), 'New Product Varieties and the Measurement of International Prices', *American Economic Review*, **84**, 15–77.

Feenstra, R.C. and J.R. Markusen (1993), 'Accounting for Growth with New Inputs', *NBER Discussion Paper*, No. 4114.

Grossman, G.M. and E. Helpman (1984), 'The Role of Saving and Investment in Exchange Rate Determination under Alternative Monetary Mechanisms', *Journal of Monetary Economics*, **13**, 307–25.

Grossman, G.M. and E. Helpman (1990), 'Comparative Advantage and Long-Run Growth', *American Economic Review*, **80**, 796–815.

Grossman, G.M. and E. Helpman (1991), *Innovation and Growth*, Cambridge, MA: MIT Press.

Honkatukia, J. (1994), 'Endogenous Growth in Finance-Constrained Economies', *Working Paper*, No. 124, Trade Union Institute for Economic Research, Stockholm.

Jones, L.E. and R. Manuelli (1993), 'Growth and the Effects of Inflation', *NBER Working Paper*, No. 4523.

Mankiw, N.G., D. Romer and D.N. Weil (1992), 'A Contribution to the Empirics of Economic Growth', *Quarterly Journal of Economics*, **107**, 408–37.

Orphanides, A. and R.M. Solow (1990), 'Money, Inflation and Growth', in B. Friedman and F. Hahn (eds), *Handbook of Monetary Economics*, Vol. I, Amsterdam: North-Holland, pp. 223–61.

Rebelo, S. (1992), 'Growth in Open Economies', *Carnegie-Rochester Series on Public Policy*, **36**, 5–46.

Romer, P.M. (1990), 'Endogenous Technological Change', *Journal of Political Economy*, **98**, 71–102.

Vartia, Y.O. (1976), 'Ideal Log-Change Index Numbers', *Scandinavian Journal of Statistics*, **3**, 121–6.

12. Trade, technology and changes in employment of skilled labour in Swedish manufacturing*

Pär Hansson

1 INTRODUCTION

The composition of employment has undergone considerable changes during the last few decades. In particular, the skill level in the labour force has risen. The share of employees with higher education (tertiary) in Swedish manufacturing rose from 2.7 per cent in 1970 to 15.7 per cent in 1993 and a similar pattern can be observed in many other OECD countries.

The two most popular hypotheses put forward to explain this development are: increased international competition from the newly industrialized and the less-developed countries (NICs and LDCs) and technical progress which reduces the need for unskilled labour, that is, unskilled labour-saving-biased technical progress. The former explanation is primarily expected to result in increased specialization in skill-intensive industries, and accordingly, to growing employment in these industries and contracting employment in industries using large shares of unskilled labour. The latter effect is mainly supposed to take place within industries and implies rising skill-intensities within industries and plants. Yet stronger exposure to trade may also raise the within-industry share of skilled labour. Wood (1994, 1995) argues that, above all, increased import competition from NICs and LDCs would raise the proportion of skilled labour within industries due to shifts from less-skill-intensive to more-skill-intensive activities and/or by search for new production methods that economize on unskilled labour ('defensive innovation').

The purpose of this chapter is to examine the importance of these factors in Swedish manufacturing industries during the 1970s and the 1980s. One approach is to decompose the changes in the share of skilled labour into between- and within-industry changes. Previously, the method has been used by Berman, Bound and Griliches (1994) for the USA and by Machin (1994) for the UK. An advantage with this study is that we have access to better data on skill and that we have data at the plant level. The latter means that we can decompose the changes in the share of skilled labour further, that is, into within- and between-plant changes. We can also look at skill shares in plants entering into and exiting from the industry and make comparisons with plants that have been in operation during the whole studied period.

Another way to investigate shifts in skill structure is to examine whether changes in the demand for skilled labour can be attributed to technical changes. There are many examples where the introduction of computers has shifted the composition of labour demand from manual production workers towards technicians and other types of skilled labour. To analyse this more systematically we follow a methodology developed by Berman, Bound and Griliches (1994). In a model derived from a translog cost function, we regress changes in the share of skilled labour on various indicators of technical change. Within this framework we also test the idea set out by Wood that increased import competition would affect the within-industry share of skilled labour.

This chapter is organized as follows: Section 2 documents some trends in Swedish manufacturing employment and trade; Section 3 gives a theoretical background; in Section 4 we present the decomposition; in Section 5, we attempt to explain the shift in the demand for skilled labour with observable measures of technical change; Section 6 provides a conclusion to the chapter.

2   TRENDS IN SKILL STRUCTURE AND INTERNATIONALIZATION

Both in the USA and the UK one can observe a steady increase in the share of skilled labour in manufacturing during the postwar period. For the period 1970 to 1990, Berman, Machin and Bound (1994) discovered a shift towards increased use of skilled workers in almost all the studied countries (both developed and developing). In theirs and many other studies, skilled labour is defined as non-production workers and a growing share of non-production workers is interpreted as increased use of relatively skilled workers. Obviously, the distinction between production and non-production workers is a crude measure of skill and some economists, for example, Leamer (1994), have asserted that it is inappropriate. A worker's skill is probably related to education, on-the-job training and work experience and, obviously, there are misclassifications with the measure since not all non-production workers are skilled and not all production workers are unskilled. For instance, low-skilled office employees are classified as non-production workers. Generally, however, non-production workers appear to have higher education.[1]

Our classification of skilled labour is based entirely on educational attainment. Of course, educational attainment is an imperfect measure of skill.[2] The main weakness is that it does not capture experience and it partially understates participation in further education and training. Another problem is variations in quality of schooling, both over time and between areas. Educational attainment seems, however, to be strongly correlated with occupation and earnings, and initial attainment is a good predictor of whether a person will participate in further education and training. We thus think educational attainment is a better measure of skill than the share of non-production workers.

We define skilled labour as employees with tertiary education, that is, most of them have at least 15 years of education. We can observe a continuous increase in the share with higher education in the whole economy from 8.6 per cent in 1971 to 25.8 per cent in 1994. The corresponding figures for the manufacturing industry (the tradables sector) is lower, but shows the same pattern of development over time. From Table 12.1 it is evident that the non-manufacturing part of the economy (the non-tradables sector) is dominated by the public sector, in which the skill share has grown considerably. A substantial increase in the share of skilled labour has also occurred in the financial sector. On the other hand, the rest of the non-tradables sector is not as skill intensive, and has experienced fewer structural changes regarding employment and skill intensity, in comparison with manufacturing.

Table 12.1   *Sector skill and sector employment shares, 1994, and changes in shares between 1971 and 1994 in Sweden (in percentage terms)*

Sector code	Sector	1994		1994–1971	
		Skill share*	Employ-ment**	ΔSkill share	ΔEmploy-ment
1	Agriculture, forestry and fishing	10.24	3.49	9.34	−4.18
2,3,4	Mining and quarrying, manufacturing, and electricity gas and water	15.39	19.51	12.62	−8.70
38	Engineering	17.44	8.76	14.76	−2.60
5	Construction	7.33	6.14	5.97	−3.63
6	Wholesale and retail trade, hotels and restaurants	14.40	14.72	10.61	0.06
7	Transport, storage and communication	12.61	6.85	8.19	0.37
8	Financing, insurance, real estate and business services	36.69	9.46	24.48	4.12
9	Other personal services	38.98	39.83	17.15	11.95
91,931–934	Public administration, education and medical service	42.41	33.02	15.89	12.20
	All sectors	25.79	100	17.23	

Notes
*   Share of skilled labour in sector employment.
**   Share of employment in all sectors.

Source: SCB Labour Force Survey (AKU).

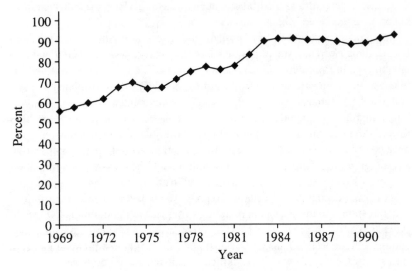

Figure 12.1   Foreign trade ratio in Swedish manufacturing, 1969–1992, in current prices

To a large extent the growing skill level in manufacturing coincided with increased internationalization, which Figure 12.1 demonstrates. Over the past 20 years international trade in Sweden has been boosted by international agreements, for example, the free trade agreement between the EC and EFTA (which came into force in 1973) and the Tokyo Round (which was completed in 1979), market liberalization in the developing world, and falling costs of communication and transport. Figure 12.1 shows the foreign trade ratio in manufacturing, that is, exports plus imports as a share of the value of sales (production). The foreign trade ratio rose from 55 per cent in 1969 to 90 per cent in 1985, but has since then been almost constant (92 per cent in 1992). Hence, it is tempting to believe that increased internationalization has, at least partially, affected the employment structure in manufacturing.

3   THEORETICAL BACKGROUND[3]

3.1   International Trade

To see how international trade may influence the composition of employment, let us consider the simple $2 \times 2 \times 2$ Heckscher–Ohlin–Samuelson (HOS) model.[4] There are two factors of production (skilled and unskilled labour) producing two goods (a skilled-labour-intensive and an unskilled-labour-intensive good) where one country has an abundance of skilled labour and therefore exports the skilled-labour-intensive good, while the other country exports the unskilled-labour-intensive good.[5]

Reciprocal reduction of tariffs and/or falling costs of communications and transport may lead to a situation where trade expands as a share of GDP without any change in the international prices of goods. The changes will, however, increase the domestic price in Sweden of the skilled-labour-intensive good and lower the domestic price of the unskilled-labour-intensive good. This will imply increased demand for skilled workers since overall production shifts towards the skill-intensive good and away from the less-skill-intensive good because of increased international specialization according to comparative advantage. In the simple Heckscher–Ohlin model, the endowments of skilled and unskilled labour are assumed to be fixed in each country as these trade and product market changes take place. To preserve the labour market equilibrium and in response to the change in relative factor prices (higher relative wages of skilled workers), there will be a substitution of unskilled labour for skilled labour within each subsector. Thus, as trade expands, there is both a *between*-industry shift in employment towards the skilled labour-intensive goods and a *within*-industry shift in both industries towards an increase in the proportion of unskilled workers.

3.2 Unskilled-labour-saving Biased Technical Progress

The increased requirement of skilled labour *within* industries could, however, be explained by skilled-biased technical progress. Technical progress means that more output can be produced with given amounts of inputs, and unskilled-labour-saving technical progress increases the marginal productivity of skilled labour more than it raises the marginal productivity of unskilled labour at a constant ratio of skilled to unskilled labour. Unskilled-labour-saving technical progress is illustrated in Figure 12.2.

$1/p_Y$ and $1/p_X$ are unit-value isoquants of the two goods produced in industry Y and industry X, where p_X and p_Y are the initial equilibrium prices. The line AB is the unit-value isocost line. Perfect competition implies that prices equal unit costs so that AB is tangent to both unit-value isoquants. The slope of AB shows the relative wages of unskilled to skilled labour, w_u / w_s, and the rays from origin to the tangency points indicate the ratio of skilled to unskilled labour used in the production of each good. Hence, the production of the good in industry Y is more skill intensive than the production of the good in industry X.

Unskilled-labour-saving technical progress in both industries means that the unit-value isoquants in Figure 12.2 shift towards the origin and change the tangency point with the unit-value isocost line in a manner such that, for given relative factor prices, that is, where the slope of the isocost CD equals the slope of AB, the ratio of skilled to unskilled labour used in producing each good

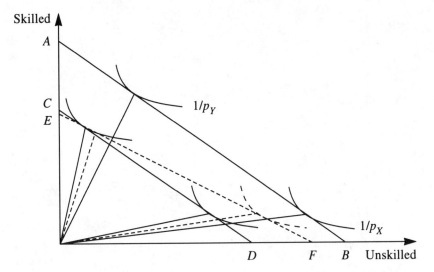

Figure 12.2 Unskilled-labour-saving technical progress

increases. The product prices p_X and p_Y are unchanged so the same output value can be produced with less-skilled and unskilled labour. This is a case where technical progress occurs to exactly the same extent in both industries. Let us now assume that the technical progress is faster in the skill-intensive industry Y. We illustrate this by the dotted lines in Figure 12.2. The slope of the unit-value isocost line EF is then flatter, that is, the relative wage w_u / w_s decreases. The relative wage of skilled labour increases, since skilled labour is used intensively in the industry with the fastest rate of technical progress.[6] Because technical progress is unskilled-labour-saving, the *within*-industry proportion of skilled labour rises in both industries. The factor endowments are given in our simple $2 \times 2 \times 2$ HOS model, which means that there will also be a *between*-industry shift of employment, namely increased employment in the unskilled-labour-intensive industry X, in order to fully employ unskilled labour.

3.3 Increased Relative Endowments of Skilled Labour

Let us now relax the assumption of fixed factor endowments. Higher relative wages of skilled labour, as a result of faster technical progress in the skill-intensive industry and/or of intensified international competition in the unskilled-labour-intensive industry, may then lead to increased supply of skilled labour. Increased supply of skilled labour relative to unskilled labour would in turn boost production in the skill-intensive industry Y relative to the unskilled-intensive industry X.

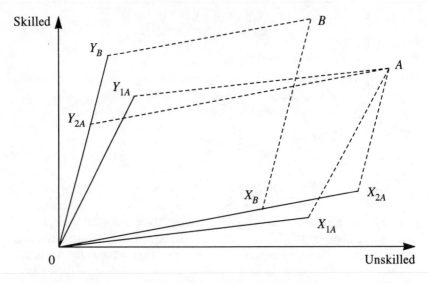

Figure 12.3   Increased relative endowments of skilled labour

Figure 12.3 exemplifies this. A is the initial endowment of skilled and unskilled labour in the economy. $0X_{1A}$ and $0Y_{1A}$ are the employment levels in industry X and Y respectively. The slopes of these rays from the origin indicate the ratio of skilled to unskilled labour in each industry (compare Figure 12.2). Technical progress which leads to a saving of unskilled labour raises the skill intensity in both industries and leads to new employment levels $0X_{2A}$ and $0Y_{2A}$. Let us now assume that the level of education in the economy rises; the number of skilled grow at the expense of the number of unskilled. Point B shows the new factor endowments and $0X_B$ and $0Y_B$ are the new employment levels.

We conclude that unskilled-labour-saving technical progress gives rise to raised *within*-industry proportions of skilled labour. A simultaneous *between*-industry shift in employment towards skill-intensive industries requires, in turn, an increased relative supply of skilled labour.

4   DECOMPOSITION OF CHANGES IN LABOUR SKILLS

We can decompose the increase in skilled labour in Swedish manufacturing into a *between*- and a *within*-industry component. The share of the employed with higher education can be expressed as:

$$P^E = \sum_{i=1}^{n} \frac{E_i^s}{E} = \sum_{i=1}^{n} \frac{E_i^s}{E_i} \frac{E_i}{E} = \sum_{i=1}^{n} P_i^E S_i \qquad (12.1)$$

where P_i^E is the share of the employees in industry i with tertiary education and S_i is industry i's share of total employment in manufacturing.

The change in the share of skilled workers can be decomposed into two parts

$$\Delta P^E = \sum_{i=1}^{n} \Delta S_i \overline{P}_i^E + \sum_{i=1}^{n} \Delta P_i^E \overline{S}_i \qquad (12.2)$$

where $\overline{P}_i^E$ and $\overline{S}_i$ are period averages. The first part captures reallocations of employment between industries, for example, from low-skill to high-skill industries. Changes in international specialization at the industry level and other factors that invoke changes in product demand between industries imply shifts in this component. Growth in relative endowments of skilled labour would, as we have shown in Section 3, be reflected as shifts in production towards skill-intensive industries. The second part measures increased skill intensities within industries. Technical changes in the production process are, among other things, expected to affect that component.

Table 12.2   Changes in the employment structure in Swedish manufacturing, 1970–1993, between- and within-industry decomposition (percentage points)

Number of industries and sample period	Total change (annualized)	Between-industry component	Within-industry component	Correlation between $\Delta S_i \overline{P}_i^E$ and Δr_i
36 1970–85	0.435	0.040	0.395	0.41 (0.01)
36 1985–90	0.418	–0.018	0.436	–0.16 (0.37)
146 1986–93	0.905	0.095	0.810	0.10 (0.28)

Note: Parentheses give significance levels of the correlation coefficients.

We have studied the changes in skill structure in 36 Swedish manufacturing industries during the periods 1970–85 and 1985–90. It is evident from Table 12.2 that the annual total change is about the same in both periods (roughly 0.4

percentage points per year). The *within*-industry component is by far the most important. The *between*-industry component is even negative during the 1985–90 period. This means that most of the shift away from relatively unskilled labour occurred *within* given industries. A result which is in line with similar US and UK work on this issue.

To examine whether changes in international specialization have been related to shifts in the employment structure between industries of different skill intensities, we correlate cross-section changes in the specialization index,[7] Δr_i, with the between-industry component, $\Delta S_i P_i^E$. An increase in the specialization index implies, given unchanged consumption, larger net exports, so a positive relationship indicates the occurrence of a shift in employment from low-skilled to high-skilled industries due to increased net exports of skill-intensive products. According to Table 12.2, the correlation coefficient is positive and clearly significant for the period 1970–85, whereas it is insignificant for the period 1985–90. Our interpretation is that the growing internationalization during the first period (see Figure 12.2) involved a shift in employment between industries towards more skill-intensive industries. During the second period, changes in international specialization seem to have been unrelated to the average skill upgrading of workers. The results are consistent with the findings in Hansson and Lundberg (1995), which indicate that the tendency towards increased specialization in skill-intensive industries may have declined in the late 1980s. The explanation we put forward is insufficient accumulation of human capital during the 1980s in Sweden relative to other countries, in particular to the NICs, but also relative to other OECD countries.

The industry data we use for the period 1970–90 are highly aggregated. For the years 1986 and 1993 we have access to plant-level data in 146 manufacturing industries. We start utilizing this data by carry out the same analysis as above. Table 12.2 shows that the total annual change is larger in this period (0.9 percentage points) than in the periods 1970–85 and 1985–90. The reason may be the sharp increase in the share of skilled labour between 1990 and 1993.[8] Table 12.2 demonstrates that the *within*-industry component is by far the largest. The *between*-industry component is positive, but uncorrelated with changes in international specialization.

Since we have access to data on plants for 1986 and 1993, we can decompose the within-industry component further, that is, into a within- and a between-plant component. We can express the share of the employees with higher education as:

$$P^E = \sum_{i=1}^{n} \sum_{j=1}^{m} \frac{E_{ij}^s}{E_{ij}} \frac{E_{ij}}{E_i} \frac{E_i}{E} = \sum_i \sum_j P_{ij}^E S_{ij} S_i \qquad (12.3)$$

where P_{ij}^E is the share of the employees in plant j in industry i with tertiary education, S_{ij} is plant j's share of employment in industry i, and S_i is industry i's share of total employment in manufacturing.

Decomposition of the change in the share of skilled labour gives

$$\Delta P^E = \sum_{i=1}^{n} \sum_{j=1}^{m} \Delta P_{ij}^E \overline{S}_{ij} \overline{S}_i + \sum_{i=1}^{n} \sum_{j=1}^{m} \overline{P}_{ij}^E \Delta S_{ij} \overline{S}_i + \sum_{i=1}^{n} \sum_{j=1}^{m} \overline{P}_{ij}^E \overline{S}_{ij} \Delta S_i \qquad (12.4)$$

The first component measures the effect of changes in the share of skilled labour within plants. The second captures reallocations of employment between plants within industries and the third is the between-industry component (compare equation (12.2)).[9] Table 12.3 reports the results of such a decomposition.

Table 12.3   Changes in the structure of skilled labour within and between plants and between industries (percentage points)

1986–93 Annulized changes in percentage points	Within-plant component	Between-plant- within-industry component	Between-industry component
0.696	0.672	0.011	0.013

The changes in employment composition are totally dominated by the *within*-plant component. The bulk of the increase in the share of skilled labour has occurred *within* plants, while shifts in employment between plants within industries and between industries have played a minor role.

The data set in Table 12.3 consists of all plants with more than five employees that appeared in 1986 and 1993 and in both years were classified to the same industry; altogether this amounts to 7,765 plants. This means that plants entering and exiting the industry are excluded. To compare the share of skilled labour in exiting and entering plants[10] with plants that have been in operation the whole period, we estimate two probit regressions:

Prob(Entry) = f *(Skill share, Industry)*
Prob(Exit) = g *(Skill share, Size, Industry)*

The variable entry (exit) is a discrete variable, which takes the value one if the plant has entered (exited) between 1986 and 1993 and the value zero if it was in operation in 1986 and in 1993. In both regressions we include the plants' skill share and dummies to control for industry effects. The exit equation also contains a size variable (employment), since virtually all empirical studies of exit have found that smaller plants fail more frequently.[11] The probit estimates are presented in Table 12.4.

Table 12.4   Probit estimates of entry and exit

	Skill share	Size	Observations
Entry = 1	0.726		13,283
	(9.43)		
Exit = 1	0.151	−0.001	14,601
	(1.63)	(−10.36)	

Note: Figures in parentheses show *t*-values.

We find that the skill share in 1993 was significantly higher in plants established between 1986 and 1993. In exiting plants, the skill share at the beginning of the period was almost the same as in surviving plants. Finally, we observe that smaller plants have a significantly larger tendency to fail. We thus conclude that entry has contributed to a higher skill share.

5   EXPLAINING SHIFTS IN THE DEMAND FOR SKILLED LABOUR

To explore factors that might explain within-industry changes in skill structure, we derive the demand for skilled labour from a translog cost function. We assume that skilled and unskilled labour are variable factors and capital is treated as fixed. We then obtain the following expression for the changes in the cost share of skilled labour in industry i[12]

$$dCS_{si} = \beta_0 + \beta_1 d \ln(w_{si} / w_{ui}) + \beta_2 d \ln K_i + \beta_3 d \ln Y_i + \varepsilon_i \qquad (12.5)$$

where K is capital, Y is real output, and w_s and w_u are wage rates of skilled and unskilled labour. If we estimate equation (12.5), the sign of β_1 depends on whether the elasticity of substitution between skilled and unskilled labour is greater than or less than one.[13] Estimates of β_2 indicate whether skilled labour and capital are complementary inputs ($\beta_2 > 0$) or substitutes ($\beta_2 < 0$) in the production process. Estimates of β_3 show whether growth in output is related to changes in the wage bill of skilled labour. Finally, we can interpret $\beta_0 + \varepsilon_i$, where ε_i is an error term, as bias in technical change at the industry level, which means that estimates of β_0 represent the average bias across industries.

We obtain direct evidence of the impact of technical change on the demand for skilled labour by including an observable measure of technical change in the regression equation in (12.5). Similar to Berman, Bound and Griliches (1994) and Machin (1994), we use the industry-level research and development (R&D) intensity defined as R&D expenditure divided by value added (average for the studied period).

As an alternative indicator we employ the share of technicians *TECH*. Presumably, technical growth is faster in industries where the share of technicians is high; the ability to develop, adopt and implement new technologies is superior for industries with a large number of technicians. Our prior belief is strengthened by the very strong correlation between the R&D intensity and the share of technicians at the industry level (0.91). The measure *TECH* has some advantages compared to the R&D intensity. First, R&D expenditures are only reported on a fairly high level of aggregation.[14] Second, the amount of R&D in small- and medium-sized firms is underestimated since the figures only include firms with more than 50 employees.

Wood (1994, 1995) asserts that increased import competition, especially from the LDCs and NICs, has contributed to skill-biased technical progress in the developed countries. By this he means that the emergence of low-wage competitors caused drastic changes in market conditions. In order to survive, firms in the developed countries have had to search for new production technologies, which generally use less unskilled labour. A theoretical underpinning for his arguments can be found in the literature on X-efficiency.[15] The basic idea here is that managers, in particular in oligopolistic industries, do not maximize profits. One reason may be that they prefer leisure before profit; another is that they appreciate the power and satisfaction an excess number of employees can afford. A rent-threatening disturbance, such as increased import competition, implies, however, that managers take action, for example, by eliminating excess labour or by introducing labour-saving techniques. To capture this effect we add the annual change in the import share of consumption $\Delta(M / C)$ to the regression in equation (12.5).

In a careful study of skill upgrading in US manufacturing during the 1970s and 1980s Bernard and Jensen (1996) found that higher employment at exporting plants contributed heavily to the observed increases in relative demand for skilled labour. One reason could be that in a skill-abundant country, like the USA, exports expand the more skill-intensive activities. In order to examine whether we could trace a similar development in Sweden we include the annual growth in the export share of sales $\Delta(X / Q)$ in our model.

We begin by estimating our model in (12.5) for 16 manufacturing industries (2- and 3-digit International Standard Industrial Classification), where we pool observations from two periods 1970–85 and 1985–90. Data on capital stocks K and R&D intensity determines the level of aggregation.[16] Unfortunately, we do not have data on wage costs for skilled and unskilled labour at the industry level so we replace the cost share of skilled labour CS_{si} with the skill share in employment. If labour is perfectly mobile across industries, the wages of the skilled and unskilled are equalized and thus $d \ln(w_{si} / w_{ui})$ is a constant. The exclusion of the relative wages will then only affect the constant β_0. According to Figure 12.1, the growth rate of the foreign trade ratio differs between the two periods – positive for 1970–85 and zero for 1985–90. One could therefore expect that the factors that led to changes in trade exposure vary between the two periods. Reduced trade barriers and increased competition from the LDCs and the NICs have probably had their largest impact during the first period and consequently we allow for shifts in the coefficients of $\Delta(X / Q)$ and $\Delta(M / C)$ between the two periods.

We estimate the same model for 107 manufacturing industries (5-digit Swedish Standard Industrial Classification) during the period 1986–93. For this period we have access to data on wage costs so our dependent variable here is the cost share of skilled labour. Yet we follow Berman, Bound and Griliches (1994) and Machin (1994) and exclude the relative wage variable, since one could expect that some of the relative wage changes depend on cross-sectional differences in skill upgrading, that is, price changes are confounded with quality changes. In other words this means that it is not reasonable to consider the relative wage changes to be exogenous. But, as we noticed above, if both types of labour are mobile across industries then there will be no variation in the price of quality-adjusted skilled and unskilled labour across industries and an exclusion of $d \ln(w_{si} / w_{ui})$ will influence only the constant β_0.

In Table 12.5, we report the results of the estimation of various specifications of (12.5). In specifications (i)–(iv) we combine data from the two periods 1970–85 and 1985–90 and include a dummy variable for the second period. The annual growth in the share of skilled labour is measured in terms of employment. In specifications (v)–(vii) we have estimated corresponding regressions for the period 1986–93 where we explain the annual growth in skilled labours' share of the wage bill.

The coefficient on the capital stock is positive and significant in all specifications. Capital-skill complementarity seems to prevail in Swedish manufacturing.[17] However, capital accumulation explains only a fraction of the observed skill upgrading. The positive and significant coefficients on output in almost all specifications are signs of higher demand for skilled labour in growing industries.[18] Yet the effect of output is not as robust as the effect of capital; it tends to disappear when we include our indicators of technical change.

Table 12.5 *Effects of increased internationalization and technical change on the demand for skilled labour in Swedish manufacturing*

Variable	(i)	(ii)	(iii)	(iv)	(v)	(vi)	(vii)
$\Delta\ln K$	0.039	0.028	0.050	0.056	0.011	0.013	0.012
	[2.69]	[2.68]	[2.32]	[2.42]	[2.16]	[2.41]	[2.14]
$\Delta\ln Y$	0.014	−0.001	0.036	0.039	0.028	0.033	0.033
	[1.56]	[−0.12]	[2.19]	[2.48]	[1.99]	[2.25]	[2.23]
R&D	0.028						
	[4.60]						
TECH		0.026			4.436		
		[6.92]			[3.63]		
$\Delta(X/Q)$ 1970–85			0.083				
			[1.59]				
$\Delta(X/Q)$ 1985–90			−0.093				
			[−1.60]				
$\Delta(M/C)$ 1970–85				0.111			
				[3.15]			
$\Delta(M/C)$ 1985–90				0.022			
				[0.54]			
$\Delta(X/Q)$ 1986–93						0.004	
						[0.28]	
$\Delta(M/C)$ 1986–93							−0.026
							[−0.87]
1985–90	−0.084	−0.036	0.036	0.013			
	[−1.56]	[−0.83]	[0.42]	[0.19]			
Constant	0.150	0.023	0.086	0.079	0.609	0.795	0.818
	[3.61]	[0.46]	[1.06]	[1.23]	[10.05]	[13.29]	[12.71]
$\bar{R}^2$	0.652	0.736	0.405	0.442	0.221	0.129	0.136
n	32	32	32	32	107	107	107

Note: The dependent variable in specification (i)–(iv) is changes in the share of skilled labour in employment 1970–90. The dependent variable in specification (v)–(vii) is the skilled labours' share of the wage bill 1986–93. Square brackets give White's (1980) heteroscedasticity consistent *t*-statistics.

We consider the unexplained shift from unskilled towards skilled labour in equation (12.5) as biased technical change in addition to the average bias across industries β_0. Hence, the positive and highly significant coefficients on average R&D intensity in specifications (i) and on the share of technicians in specifications (ii) and (v) indicate that the technical change is skill biased.

The growth in the foreign-trade ratio between 1970 and 1985 seems to have influenced the within-industry share of skilled labour. It applies in particular to increased import penetration, for which the coefficient is strongly significant. During the period after 1985 changes in trade are unrelated to changes in skill shares. Our results thus give some support to the hypothesis that increased import competition caused producers to invest in labour-saving techniques thereby increasing the proportion of skilled labour within industries.

6 CONCLUDING REMARKS

During the last 20 years we have observed an uninterrupted increase in the share of skilled labour in Swedish manufacturing. To scrutinize that development we have decomposed the increase into a within-industry and a between-industry component. Until 1985 the between-industry component, which captured the shift in employment from low-skill industries to high-skill industries, coincided with increased international specialization in skill-intensive industries. After 1985, however, no relationship between changes in international specialization and between industry shifts could be established. One reason may be that the continuous shift towards increased international specialization in human-capital-intensive industries in the 1970s and the beginning of the 1980s was interrupted because of a relatively slow accumulation of human capital in Sweden during the 1980s.

The bulk of the observed shifts towards skilled labour has taken place within industries, or rather within plants. Capital-skill complementarity is one explanation for that development. Another is biased technical change. R&D-intensive industries and industries with high shares of technicians have been more likely to increase their shares of skilled labour. We regard this as direct evidence of the presence of skill-biased technical change in Swedish manufacturing industries during the 1970s and 1980s. Our findings conform with similar studies for the USA and the UK. The tendency that industries characterized by high rates of innovation, adoption and implementation of new technologies create the most opportunities for highly educated workers is thus an international phenomenon. We also find that increased import competition contributed to higher skill shares within industries during the period when competition from abroad intensified the most.

NOTES

*   Paper prepared for the conference on Technology and International Trade at Leangkollen, Oslo, 6–8 October 1995. Financial support from the Swedish Council for Research in the Humanities and Social Sciences is gratefully acknowledged. I have benefited from comments by Gert

Villumsen and my fellow editors, and the competent research assistance of Cesar Fuentes-Godoy and Paul Hansson.

1. See, for example, Berman, Machin and Bound (1994).
2. Howell and Wolff (1991) use many different indicators of skills to examine skill changes in the US workplace.
3. For a more thorough exposition see Baldwin (1994) and Deardorff and Hakura (1994).
4. One may question the relevance of using a HOS framework for the analysis since most of the increased trade during the last few decades has been intra-industry trade. On the other hand, it is unclear how the models developed to explain intra-industry trade – where product differentiation and economies of scale are the driving forces behind trade – will affect the composition of employment.
5. Sweden's relative endowment of skilled labour, measured in terms of educational attainment in the labour force, is about the same as in other OECD countries. In comparison with less-developed and newly industrialized countries, that is, the LDCs and the NICs, Sweden is relatively abundant in skilled labour (Hansson and Lundberg, 1995, Table 2.5). Sweden also seems to have a comparative advantage, particularly in trade with LDCs, in human-capital-intensive industries, that is in industries where the employees' average years of schooling is high (Hansson and Lundberg, 1995, Table 3.2).
6. The firms in the unskilled-labour-intensive industry have to offset their growing technical disadvantage by holding back the wages of the majority of their workers.
7. We define the specialization index as:

$$r_i = \frac{Q_i}{C_i} = \frac{C_i - M_i + X_i}{C_i} = 1 + \frac{X_i - M_i}{C_i}$$

where Q_i, C_i, M_i and X_i are production, consumption, import and export in industry i.

8. The share of skilled labour was 9.1 per cent in 1985 and increased to 11.2 per cent in 1990 and jumped to 15.7 per cent in 1993. At this time employment in Swedish manufacturing dropped substantially. The employment was 0.93 million in 1990 and decreased to 0.74 million in 1993. This implies that most of the employees who were laid off from manufacturing were unskilled.
9.

$$\sum_{i=1}^{n} \sum_{j=1}^{m} \overline{P}_{ij}^{E} \overline{S}_{ij} \Delta S_i = \sum_{i=1}^{n} P_i^{E} \Delta S_i$$

10. Plants entering after 1986 and which have exited before 1993 are not included.
11. See, for example, Doms et al. (1995) and Evans (1987).
12. Hansson (1996) gives the complete derivation. See also, for example, Berndt (1991, Chapter 9).
13. See, for example, Hamermesh (1993, p. 41).
14. In Swedish manufacturing for 18 industries.
15. See, for example, Leibenstein (1966), Corden (1974) and Caves and Krepps (1993).
16. Hansson (1996) gives a detailed description of data, sources and how variables have been generated.
17. Bergström and Panas (1992) gain a similar result.
18. Our result differs in that respect from Berman, Bound and Griliches (1994) and Machin (1994) who gain a negative coefficient on output growth.

REFERENCES

Baldwin, R.E. (1994), 'The Effect of Trade and Foreign Direct Investment on Employment and Relative Wages', *OECD Economic Studies*, **23**, 7–54.
Bernard, A. and J.B. Jensen (1996), 'Exporters, Skill Upgrading, and the Wage Gap', *Journal of International Economics*, forthcoming.

Bergström V and E.E. Panas (1992), 'How Robust is the Capital-Skill Complementary Hypothesis?', *Review of Economics and Statistics*, **74**, 540–46.

Berman, E., J. Bound and Z. Griliches (1994), 'Changes in the Demand for Skilled Labor Within U.S. Manufacturing: Evidence From the Annual Survey of Manufactures', *Quarterly Journal of Economics*, **109**, 367–98.

Berman, E., S. Machin and J. Bound (1994), 'Implications of Skilled Biased Technological Change: International Evidence', Mimeo.

Berndt, E.R. (1991), *The Practice of Econometrics. Classic and Contemporary*, New York: Addison-Wesley.

Caves, R. and M. Krepps (1993), 'Fat: the Displacement of Nonproduction Workers from US Manufacturing Industries', *Brookings Papers: Microeconomics* **2**, 227–88.

Corden, W.M. (1974), *Trade Policy and Economic Welfare*, Oxford: Clarendon Press.

Deardorff, A.V. and D. Hakura (1994), 'Trade and Wages: What Are the Questions?', in J. Bhagwati and M.H. Kosters (eds), *Trade and Wages*, Washington DC: AEI Press.

Doms, M., T. Dunne, and M.J. Roberts (1995), 'The Role of Technology Use in the Survival and Growth of Manufacturing Plants', *International Journal of Industrial Organization*, **13**, 523–42.

Evans, D.S. (1987), 'The Relationship Between Firm Growth, Size, and Age: Estimates for 100 Manufacturing Industries', in T.F. Bresnahan and R. Schmalensee (eds), *The Empirical Renaissance in Industrial Economics*, Oxford: Blackwell.

Hamermesh, D.S. (1993), *Labor Demand*, Princeton: Princeton University Press.

Hansson, P. (1996), 'Trade, Technology and Changes in Employment of Skilled Labor in Swedish Manufacturing', *FIEF, Working Paper*, No. 131.

Hansson, P. and L. Lundberg (1995), *Från basindustri till högteknologi? Svensk näringsstruktur och strukturpolitik*, Stockholm: SNS–förlag.

Howell, D.R. and E.N. Wolff (1991), 'Trends in the Growth and Distribution of Skills in the U.S. Workplace', *Industrial and Labor Relations Review*, **44**, 486–502.

Leamer, E.E. (1994), 'Trade, Wages and the Revolving Door Ideas', *NBER Working Paper*, No. 4716.

Leibenstein, H. (1966), 'Allocative Efficiency versus "X-efficiency"', *American Economic Review*, **56**, 392–415.

Machin, S. (1994), 'Changes in the Relative Demand for Skills in the UK Labour Market', *CEPR Discussion Paper*, No. 952.

White, H. (1980), 'A Heteroskedasticity-Consistent Covariance Matrix Estimator and a Direct Test for Heteroskedasticity', *Econometrica*, **48**, 817–38.

Wood, A. (1994), *North–South Trade, Employment and Inequality: Changing Fortunes in a Skill-Driven World*, Oxford: Clarendon Press.

Wood, A. (1995), 'How Trade Hurt Unskilled Workers', *Journal of Economic Perspective*, **9**, 57–80.

Index